WALKING PARIS

WALKING PARIS

GILLES DESMONS

30 ORIGINAL WALKS
IN AND AROUND PARIS

NEW
HOLLAND

This edition published in 2008
by New Holland Publishers (UK) Ltd
London • Cape Town • Sydney • Auckland
First published 1994

2 4 6 8 10 9 7 5 3 1

www.newhollandpublishers.com

Garfield House, 86–88 Edgware Road, London, W2 2EA, United Kingdom

80 McKenzie Street, Cape Town 8001, South Africa

Unit 1, 66 Gibbes Street, Chatswood, NSW 2067, Australia

218 Lake Road, Northcote, Auckland, New Zealand

ISBN 978 1 84773 061 9

Publishing Manager: Jo Hemmings
Senior Editor: Kate Michell
Assistant Editor: Rose Hudson
Designer/Cartographer: Paul Wood
Cover Design: Alan Marshall
Production: Ben Byram-Wigfield

Reproduction by Pica Colour Separation Overseas (Pte) Ltd, Singapore
Printed and bound in Singapore by Kyodo Printing Co (Singapore) Pte Ltd

Photographic acknowledgements
Front cover: Street in Montmartre © Ric Ergenbright/CORBIS
Back cover: The Seine Running Under Pont Neuf © Dave G. Houser/CORBIS
Spine: Sacré Coeur © Laurence Poos
Aspect/Adrian Greeman: Plate 25; Aspect/J. Alex Langley: Plates 18, 28;
J. Allan Cash: Plates 1, 2, 8, 11, 13, 14, 19, 26, 31, 34, 35, 36;
Peter Feeny: Plates 3, 4, 5, 6, 7, 9, 10, 12, 17, 20, 22, 24, 27, 29, 30, 32, 33, 37, 38;
Paris Travel Service: Plate 23; Barrie Smith: Plate 15; Ken Wright: Plates 16, 21.

The publishers gratefully acknowledge the generous assistance of Nikon UK Ltd
and the loan of a Nikon F601M to Peter Feeny.

Contents

Preface

There is never any ending to Paris, and the memory of each person who has lived in it differs from that of any other . . .

Ernest Hemingway, *A Moveable Feast* (1964)

Paris ne se livre guère aux gens pressés.

Julien Green, *Paris* (1983)

Paris, c'est le décor d'un roman que personne n'écrira jamais.

Julien Green, *ib.*

Walking is probably the best way to discover a city, and Paris is the capital *par excellence* where this old adage is true – yet a modern-day walking book on Paris is almost impossible to find. Many figures of the French literary scene have written about the charms of such walks, from Romain Rolland – an inveterate Paris walker – to Armand Lanoux, Julien Green and of course the Surrealists, who made walking an almost ideological necessity in the quest for the impromptu and the elusive within a diffuse network of subtle resonances and connections.

Time is necessary to seek out the hidden charm and the secret voices of so large a city. Probably you really need to lose yourself in the city to gain the full benefits of the 'pleasure of the unexpected and the subtle fear of the unknown' (Julien Green's *Paris*), but this guide hopes to provide you with the next best thing, and so to help you make your own personal discoveries. The tempo of discovery is gentle – none of the walks is too long – and, while culture in all its forms is never far from the surface, life itself looms large: you will be walking through, not a city petrified in its past, but one that is abundantly alive.

I discovered Paris by walking and walking, criss-crossing the city in all directions, getting lost and finding my way, slowly working out different itineraries that would present allusive perspectives and visual pleasure. A new detail, an unknown *passage*, an as yet undiscovered sign on a shop, a new café – all were causes for joy. In those days, the 1960s and 1970s, there was a latent excitement everywhere – an aura of change and of impending revolution, but also one of personal discovery. For this book I revisited those walks of the past while also discovering a number of new ones. I have often strayed away from the obvious. I have crossed the barriers – both artificial (e.g., the Haussmann boulevards) and natural (e.g., the Seine) – that split the city into so many small fragments. I have sought an understanding of the physiology of Paris beyond the boundaries, beyond the mosaic-like fabric that so often awes the visitor.

No city is static. Paris has changed, and I have chronicled those changes carefully over the years, watching Paris evolving, as always, according to its own strong sense of fate.

Gilles Desmons

Introduction

It is a good idea to read the historical section (p13) first, as inevitably there are references in the main text that cannot be explained in full every time. Reading this section will also give you a general flavour of the city and help you understand how Paris came to be.

If you are unfamiliar with the city, read the summaries at the head of each walk to get the feel of the area concerned. There you will find information about the main monuments, museums and other sites of interest, as well as tabulated practical details. Each walk is accompanied by a map on which the route is clearly marked in green.

While this book gives you a fair amount of information about each of the locations visited, it cannot hope to be fully comprehensive. There are plenty of guidebooks available for Paris, and new ones seem to appear each year. There are specialist booklets and even books about many of the major places of interest; these are usually on sale at the place itself. Restaurants, clubs and the latest 'in' places can be checked out on the Internet, *in situ*, in *Time Out Paris* or other guides.

None of the walks is particularly long, and it is assumed you will want to pause in a café now and again. I have given approximate times for each walk, but of course these do not allow for stops. Generally you should reckon to be able to do two walks easily in a day. Some walks can be connected with others to make a longer outing: consult the list on page 10 and the details given at the ends of the texts on the walks concerned.

The index is not merely a decoration! Use it to guide yourself around this book as much as you use the book itself to guide you around Paris.

Author's Acknowledgements

I want to thank the former commissioning editor at New Holland, Charlotte Parry-Crooke, who asked me to write this book and who bore with me through the inevitable delays; my editor, Paul Barnett, who did a brilliant job; and my wife, Maryrose, who suffered through the various stages of the manuscript's preparation. Special thanks go to my walking friends François de Boisseuil, Hervé Gras and Paul Watson, whose comments were invaluable.

Author's Note

For this third edition, like the previous one, I have re-walked the walks in this book. Shops, cafés and restaurants come and go, and the odd monument or museum closes for restoration. The fully revised text takes account of all such changes (as well as of all new telephone numbers, altered opening times and so forth). But the fabric of the city does not change and Paris retains its integrity, the visual identity and organic design that make it such a rewarding place to walk and wander in.

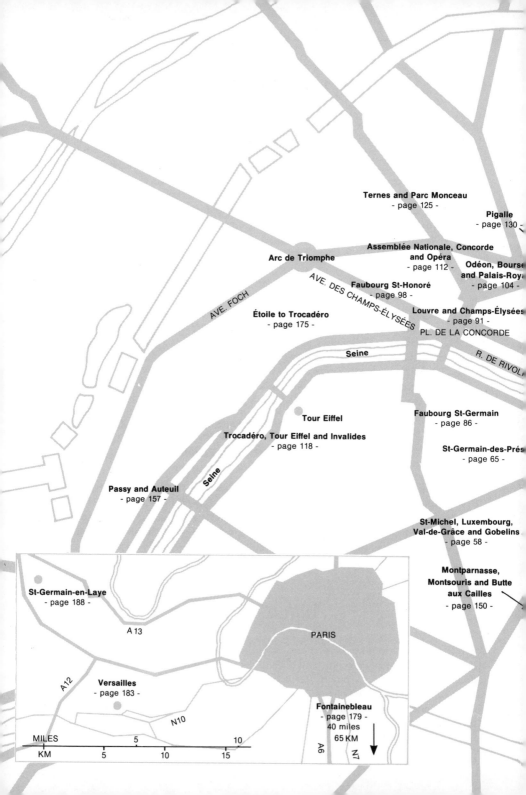

PL. DE LA RÉPUBLIQUE

BVD. VOLTAIRE

PL. DE LA BASTILLE

PL. DE LA NATION

VD. ST-MICHEL

PL. D'ITALIE

Seine

Categories of Walks

RIVER WALKS
The Îles St-Louis and de la Cité
The *Quais*
Trocadéro, Tour Eiffel and Invalides

SHOPPING WALKS
St-Michel, Luxembourg, Val-de-Grâce
 and Gobelins
St-Germain-des-Prés
Les Halles
Faubourg St-Honoré
Odéon, Bourse and Palais-Royal
Assemblée Nationale, Concorde and
 Opéra
The *Passages*

WALKS WITH MUSEUMS
The *Quais*
Le Marais
République and Temple
Cluny, the Sorbonne and Montagne Ste-
 Geneviève
Arènes, Mouffetard and the Jardin des
 Plantes
St-Germain-des-Prés
Beaubourg and Châtelet
Maubert to Orsay
Faubourg St-Germain
Louvre and Champs-Élysées
Trocadéro, Tour Eiffel and Invalides
Ternes and Parc Monceau
Pigalle
Montmartre
Passy and Auteuil
The *Passages*
Étoile to Trocadéro

PARKS AND GARDENS WALKS
Arènes, Mouffetard and the Jardin des
 Plantes

St-Michel, Luxembourg, Val-de-Grâce
 and Gobelins
Faubourg St-Germain
Louvre and Champs-Élysées
Ternes and Parc Monceau
Montparnasse, Montsouris and Butte aux
 Cailles
Père-Lachaise to Buttes Chaumont
Fontainebleau
Versailles
St-Germain-en-Laye

CHÂTEAU WALKS
Fontainebleau
Versailles
St-Germain-en-Laye

CIRCULAR WALKS
The *Quais*
Arènes, Mouffetard and the Jardin ˙des
 Plantes
St-Germain-des-Prés
Les Halles
Bastille and Faubourg St-Antoine
Fontainebleau
Versailles
St-Germain-en-Laye

CONNECTING WALKS
The Îles St-Louis and de la Cité **to** The
 Quais
The *Quais* **to** Louvre and Champs-Élysées
République and Temple **to** Le Marais
Cluny, the Sorbonne and Montagne Ste-
 Geneviève **to** Îles St-Louis and de la
 Cité **or to** Arènes, Mouffetard and the
 Jardin des Plantes
St-Germain-des-Prés **to** St-Michel,
 Luxembourg, Val-de-Grâce and
 Gobelins

Beaubourg and Châtelet **to** Les Halles
Maubert to Orsay **to** St-Germain-des-
Prés
Louvre and Champs-Élysées **to** Ternes
and Parc Monceau **or to** Étoile to
Trocadéro
Faubourg St-Honoré **to** Assemblée
Nationale, Concorde and Opéra
Assemblée Nationale, Concorde and
Opéra **to** Faubourg St-Germain **or to**
Louvre and Champs-Élysées
Trocadéro, Tour Eiffel and Invalides **to**
Assemblée Nationale, Concorde and
Opéra
Ternes and Parc Monceau **to** Faubourg
St-Honoré
Étoile to Trocadéro **to** Trocadéro, Tour
Eiffel and Invalides

WALKS IN ORDER OF LENGTH
The lengths given here are approximate,
for obvious reasons.

3 km (2 miles)
Étoile to Trocadéro
République and Temple

3.5 km (2¼ miles)
Le Marais
St-Germain-des-Prés
Odéon, Bourse and Palais-Royal
Assemblée Nationale, Concorde and
Opéra

4km (2½ miles)
The Îles St-Louis and de la Cité
The *Quais*
Cluny, the Sorbonne and Montagne
Ste-Geneviève

Maubert to Orsay
Fontainebleau

4.25 km (2⅔ miles)
Faubourg St-Honore

4.5 km (2¾ miles)
Les Halles
Faubourg St-Germain
Trocadéro, Tour Eiffel and Invalides
St-Germain-en-Laye

5 km (3 miles)
Louvre and Champs-Élysées
Montmartre
Bastille and Faubourg St-Antoine

5.5 km (3½ miles)
St-Michel, Luxembourg, Val-de-Grâce
and Gobelins
Beaubourg and Châtelet
Pigalle
Passy and Auteuil
Père-Lachaise to Buttes Chaumont
The *Passages*

6 km (3¾ miles)
République to La Villette

6.5 km (4 miles)
Arènes, Mouffetard and the Jardin des
Plantes
Ternes and Parc Monceau

7 km (4¼ miles)
Montparnasse, Montsouris and Butte aux
Cailles

8.5 km (5¼ miles)
Versailles

11

Key to Maps

═══	Route of walk	Abbreviations	
┅┅┅	Path	ALL.	*allée*
═══	Railway line	AVE.	*avenue*
▤	Steps	BVD.	*boulevard*
		G.	*galerie*
Ⓜ	Métro station	PASS.	*passage*
Ⓡ	RER station	PL.	*place*
Ⓐ	Autobus: bus stop	PT.	*pont*
		PTE.	*porte*
†	*Église*: Church	Q.	*quai*
Ⓗ	*Lieu historique*: historic building or monument	R.	rue
Ⓜ	*Musée*: museum, art gallery, display or exhibition open to the public	SQ.	*square*
		V.	*village*
Ⓟ	*Parc*: park, garden or open space open to the public		

Historical Background

The growth of Paris has been outward from the centre – Lutèce (Lutetia) and the Île de la Cité – in successive concentric circles or ellipses, absorbing small villages on the way. Absorption meant acquisition: those villages quickly lost their identity and became integral parts of the city. The growth was not only organic but 'pyramidal': successive layers were added upon one another, with the medieval city succeeding the Roman, then the Classical city the medieval, the Haussmannian city the Classical . . .

The river
Like almost all major cities Paris was built upon a river. The Seine is on a much more human scale than, for example, the Thames or the Hudson, and it was natural that – from the time of the Parisii onwards – people should settle on its banks and islands, and that those settlements should grow.

The Seine, then, has been the main artery of the city for centuries, and it is still an essential ingredient of the city's life. It was even more so until relatively recently: wood, stones, hay and grains were carried downstream to build and feed the city. Crossing the river was by ferry: in medieval times there were only two (wooden) bridges over the Seine, the Grand Pont and the Petit Pont; Henri III (reigned 1574–89) and Henri IV (reigned 1589–1610) gave a new impetus to the city by constructing Pont Neuf, and thereafter more bridges appeared. A decree of Louis XVI (reigned 1774–93), that all houses on bridges should be demolished, gave the city a completely new look: the river, now visible, added an aesthetic role to its commercial one. From the 18th century until the first half of the 20th there was a regular passenger service from Pont Royal, near the Louvre, to the villages of Sèvres and St-Cloud – today fashionable suburbs of Paris. Guy de Maupassant (1850–1893) records that the traditional Sunday outing was to go by riverboat – a *bateau mouche* – to frolic in the woods of Sèvres, St-Cloud or Meudon. Today's *bateaux mouches* are not much like the originals, but they still offer pleasant trips on the river.

The walls
From very early days Paris felt a need to protect herself. In Gallo-Roman times the Seine was protection enough for the small community that lived on the island. The city's first expansion onto the Left Bank and the Montagne Ste-Geneviève (the Right Bank was then too boggy for settlement) was interrupted by successive barbarian invasions; Roman Paris was practically eradicated, and its memory lost for centuries.

Security was also paramount to the medieval city, and Philippe-Auguste (Philip II; reigned 1180–1223), on his way to the Crusades, decided to protect the 200,000 inhabitants by building a fortified wall around Paris (1190–1213). 150 years later Paris had outgrown its boundaries, and Charles V (reigned 1364–80) initiated a new wall on the Right Bank and fortified the existing Philippe-Auguste wall on the Left. There were then five gates (*portes*) on the Left Bank and seven on the Right. In the 17th century Louis XIII (1601–1643) decided to extend Charles V's wall to the west, where the city was growing fastest; the task was accomplished in 1633–6.

This was Paris's last fortified wall, and Louis XIV (reigned 1643–1715) razed all three to the ground 30 years later. However, in the late 18th century the Fermiers Généraux wall was built. The Fermiers Généraux (Farmers-General) were government tax collectors, and this wall was a tax barrier that enabled the collection of tax from anyone entering the city; there were 60 gates along 23km (14.5 miles) of a wall that encircled a city of 600,000 people. Lastly there were the military fortifications erected in 1841–5 by Louis Adolphe Thiers (1797–1877).

There are important remains of the Philippe-Auguste wall and of the Fermiers Généraux wall, but nothing is left of the others.

The Church

The Roman Catholic Church was also important in the growth and development of Paris. The French capital was the seat of the crown, of power and of influence, and a major centre for educational, intellectual and artistic pursuits – and it drained the country of its talents, a state of affairs that continues. It was clearly vital to the expansionist policies of the Church that it be established near the corridors of power. During the Middle Ages, when Christian mystic fervour was at its peak, Paris became a city of monasteries, abbeys, convents and churches. There were religious institutions that not only occupied large areas of land but exerted enormous temporal and spiritual power; e.g., the abbeys of St-Germain-des-Prés, St-Martin-des-Champs, Ste-Geneviève and St-Victor. Almost all orders were represented – many warring with one another – including Dominicans, Jesuits, Augustines, Cistercians and Knights Templar.

Urbanization

After the Roman city had been destroyed by the Barbarians, the memory of Roman order and town-planning skills was lost during the Dark Ages, and it was not until the 17th century that there re-emerged any awareness of urban design. While the medieval city looked inwards, and in some respects the Renaissance city did so as well, the Classical city of Louis XIII (reigned 1610–43) and especially of Louis XIV (reigned 1643–1715) became extrovert.

The medieval city was concerned with protection, with warren-like streets and fortified walls and palaces: the Louvre was then merely a military fortress. The only variation lay in the monuments to God, where a tremendous popular élan expressed itself: structures like Notre-Dame, the Sainte Chapelle and St-Martin-des-Champs are testimony to this essential preoccupation of the Middle Ages. François I (reigned 1515–47) was probably the first to introduce a sense of decoration, even of aesthetics: he renewed the Louvre and introduced the Italian Renaissance artists. He was followed by his son, Henri II (reigned 1547–59), and Henri's wife, the formidable Catherine de' Medici (1519–1589), but it was really with Henri IV (reigned 1589–1610) that the city ceased to be just a tangle of streets and started to show a strong feeling of identity: there was the beginning of a will to create a new urban design. During the reigns of Louis XIII and Louis XIV expansion knew few bounds. The Île St-Louis was developed over 30 years by Louis Le Vau (1612–1670) and others, and became a jewel of 17th-century architecture. The Places Royales – Place des Vosges (initiated by Henri IV), Place des Victoires, Place Vendôme and later Place de la Concorde – were born of a sense of theatre and staging and of a desire to show off the glory of the monarch. Domestic architecture became ornate, pleasing not only to the occupant but also to his fellow-citizens. The kings led the way, with their fine *châteaux* and grand gardens, there to be admired by all.

But the city was still ensconced within its walls. Louis XIV had the grand vision to open it out, to pull down the defensive walls and create instead large avenues (the *cours*) bordered with trees, and soon these became the most fashionable places of entertainment. Every new monument now needed to be enshrined in a grand décor – the Invalides is a perfect example. This tradition prevailed for generations: Jacques Germain Soufflot (1709–1780), for example, created a grand avenue to highlight his church (now the Panthéon), and Charles Garnier (1825–1898) built his Opéra in alignment with Georges Haussmann's avenue.

Montmartre
The villages bordering Paris were integrated with it in 1860. Of these, Montmartre is the only one to have kept its autonomy (it seceded from Paris for about 70 days during the Commune in 1871) and its quaint rural charm. It has also been more fortunate than the others – e.g., Ménilmontant, Belleville and Charonne – in that it has somehow escaped the bulldozer.

As the highest point near the city (129m [424ft]), it was only natural that the *butte* should be seen as sacred, attracting first the Druids, then the Romans, who had two temples there – dedicated to Mercury and to Mars – and finally Louis le Gros (Louis VI; reigned 1108–1137), who had an abbey built there in 1133 at the behest of his wife, Adélaide de Savoie (d1154), who was sister to the Pope, Calixte II (reigned 1119–24).

The name 'Montmartre' probably comes from *mons martyrium* (hill of the martyrs). St Denis was beheaded halfway up the *butte* by the Romans in the 3rd century. The legend is that he then picked up his head and walked 6km ($9\frac{3}{4}$ miles) down the northern side of the *butte* before collapsing in the plain, at which a spring appeared and flowers bloomed. At the end of the 5th century St Geneviève (*c*422–512) founded at this spot the St-Denis basilica, which became the burial ground of the kings of France.

After three centuries of quiet influence, the Abbaye des Dames-de-Montmartre fell into physical and moral disrepair. When Henri IV, then King of Navarre, came to besiege Paris in 1590 – he had already been proclaimed King of France but Paris denied him as a Protestant – he and his lieutenants came to stay at the abbey. He failed to take the city but, by way of compensation, the youthful Mother Abbess, Claude de Beauvilliers (b1573), became his 'favourite', while many of her nuns became 'favourites' of his officers. The abbey was eventually put to rights by Claude's sister, Marie de Beauvilliers (b1574), and in the 17th century the nuns built a more manageable abbey further down the hill (near Place des Abbesses).

As to the village of Montmartre, as early as the 6th century there was a hamlet at the top of the hill, centred on a chapel. The village, originally just a small community of farmers, grew in the shadow of the abbey. When the abbey was demolished in the Revolution its grounds were partitioned and sold off, and it was at this stage that the expansion of Montmartre really began. The population changed over the years; the mid-19th-century brought bohemia to Montmartre, and, when the Impressionists moved in, it was really on the map.

Destruction
Destruction, too, is engraved in the history of Paris – to an extent that is not always realized. The Barbarians annihilated the Roman city. The Revolutionaries targeted their anger chiefly on the Church and the crown, with hundreds of churches and abbeys

being pulled down or sold off and symbols of autocracy (e.g., the Bastille) being razed. Less than a century later the Communards focused their wrath on the government: the law courts and the 17th-century Hôtel de Ville (city hall) were burnt down.

The other major factor in destruction, especially of living areas, was urbanization. We have mentioned the creation of the Place Royales and avenues; the Classical city was in effect born at the expense of the medieval city. But the city's most radical landscaper was Georges Eugène Haussmann (1809–1891); appointed Prefect of Paris by Napoleon III (reigned 1852–70), he remodelled the city, effectively getting rid of what was left of the medieval heritage. Haussmann had two aims in his reshaping of the city: the burgeoning bourgeoisie were to be able to expand in a climate of terrific economic growth, and the military were to be aided in the prevention of the kind of rioting that had been seen in the short-lived revolutions of 1830 and 1848. Thus large avenues and boulevards were carved through Paris, easing traffic and opening the city.

Key dates and people

Gallo-Roman Period
- 3rd century BC: the Parisii settled on the Île de la Cité
- 52BC–AD280: the Romans in Lutetia
- 280: the city sacked by the Barbarians

Dark and Middle Ages
- *451: St Geneviève (c422–512) saves Paris from the Huns*
- 751–68: reign of Pépin III, the Short
- 768–814: reign of Charlemagne (with Carloman to 771)
- 814–40: reign of Louis I
- 840–77: reign of Charles I
- 877–9: reign of Louis II
- 879–84: reign of Carloman (with Louis III to 882)
- 884–7: reign of Charles II, the Fat
- 887–98: reign of Eudes
- 898–922: reign of Charles III
- 922–3: reign. of Robert I
- 923–36: reign of Raoul (also known as Rudolf or Rodolphe)
- 936–54: reign of Louis IV
- 954–86: reign of Lothaire
- 986–7: reign of Louis V
- 987–96: reign of Hugues Capet
- 996–1031: reign of Robert II
- 1031–60: reign of Henri I
- 1060–1108: reign of Philippe I
- 1108–37: reign of Louis VI

- 1137–80: reign of Louis VII
- 1180–1223: reign of Philippe II
- 1223–6: reign of Louis VIII
- *Early 12th century: birth of the University on the Left Bank; Peter Abélard (1079–1142) leads the student exodus from the Île de la Cité to the other side of the river*
- 1226–70: reign of Louis IX (St Louis)
- 1270–85: reign of Philippe III
- 1285–1314: reign of Philippe IV
- 1314–16: reign of Louis X
- 1316: reign of Jean I
- 1316–22: reign of Philippe V
- 1322–8: reign of Charles IV
- 1328–50: reign of Philippe VI
- 1350–64: reign of Jean II
- 1364–80: reign of Charles V
- 1380–1422: reign of Charles VI
- 1422–61: reign of Charles VII
- 1461–83: reign of Louis XI
- 1483–98: reign of Charles VIII
- 1498–1515: reign of Louis XII

The French Renaissance and the 16th century – The House of Valois
- 1515–47: reign of François I
- *1530 onwards: Italian artists in France*
- *1533: creation of the Jesuit order by Ignatius de Loyola (1491–1556)*
- *The Humanists: Guillaume Budé (Budaeus; 1467–1540), Pierre de*

Ronsard (1524–1585), Clément Marot
(c1497–1544), etc.
- 1547–59: reign of Henri II, his queen
being Catherine de' Medici (1519–
1589)
- 1559–60: reign of François II
- 1560–74: reign of Charles IX
- *1572: St Bartholomew Massacre*
- 1574–89: reign of Henri III

17th century – The House of Bourbon
- 1589–1610: reign of Henri IV, his
queen being Marie de' Medici (1573–
1642)
- 1610–43: reign of Louis XIII, his
queen being Anne of Austria (1601–
1666)
- 1629–42: Cardinal Richelieu (1585–
1642) effective ruler of France
- 1643–1715: reign of Louis XIV, with
Cardinal Mazarin (1602–1661) and
Anne of Austria as regents
- *1661: death of Mazarin; Jean Baptiste
Colbert (1619–1683) becomes Louis's
chief minister*
- *1660s–70s: Fortified walls pulled down
and the* cours *created*
- *The Classicists: Pierre Corneille (1606–
1684), Jean Racine (1639–1699),
Molière (1622–1673), etc.*

*18th century – The Age of Enlightenment –
The House of Bourbon*
- 1715–74: reign of Louis XV
- *1715–23: regency of Philippe d'Orléans
(1674–1723)*
- *1717–20: John Law's bank*
- *Voltaire (1694–1778)*
- *Jean-Jacques Rousseau (1712–1778)*
- *The* Encyclopédistes: *Denis Diderot
(1713–1784), Jean le Rond D'Alembert
(1717–1783), etc.*
- 1774–93: reign of Louis XVI
- *1784–91: erection of the Fermiers
Généraux wall*

The Revolution (1789–99)
- *14 July 1789: Fall of the Bastille*
- *1789 onwards: Dissolution and destruction
of church properties*
- *21 January 1793: Louis XVI guillotined*
- *1792–5: National Convention*
- *1793–4: the Terror, under Maximilien
Robespierre (1758–1794)*
- *1795–9: Directoire*

*The Consulate (1799–1804) and the First
Empire (1804–15)*
- 1804–14 *and* 1815: reign of Napoleon I
- *1815: Napoleon defeated at Waterloo*
- 1815: reign of Napoleon II

*The Restoration – The Houses of Bourbon
and Orléans*
- 1795–1824: reign of Louis XVIII (in
effect from 1814)
- *1824–30: reign of Charles X*
- *1830: the Revolution of 27, 28, 29 July
ends the Bourbon hold on the throne*
- 1830–48: reign of Louis-Philippe, son
of Philippe Égalité (1747–1793)
- *1841–5: Thiers erects a new set of
fortifications around Paris*
- *February 1848: revolution and effective
end of the monarchy*

*The Second Republic (1848–52) and
Second Empire (1852–70)*
- 1848–52: presidency of Louis-
Napoleon Bonaparte
- 1852–70: reign of Louis-Napoleon
Bonaparte as Napoleon III
- *1853–70: Haussmann creates a new Paris*
- *1855: first of the great Expositions
Universelles; others of note were those of
1867, 1878, 1889, 1900, 1925, 1931
and 1937*
- *1860: absorption of the villages bordering
Paris*

The Third Republic (1870–1940)
- 1871–3: presidency of Adolphe Thiers (1797–1877)
- 1871: *the Commune*
- 1873–9: presidency of Marie Edmé Patrice Maurice, Cornte de MacMahon (1808–1893)
- 1879–87: presidency of Jules Grévy (1807–1891)
- 1887–94: presidency of Sadi Carnot (1837–1894)
- 1894–5: presidency of Jean Casimir-Périer (1847–1907)
- 1895–9: presidency of Félix Faure (1841–1899)
- 1899–1906: presidency of Émile Loubet (1899–1906)
- 1906-1913: presidency of Armand Falliéres (1841–1931)
- 1913–20: presidency of Raymond Poincaré (1860–1934)
- 1920: presidency of Paul Deschanel (1855–1922)
- 1920–24: presidency of Alexandre Millerand (1859–1943)
- 1924–31: presidency of Gaston Doumergue (1863–1937)
- 1931–2: presidency of Paul Doumer (1857–1932)
- 1932–40: presidency of Albert Lebrun (1871–1950)
- *Art Nouveau; Art Deco; birth of Modernism*

Vichy Government
- 1940–44: Marshalship of Henri Petain (1856–1951)

The Fourth Republic (1944–58) and Fifth Republic (1958–)
- *1944–7: provisional government*
- 1947–54: presidency of Vincent Auriol (1884–1966)
- 1954–8: presidency of René Coty (1882–1962)
- 1959–69: presidency of Charles de Gaulle (1890–1970)
- 1969–74: presidency of Georges Pompidou (1911–1974)
- 1974–81: presidency of Valéry Giscard d'Estaing (b1926)
- 1981–96: presidency of Franqois Mitterand (1916–1996)
- 1996–2007: presidency of Jacques Chirac (b1932)
- 2007 onwards: presidency of Nicolas Sarkozy (b1955)

The Îles St-Louis and de la Cité

Probably the most stunning walk in Paris, this takes you across the beautiful Île St-Louis with its fine 17th-century *hôtels* – the whole island has hardly changed in 400 years – and the Île de la Cité with Notre-Dame, the remains of a medieval royal palace, the stunning Gothic Sainte Chapelle and the delightful early-17th-century Place Dauphine. The Seine, never far away, adds its own charm to this walk.

Start: **Métro Sully-Morland; buses 67, 86, 87.**
Finish: **Métro Pont-Neuf; buses 58, 67, 69, 72, 75.**
Length: **4km (2½ miles).**
Time: **1½hr.**
Refreshments: **Many cafés and restaurants in the Île St-Louis and at the end of the walk near Pont Neuf and in Place Dauphine.**
Which day: **Any day.**
To visit:
- **Notre-Dame: daily 08.00–19.00; treasure Monday-Saturday 10.00–18.00 and Sunday 14.00–18.00; towers daily 10.00–17.00.**
- **The Conciergerie: daily 09.30–19.00 (1 April to 30 September) or 10.00–17.00 (1 October to 30 March).**
- **The Sainte Chapelle: daily 09.30–18.30 (1 April to 30 September) or 10.00–16.30 (1 October to 30 March).**

A bakers' union
Leave Sully-Morland métro and cross the river by Pont de Sully, built 1876, to Île St-Louis. Behind you are the broad Boulevard Henri-IV, a late-19th-century creation (post-Haussmann), and, at its far end, the column of Place de la Bastille. Facing you, up on Montagne Ste-Geneviève on the far side of the river, is the splendid dome of the Panthéon (see p49).

While the Île de la Cité was the original seat of the city, the Île St-Louis was developed only in the 17th century. Originally one island, it was split into two during the reign of Charles V, with a canal separating the upstream island, the Île aux Vaches, from the other, the Île Notre-Dame. Henri IV decided to reunite the islets and to create of the result a *beau quartier*, but was murdered before building started; his widow, Marie de' Medici (1573–1642), and his son, Louis XIII, took over the project. The island was developed in 1620–50. The person most instrumental in this transformation was Louis Le Vau (1612–1670), later the architect of Vaux le Vicomte, the Louvre, the Collège des Quatre-Nations (now Institut de France) and Versailles. Wealthy magistrates, financiers and members of the aristocracy became the first tenants.

The Île St-Louis thus became a kind of annexe to the Marais, the area on the other side of the river which was likewise undergoing serious development (see p32). As in the

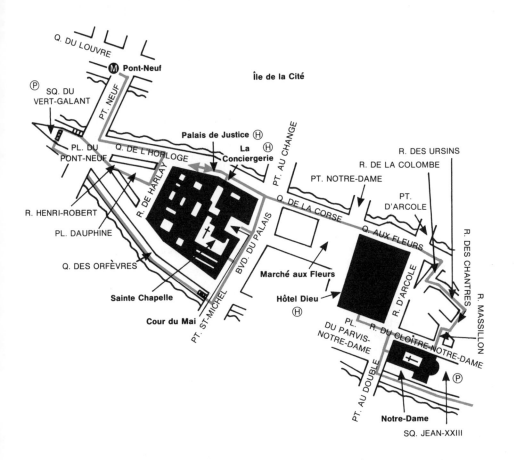

Marais, but less so because of the more limited space, it was felt that part of the function of domestic architecture was to contribute to the area's general splendour, and thus many of the Île St-Louis's *hôtels* display fine features that were designed to be enjoyed by the public at large.

Just over the river, turn right into Quai d'Anjou, named for François (1554–1584), Duc d'Anjou, fifth son of Henri II. The first house, with its unusual round turret, is the magnificent Hôtel Lambert, built by Le Vau; its entrance is on the other side, in Rue St-Louis-en-l'Île. In 1742 Voltaire (1694–1778) lived in the *hôtel*, then owned by his mistress, Gabrielle Le Tonnelier de Breteuil. On the wall of the parapet opposite is a plaque – '*Crue Janvier 1910*' – indicating the level of Paris's worst flood, when half the city could move only by boat.

At no 5 is the Hôtel de Marigny, built in 1640. No 7, built two years later, has been the seat of the Syndicat des Boulangers (bakers' union) since 1843. Do go in: the entrance is decorated with plates from Diderot's *Encyclopédie* showing various bakers' tasks. At no 9 lived Honoré Daumier (1808–1879), the great caricaturist; like nos 11, 13 and 15, this house belonged to the Lambert family.

The Hôtel de Lauzun at no 17 is probably the most ravishing *hôtel* of the period. Built by Le Vau in 1656–7 for a rich café-owner, it passed into the hands of the Comte de Lauzun (1633–1722) in the 1680s. It was sold and resold before becoming, in the late 19th century, the property of a collector and bibliophile who restored the house completely while hosting tenants such as Charles Baudelaire (1821–1867) and Théophile Gautier (1811–1872). The wrought-iron balcony is remarkable, as are the gutters decorated with dolphins – the gilding was added at the turn of this century. You can visit the interior at weekends: the painted panels and ceilings are superb, and there are pieces of furniture and *objets* from the 17th, 18th and 19th centuries.

Continue and cross Rue des Deux-Ponts with, on your right, one of the oldest bridges of Paris (built 1618–30), Pont Marie. The entrepreneur Christophe Marie built it at his own expense in exchange for some land on the island. Marie was responsible also for what became a Parisian institution, the *bateau-lavoir* ('washing-boat'), where people would come and do their laundry – hot water was provided, while rinsing was in Seine water; the one moored at the Île St-Louis was destroyed in 1942. As you pass the bridge you can see the roofs of the Hôtel de Ville to the right.

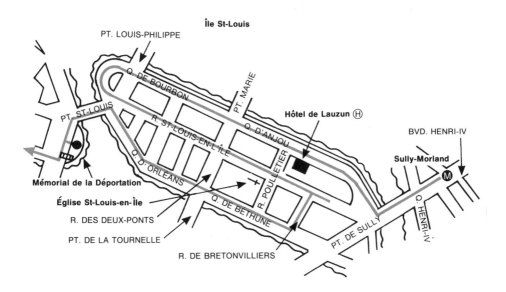

A Baroque church

The *quai* now changes name, becoming Quai de Bourbon. Built 1614–46, it owes its name to the French royal family of Bourbon. At no 1 is a very old café, Au Franc Pinot. No 11 was built for Philippe de Champaigne (1602–1674), valet to Marie de' Medici and royal painter – his portrait of Cardinal Richelieu (1585–1642), now at the National Gallery, London, is a masterpiece of French Baroque art. The Hôtel Le Charron at nos 13–15, built in the 1640s, boasts fine tall windows, a turret, an unusual door (with mascaron) and an especially lovely courtyard. The monumental Hôtel de Jassaud at no 19 dates from 1650; the pediments of its ornate façade are decorated with sculpted garlands, and the balcony is also fine. The sculptor Camille Claudel (1864–1943) had her *atelier* here for many years (1899–1913), and on the plaque is a quotation from one of her letters to her lover, Auguste Rodin (1840–1917): '*Il y a toujours quelquechose d'absent qui me tourmente*' – which is especially poignant because the last 30 years or so of her life were spent in madness.

Cross the end of Rue Le Regrattier and continue along the river. There is a stunning door at no 29, whose windows are decorated with sculpted garlands. Pass Pont Louis-Philippe, built 1860–62, in the days of Napoleon III. There is a pleasant view from here over the two sides of the city: to your left is the Left Bank, with Église St-Étienne-du-Mont (see p50) in the distance, while on the right is the Right Bank, with Église St-Gervais (see p74) not far away.

Carry on to the tip of the island, a peaceful place with a great view over the Île de la Cité. It was here that Julio Cortazar (1914–1984) set his short story 'The Son of the Virgin' (1963), which inspired that seminal film of the 1960s *Blow-Up* (1966). Behind you as you look out over the river are three fine *hôtels* (nos 45, 47, 49 Quai de Bourbon) built by and for the Le Vau family; at no 45 lived Princess Bibesco (d1945) – a writer and a great friend of Marcel Proust (1871–1922) – and later André Breton (1896–1966), the theoretician of Surrealism, who wrote *Les Champs Magnétiques* (1921) here.

Carry on around the tip until you reach the Brasserie de St Louis en l'Île (excellent beer and food); to your right are Pont St-Louis and a splendid perspective over the Panthéon and Left Bank. Cross the road to Rue St-Louis-en-l'Île, which splits the island in half lengthwise. Very straight, and a shopping street since its inception, this has changed in recent years: although there are still plenty of old houses and shops of interest, many art galleries have appeared, sometimes showing interesting work. At no 51 is the Hôtel Chenizot, a 17th-century *hôtel* transformed in the 1720s by a tax collector, Jean François de Chenizot; its post-Baroque façade is most extraordinary, with a mascaron, puttis, rocaille, superb ornamented door, wrought-iron balcony and ornate pediment.

Keep on, passing Rue Budé on your right, until you cross Rue des Deux-Ponts; this street dates from 1614, but was enlarged in 1913, with the loss of many of the original houses. At no 31 Rue St-Louis-en-l'Île is the wonderful ice-cream and sorbet maker Berthillon (long queues).

At no 21 is Église St-Louis-en-l'Île. Based on plans by Le Vau, the church took 62 years to build (1664–1726). It is a typical village *église*, built on the street with no room for display, and a contrast to the overt splendour of other contemporary and later Parisian churches. Walk in: there is no front door as such (it just never got built), so you use a side entrance. In spite of the squeezed-in appearance, this is a light and gracious building, a fine example of French religious Baroque, with a semicircular vault resting on Corinthian pilasters, although most of the murals are later, dating from the 19th-century renovation.

On leaving the church, carry on along Rue St-Louis-en-l'Île and cross Rue Poulletier, built on the site of the medieval canal that separated the two islets. When you reach no 9, go under the arch into Rue de Bretonvilliers, but not before you take a look at the superb entrance of the Hôtel Lambert at no 2, with its remarkable door and superb courtyard; now owned by the Rothschild family, the *hôtel* is not visitable. Nos 5, 7 and 9 are the remains of the outbuildings of the Hôtel Bretonvilliers, demolished in the 19th century.

A gipsy legend
Walk down the small Rue de Bretonvilliers and turn right into Quai de Béthune, created 1614–48. It was Le Vau's idea to adorn the *hôtels* on this side of the island with wrought-iron balconies, and almost all the houses on the *quai* boast them, with that at no 22 being especially fine. Except for no 24, which is a 1930s reconstruction, the houses date from the 1640s. At no 16 lived Louis de Vignert du Plessis (1696–1788), Duc de Richelieu, one of the great marshals of 18th-century France; he spent a lot of time in the Bastille because of his unfortunate habit of taking the Regent's mistresses as lovers. Charles Baudelaire (1821–1867) lived for a while at no 22 and Marie Curie (1867–1934) for 22 years (1912–34) at no 36.

Pass Pont de la Tournelle, enlarged in the 19th century but originally built, at the same time as the rest of the island, over the site of a bridge that dated from 1369. The statue is of St Geneviève, the patron saint of Paris. Cross Rue des Deux-Ponts into Quai d'Orléans, where there are more old houses, including the 18th-century Hôtel Rolland at nos 18–20. The *quai* now bends a little to the right; just after the curve you find the best view over the apse of Notre-Dame and can also see Tour St-Jacques. Soon you reach Pont St-Louis again; opposite the Brasserie de St Louis and the bridge you have another chance to buy a Berthillon ice-cream.

Leave the island by Pont St-Louis (formerly Pont Rouge). An interesting legend attaches to the bridge. In the 17th century the city authorities tortured a gipsy woman for some crime apparently committed nearby. Her grief-stricken mother put a curse on the bridge, so that it would periodically collapse. And collapse it has, at least seven times. The present single-span bridge dates from 1970.

Crypte de la Déportation
On the far side of Pont St-Louis you enter the Île de la Cité, a stark contrast with what you have just left. At the end of the bridge, turn left into a small garden, where two lateral flights of steps take you down to a sunken courtyard leading to a crypt. This is a discreet, sober and moving monument built in 1961 by Georges Pingusson (1894–1978) to the memory of the 200,000 French people sent to Nazi camps. It is in the shape of a large hexagon with, in one apex, a long gallery lit up by thousands of small glass batons (one for each prisoner); on the walls are quotations from Robert Desnos (1900–1945), Louis Aragon (1897–1982), Jean-Paul Sartre (1905–1980) and others.

Notre-Dame de Paris
Leave the memorial and enter Square Jean-XXIII, which borders the apse and the south wall of Notre-Dame Cathedral; this is a good spot to admire the light flying buttresses and also to smile at the gargoyles. Notre-Dame is vast: 130m (142yd) long and 48m (53yd) wide. Pass the south door, Porte St-Étienne (no entry), and continue until you reach the cathedral *parvis*, now, thanks to Georges Haussmann (1809–1891), six times larger than the original; it was entirely relaid in the 1970s to make way for an underground carpark. The architectural genius responsible for the cathedral is unknown.

Like many other Christian monuments, it was built on an earlier religious site – in this instance, that of a Roman temple. Without doubt one of the most glorious Christian edifices, it marks the transition from Romanesque to Gothic, though the latter prevails. The main body of the church took remarkably little time to complete, just under 90 years (1163–1250); the then bishop of Paris, Maurice de Sully (1128–1196), was the man responsible for this amazing undertaking. The buttresses, the transept doors, some of the interior decoration and other features were added until 1330. Like many buildings in Paris, Notre-Dame was severely altered during the 17th and 18th centuries (e.g., the spire and the rood-screen were destroyed). The Revolution continued the disfigurement, and it was not until Victor Hugo (1802–1885) wrote his famous *Notre-Dame de Paris* (1831) that the authorities reacted, the brilliant restorer/architect Joseph Duc (1802–1879) being appointed to return the cathedral to its former glory. He got rid of the post-medieval additions and restored what had been destroyed or lost.

Nearly 12 million people visit the cathedral annually, so it is worth going early in the day to avoid the crowds. The building has recently been completely cleaned up and restored to its medieval glory. As a result all the sculptures of the western façade are now perfectly identifiable. As you face the cathedral, the left portal (1210) is that of the Virgin, the large central one is that of the Last Judgement (mostly restored by Duc), and the right portal is that of Ste Anne. Inside, the vastness will awe you. The three stained-glass rose windows are simply magnificent, as is the treasure, in the sacristy in the choir to the right. For a serious tour of the interior I strongly recommend that you hire a walking tape at the entrance. From the towers there is a remarkable view over Paris (but you have to climb more than 350 steps!), and there you can also see the bells, one of which weighs over 13 tonnes.

On leaving the cathedral, cross the *parvis* to the Hôtel Dieu on the right. Founded in the 7th century, this was the first hospital in Paris. Haussmann had the existing building razed; the current one, erected in the 1870s, was designed by the architect Arthur Diet (1829–1880). If you walk in through the glass doors and foyer you will find yourself in the slightly bizarre-looking neo-Florentine quadrangle. There is rarely anyone here, and it is a good place to rest after the cathedral crowds.

The medieval city
Leave the hospital and retrace your steps towards Notre-Dame; cross Rue d'Arcole into Rue du Cloître-Notre-Dame, to the left of the cathedral. You are now entering the oldest part of the *île*. The cathedral close occupied the entire space east of Rue d'Arcole and was really a city within the city, with three more churches, the cathedral school and the celebrated choir school, founded 1455. There are good views along Rue du Cloître over the northern wall of the cathedral

Take the first left, Rue Massillon, which still has a few old houses (the even numbers). At no 8 is the fine Hôtel Roger-de-Gaillon, built in the 18th century and still housing the choir school. Turn right into Rue Chanoinesse, once the principal artery of the close. On the corner stood the house where Joachim du Bellay (1522–1560), the Renaissance poet, died. Almost facing you at no 12 is a fine 17th-century *hôtel* with a wrought-iron balcony and a studded door.

Turn left almost immediately into Rue des Chantres and left again into 14th-century Rue des Ursins, where there are many ancient houses. Jean Racine (1639-1699) lived at no 7 and St Bernard of Clairvaux (1090–1153), who reformed the Cistercians, preached

Plate 1: *One of the distinctive Paris métro entrances designed by Hector Guimard (see the Passy and Auteuil walk, page 159).*

Plate 2: The clock tower of the Conciergerie (see the Îles St-Louis and de la Cité walk, page 25).

Plate 3: Notre-Dame seen from across the Seine (see the Îles St-Louis and de la Cité walk, page 23).

Plate 4: View from Pont des Arts to Pont Neuf and the Île de la Cité beyond (see the Îles St-Louis and de la Cité walk, page 27).

Plate 5: *The elegant Place des Vosges in the heart of the Marais district (see the Le Marais walk, page 34).*

Plate 6: *At the sign of the 'Nègre Joyeux' in the Place de la Contrescarpe (see the Arènes, Mouffetard and the Jardin des Plantes walk, page 53).*

Plate 7: *Early morning activity in the bustling Rue Mouffetard market (see the Arènes, Mouffetard and the Jardin des Plantes walk, page 56).*

Plate 8: *The Palais du Luxembourg (see the St-Michel, Luxembourg, Val-de-Grâce and Gobelins walk, page 61).*

Plate 9: *The splendid Fontaine de l'Observatoire at the junction of the Jardins de l'Observatoire and the Boulevard St-Michel (see the St-Michel, Luxembourg, Val-de-Grâce and Gobelins walk, page 62).*

in a little chapel in the courtyard of no 9 (the remains are not on public view). Continue along Rue des Ursins – notice how it is lower than the *quai* on your right – until you reach its intersection with Rue de la Colombe, so-named since the 13th century. Although this street still has a few old houses, it was widened in the 19th century; an inscription at no 6 indicates the limit of the old Roman city wall. Turn right along the Rue de la Colombe until you reach Quai aux Fleurs, which you take to the left.

La Conciergerie

Pass Pont d'Arcole (the *quai* becomes Quai de la Corse) and continue with the back of the Hôtel Dieu to your left and views over the Hôtel de Ville, the Châtelet, etc., to your right. Pass Rue de la Cité and Pont Notre-Dame. On your left is the charming Marché aux Fleurs. The Tribunal de Commerce (Industrial Court) follows on from the marché. Cross Boulevard du Palais, with Pont au Change on the right. That enormous building on your left is the Palais de Justice (law courts), built on the site of the palace of the Capetian kings.

The *palais* is a vast edifice which goes from one side of the *île* to the other. Almost certainly Gaulish chieftains and Roman governors had a palace here, and we know that successive Merovingian and Carolingian kings had one for when they were in Paris. The big change came in the 10th century, when the Capetian dynasty decided to have a new palace. It took a long time to erect, and Louis IX greatly embellished it, notably adding the Sainte Chapelle. It was enlarged even more the following century under Philippe IV; the superb Salle des Gens-d'Armes (see below) dates from this period. When the kings left the palace for the Louvre in the mid-14th century it became the seat of Parliament. Fires in 1618, 1776 and 1871 (the latter set off during the Commune) damaged the *palais*, and today we see an amalgam of styles, with Joseph Duc (1802–1879) being responsible for about three-quarters of the 19th-century reconstruction.

Keep straight ahead along the northern wall of the *palais* on Quai de l'Horloge, built 1580–1611; before then the river, twice as wide as today, came right up to the wall. The towers survive from the original 14th-century Capetian castle, but most of the rest of the façade is the work of Joseph Duc.

Before you reach the first tower (Tour de César) you will find the entrance to the Conciergerie, the oldest relic of the Capetian palace. The Concierge was a high-ranking nobleman who enforced the law; he also had the right to tax all the shops on the ground floor of the *palais*. When part of the building became a prison he became entitled to rent from the prisoners' cells and for the loan of furniture. The superb Salle des Gens-d'Armes (1301–15), reckoned to be one of the finest examples of medieval architecture of its type, is the first room you go into. It is very large – nearly 70m x 27.5m (230ft x 90ft) – and comprises four ribbed vaults separated by three lines of columns and four enormous chimneys; it underlay the Grande Salle, destroyed in 1618 but rebuilt in the 19th century as the Salle des Pas-Perdus of the Palais de Justice (see below). From the left-hand corner a spiral stairway leads to another impressive room, the kitchen, which has four vast chimneys, one in each corner.

Come back down the stairway and enter the prison, well known for the famous captives it held during the Revolution: here Marie Antoinette (1755–1793), Louis Antoine de Saint-Just (1767–1794), André Chénier (1762–1794) and many others were incarcerated before going to the guillotine. The Conciergerie now features reconstructed rooms, many with wax figures, including Marie Antoinette's cell.

On leaving the Conciergerie, go left along Quai de l'Horloge for a closer look at the medieval towers, then come back to Boulevard du Palais and turn right. On the corner of the building is the celebrated 13th-century clock tower, featuring the city's first public clock (1371).

The Sainte Chapelle

Continue down the boulevard and pass the Cour du Mai, bordered with grand wrought-iron railings and gates which date from Louis XVI's days, as do the façade and the monumental stairs. Keep going until you see a signpost for the entrance to the Sainte Chapelle, a little further along and to the right. It seems odd that the most glorious and refined example of Gothic art in all France should be hidden away like this, its outside walls barely visible.

Nothing can quite prepare you for the shock of this incredible double-floored chapel. It was built in only two years (1246–8), probably by Pierre de Montreuil (d1267), fresh from the Abbaye St-Germain-des-Prés (see p66): Louis IX required a monument substantial enough to house the important relics (the crown of thorns, pieces of the Cross, and other relics – those that escaped the destruction of the Revolution are now at Notre-Dame) he had obtained from the French Emperor of Constantinople, who was short of money. The chapel, partly burnt in 1630, was rebuilt over the next 100 years and completely restored by Viollet-Le-Duc and others in the 19th century.

The lower chapel, with the stone painted in red and blue and fleur-de-lys (heavily restored in the last century) and tombstones on the floor, was for the palace servants; the upper chapel was for the king and his entourage. Prepare for a shock as you arrive in the upper chapel after climbing the small dark steps. This is truly a miracle of light, grace and balance: it is glass and glass and glass, restored in the last century from existing medieval fragments. The pillars supporting the vault seem invisible (in fact, the whole edifice is supported by the outside buttresses). What gives the chapel its remarkable airiness and glow are 15 stained-glass windows (plus the rose window at the back), partly original (nearly half) and showing over 1100 scenes from the Old and New Testaments.

There are concerts in the chapel in summer.

The Palais de Justice

Leave the chapel and retrace your steps into the Palais de Justice; it is a public place, and you are welcome to wander. Although it is obviously not as lively as when shops and merchants of all sorts were there, there is still plenty to see. Take a left into the Cour du Mai and climb the steps into the Galerie Marchande, now just a glorified foyer. Go right and then down a few steps to the Salle des Pas-Perdus, built by Joseph Duc and Pierre Daumet (1826–1911) in the style of an earlier 17th-century reconstruction that replaced the medieval Grande Salle, burnt in the 1618 fire. This huge room leads to various law courts. The *1ère chambre civile* (civil court) – to your left and up a few steps – was likewise restored in the last century, but is an exact replica of the 1502 Chambre Dorée where the Revolutionary Tribunal sat during the Terror.

Leaving the Salle des Pas-Perdus, turn right into the Galerie des Prisonniers. Halfway down on your right is the Galerie St-Louis, redone by Duc; the décor is extraordinary, as is that of the Criminal Chamber on the left. Returning to the Galerie des Prisonniers, you will see, almost straight ahead, the Galerie Duc. At the end turn left again into the Galerie de la Sainte-Chapelle, which borders the northern wall of the chapel – all these galleries open onto various chambers, law courts and lawyers' rooms. Finally, go down the steps into the Cour du Mai and exit onto Boulevard du Palais.

The river and the Vert Galant

Turn right and walk down the boulevard. When you reach Pont St-Michel (1857) – there is a good view over Place St-Michel and the Fontaine St-Michel – take the narrow flight of steps from Quai des Orfèvres down to the riverbank and keep on westward until you go under Pont Neuf and into Square du Vert-Galant (Henri IV's nickname, the 'sprightly gallant'). This garden, with its ancient willow trees, is almost exactly at the original level of the island. At the island's tip is a fine view over the west of the city, with Pont des Arts in the foreground, the immense Louvre to the right, the Institut de France to the left and, in the far distance, the glass roofs of the Grand Palais.

Walk around to the other side, pass the Vedettes du Pont-Neuf and take the central steps up onto Pont Neuf, Paris's oldest surviving bridge (see p31). Cross Place du Pont-Neuf; on the *place* is the Taverne Henri-IV, one of the best winebars in Paris, with delicious, simple food. Opposite is the celebrated statue of Henri IV, which dates from the Restoration, Louis XVIII deciding in 1818 to replace an original destroyed during the Revolution. The horse part of the earlier statue was a present from Cosimo I de' Medici (1519–1574) to Marie de' Medici (1573–1642); in 1635 Louis XIII decided to seat his father on it. The 19th-century caster, an ardent imperialist, secreted a statuette of Napoleon in the king's right arm and Bonapartist pamphlets in the horse's belly!

Now go through Rue Henri-Robert into the attractive Place Dauphine, created by Henri IV and named after his son, the future Louis XIII. It is a peaceful, magical little *place* bordered by 17th-century *hôtels*, many with later alterations, especially at the roofline. It used to be enclosed on all three sides of the triangle, but one, on Rue de Harlay, was taken down in 1874 to make way for the western end of the Palais de Justice. André Breton set an important scene in *Nadja* (1928) at the Hôtel Henri-IV and at the house facing it.

Cross to the *palais* and turn left into Rue de Harlay, then left again into Quai de l'Horloge, onto which back the *hôtels* of the *place*. Keep going until you reach Pont Neuf, then cross the river with the large Art-Nouveau department store, La Samaritaine, facing you. At the end of the bridge are your métro station, Pont-Neuf, and buses.

You can connect from here to the next walk, a delightful complement to what you have just done.

The Quais

A pleasant meandering walk in the heart of the city, one that will have you browsing through the famous *bouquinistes* stalls and gazing at some splendid views.

Start and finish: **Métro Pont-Neuf; buses 58, 67, 69, 72, 75.**
Length: **4km (2½ miles).**
Time: **1½ hr.**
Refreshments: **Many cafés on the way, especially at Place du Châtelet and at Place St-Michel; restaurants on Quai de l'Hôtel de Ville and Quai de la Tournelle, and an excellent winebar (Taverne Henri-IV) on Place du Pont-Neuf at the end of the walk. From the cafeteria at the top of the Samaritaine store you can enjoy a great view over Paris (now closed for renovation – check status before visiting).**
Which day: **Any day; late morning/afternoon is best, as otherwise many of the shops and *bouquinistes* are closed.**
To visit:
• **Musée de l'Assistance Publique: daily (not Monday, Tuesday) 10.00–17.00.**

La Samaritaine
Leave Pont-Neuf métro and walk down to Quai du Louvre. As you reach it, Pont Neuf is on your right and the Samaritaine, one of the largest department stores in Paris and a monument to Art Nouveau and Art Deco, is on your left. The Samaritaine was set up by Ernest Cognacq (1839–1928) and was so successful that he managed not only to expand the store considerably but also to amass a superb art collection, now the basis of the delightful Cognacq-Jay Museum (see p37). The store was improved and enlarged by Frantz Jourdain (1847–1935) and by Henri Sauvage (1839-1928), at the turn of the century and in the 1920s respectively; the steel riveted frame, enhanced by ceramics panels, was particularly innovative. The most interesting facade is the one on Rue du Pont-Neuf, at a right angle from the *quai*. (Closed for intense refurbishment, check status.)

Tanners and money-changers
Cross Rue du Pont-Neuf into the 14th-century Quai de la Mégisserie. All the buildings date from the 19th century. The shops echo another Paris: pet shops, stuffed animals, flowers, hunting and fishing . . . The *mégissiers* (leather-dressers) to which the *quai* owes its name worked here before the expansion of the city drove them further south on the Bièvre River (see pl56). There is a fine view to the Ile de la Cité and the towers of the 14th-century Capetian palace (now part of the Palais de Justice).

Walk along the *quai*, passing in front of the Théâtre du Châtelet, until you reach Place du Châtelet. On the far side of the *place* is the Théâtre de la Ville. The *place* was created in Napoleon's reign on the site of a medieval *châhelet* (fortress) that had become an

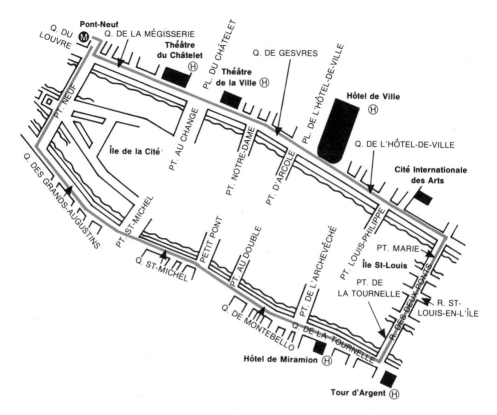

insalubrious prison and morgue; it was greatly enlarged later by Georges Haussmann (1809–1891). The fountain dates from the First Empire and the two theatres from the 1860s. The *place* has typical cafés with terraces.

On your right is Pont au Change, a Haussmann creation to replace a fine 17th century bridge by Jean Androuet du Cerceau (1585-1649), which itself replaced a wooden medieval bridge. The name Pont au Change came into use because money-changers used to have their shops on the bridge.

Keep on along what is now Quai de Gesvres, established in the 17th century and enlarged in 1875. Tanners and butchers used to work here. The roofs of the Hôtel Dieu hospital on the Île de la Cité are on your right.

Pass the 19th-century Pont Notre-Dame – which replaced an apparently superb Renaissance bridge built in 1500 by Fra Giaconda de Verona – with houses and shops on either side. Pass Pont d'Arcole (erected 1858) and continue along the *quai to* the Hôtel de Ville, where the mayor presides over the capital's destiny. The building dates from the late 19th century, replacing the original burnt during the Commune. The *place* – completely renovated in 1982 on the centenary of the completion of the building – is on the site of a medieval square, the (much smaller) Place de la Grève (bank), where at one time all Parisian executions were carried out.

Île St-Louis

Continue along Quai de l'Hôtel-de-Ville, which was built in 1673–5 and enlarged in the 19th century. The lovely 17th-century *hôtels* of the Île St-Louis (see p20) are beginning to appear behind the Île de la Cité. The block after the Hôtel de Ville has pleasant cafés and restaurants and a couple of interesting curio shops; the church behind is Église St-Gervais (see p74). Pass Pont Louis-Philippe (erected 1862) and you will see on your left, beyond a small garden, the Cité Internationale des Arts, an artists' residence, which was built in the 1960s. Next comes the fine Hôtel d'Aumont (set back behind a garden *à la française*), begun by Louis Le Vau (1612–1670) and finished by François Mansart (1596–1666).

Now cross the river by Pont Marie to the Île St-Louis; there is a glorious view over one of the most remarkable spots in Paris, a piece of the 17th century almost completely preserved. (For a full discussion of the Île St-Louis see p19.) Go across Quai de Bourbon and into Rue des Deux-Ponts; go down this and cross the river by Pont de la Tournelle. The bridge and Quai de la Tournelle, at its Left-Bank end, take their name from a tower that was part of the Philippe-Auguste wall. On the bridge is a statue (1928) by Paul Landowski (1875–1961) of St Geneviève, patron saint of Paris.

You are now on the Left Bank, or Rive Gauche. The prerogative of the university and of various religious institutions since the 12th century, the Left Bank was left unscathed by the great urban development of the city in the Middle Ages and afterwards on the reclaimed marshes of the Right Bank. The equation of the term *rive gauche* with intellectualism persists to this day. (See p45 for more on the Left Bank and the early days of the university.)

At the end of Pont de la Tournelle is the celebrated Restaurant de la Tour-d'Argent, said to date back to 1582. On reaching the *quai*, turn right; there is a spectacular view over the back and the south wall of Notre-Dame. Quite a few of the *bouquinistes* nearby have English paperbacks. On the inland side of the *quai* are some fine *hôtels*. The 13th-century Collège des Bernardins (see p45) once occupied a vast tract of land here.

Note that, instead of staying up on the *quai*, you can walk along the bank of the river, almost at water-level.

Dire health

There is a fine house at no 29/27, built in the 17th century by Leduc, and another of the same period at no 37, the Hôtel Rolland. No 47, on your left some way along the *quai*, is now the Musée de l'Assistance-Publique, occupying the Hôtel de Miramion, built in 1637, probably by Le Vau, and later completely renovated to house the museum. The building itself is fascinating and the collections – on the development of health care and the history of Paris – are equally so. Noteworthy are a reconstruction of a 19th-century hospital room, a superb illuminated antiphon of 1700, engravings of Paris and many portraits, plus medical instruments, china, etc. At no 55 is the Hôtel de Nesmond, built 1636, which houses the offices of *La Demeure Historique*.

Pass Pont de l'Archevêché, built 1826–8; from here the perspective on the cathedral is slightly different but no less superb.

Continue on Quai de Montebello until you reach Pont au Double, built in 1882 to replace a bridge privately constructed in 1631 by the Hôtel Dieu hospital. Even split in two, with buildings on the island and on the Left Bank, the hospital was finding itself suffering such overcrowding that the administration decided to build a bridge linking the two parts. No space was wasted: the bridge itself was covered with hospital rooms, and, hygiene not being a priority, all the hospital waste was conveniently dropped into the river. In order to finance the bridge, the hospital had patients pay twice – *au double* – once to get in, and again to get out.

On the other side of the *quai* is the recently created Square Viviani, with a view of one of Paris's oldest churches, St-Julien-le-Pauvre (see p83). Just at the end of the garden is Shakespeare & Co., the best Anglo-American bookshop in Paris, a necessary stop for all young Americans in the city. The original Shakespeare & Co, run by Sylvia Beach (1887–1962), was not here but in Rue de l'Odéon (see p60).

Pass Petit Pont, the shortest bridge in Paris (40m [130ft]). The narrowness of the channel here has made this a natural crossing-place since Roman times; the present bridge dates from 1852. Continue to Quai St-Michel, built in the early 19th century. To your left Rue du Chat-qui-Pêche, the narrowest street in Paris (2.5m [8ft]), leads to Rue de la Huchette (see p84), but keep to the *quai*, reaching Place St-Michel, also developed in the 19th century and now full of cafés and book- and record-stores. The famous Fontaine St-Michel, erected in 1856–60 by Gabriel Davioud (1823–1881), is a traditional meeting-place.

Pass Pont St-Michel, built in Haussmann's days on the site of an ancient bridge. On your right you can see the Palais de Justice and the spire of the Sainte Chapelle on the Île de la Cité.

Augustinian memories
Keep following the *quai*, now Quai des Grands-Augustins, the first *quai* built in Paris (1313; it was greatly enlarged under Napoleon). The name comes from the monastery established over a wide area of the city along the river since the 14th century. The Augustinians, one of the major medieval orders, were reformed by Pope Pius V (1504–1572) in the 16th century, and a century later you could find four different Augustinian monasteries in Paris: the Augustins Déchaussés, Petits and Grands, plus the Couvent des Grands-Augustins, which was destroyed during the Revolution. At no 51 is the Restaurant Lapérouse: it was one of the great restaurants of the 19th century but today the décor is more interesting than the cuisine. At no 55 was the *couvent*'s main entrance. Many of the houses date from the 18th and early 19th centuries. Note the artists' studios on the top floors of some of them. Continue until you reach Pont Neuf.

Pont Neuf ('new bridge') is the oldest extant bridge in Paris. Henri III had it built to facilitate communication between the Louvre and the Abbaye St-Germain-des-Prés on the Left Bank (despite Henri's devoutness, it was a monk, Jacques Clément [1564–1589], who assassinated him). Henri IV saw it through and christened it in 1605. Pont Neuf was the first bridge built unencumbered by houses: for the first time the Parisians could see the river and the *hôtels* and palaces bordering it. From the start it enjoyed tremendous success, and was a place where acrobats, tumblers, singers and merchants of all sorts plied their trades.

Cross the bridge, passing Square du Vert-Galant (see p27) on the Île de la Cité, and so reach Pont-Neuf métro station. Although this walk ends here, you can easily connect it with the Louvre and Champs-Élysées walk (see p91): turn left into Quai du Louvre (cross at the earliest opportunity) and then take second right into Rue de l'Amiral-de-Coligny, which will lead you to Place du Louvre.

Le Marais

Essentially a historical walk in one of the oldest and best preserved areas of Paris, this takes you past many remarkable 16th- and 17th-century *hôtels, places* and museums. You will discover narrow, beautiful streets, steeped in the past, as well as trendy shops and bars.

Developed on the reclaimed marshes of the Right Bank from the 13th century by the Church and by members of the aristocracy, this area really took off when, in 1605, Henri IV decided to create the Place Royale (now Place des Vosges). Fine *hôtels* and churches sprang up all over, and the area became a 'place to be', remaining so until the Revolution. Slowly the Marais started to change: *couvents* and the like were demolished, the smart *hôtels* were run down or given over to trade, and carriages disappeared completely; it became a poorish working quarter. Over the past two decades things have been changing again. Most of the *hôtels* have been renovated to become museums, city offices or smart flats; the poorer inhabitants are having to leave and the middle classes are moving in. The Marais is once again a 'place to be'.

Start: **Métro Pont-Marie; bus 67.**
Finish: **Métro St-Paul; buses 69, 76, 96.**
Length: **3.5km (5½ miles).**
Time: **2hr.**
Refreshments: **There are many cafés and restaurants in the Marais. The ones on Place des Vosges, under the arcades, are picturesque but not cheap. Place du Marché-Ste-Catherine has a couple of good restaurants. There are occasional tearooms, sometimes coupled with a bookshop or an art gallery, in Rue du Parc-Royal, Rue des Rosiers and elsewhere.**
Which day: **Wednesday to Sunday if you want to maximize museum time (most museums are free on Sundays); Sunday afternoons are very busy, with many shops staying open all day and artists coming to exhibit their wares on the railings of Place des Vosges, but Sunday mornings are quiet. Many of the fine houses are occupied by offices, etc., and so are shut at weekends.**
To visit:
- **Maison Victor Hugo: daily (not Monday) 10.00–17.40.**
- **Hôtel Carnavalet: daily (not Monday) 10.00–17.40.**
- **Musée Picasso: daily (not Tuesday) 9.45–17.15.**
- **Musée Cognacq-Jay: daily (not Monday) 10.00–17.40.**
- **Musée de la Chasse: daily (not Tuesday) 10.00–12.30 and 13.30–17.30.**
- **Musée de l'Histoire-de-France: daily (not Tuesday) 13.30–17.45.**

Queen Margot
Leave the métro and walk along Quai de l'Hôtel-de-Ville, with the Seine on your right and, on your left, the Cité Internationale des Arts, built in the 1960s for foreign artists, until you reach Rue des Nonnains-d'Hyères. Turn left into it, and then immediately

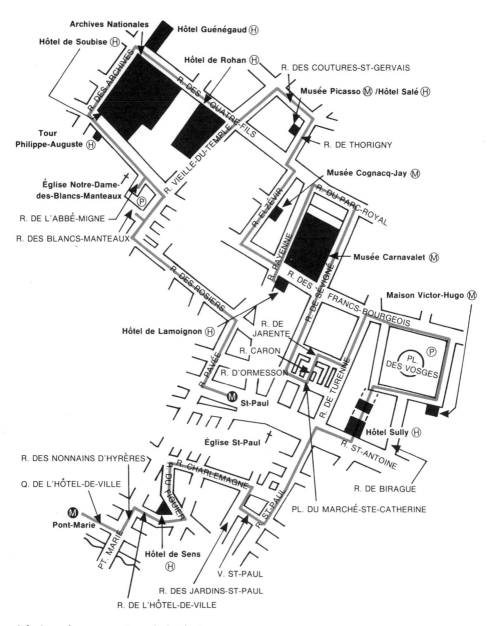

right into the narrow Rue de l'Hôtel-de-Ville. As you stand on the corner of the two streets, the elegant small *jardin à la française* of the Hôtel de Sens is on your right, and slightly further away, on the other side of Rue des Nonnains-d'Hyères (on the far side of a garden square where there are usually small children playing), is the fine late-17th-century Hôtel d'Aumont.

Go down Rue de l'Hôtel-de-Ville and, at the bottom, take a sharp left into Rue du Figuier, so-named for the fig-tree that used to flower outside the Hôtel de Sens until Queen Margot (Margaret de Valois; 1553–1615) had it uprooted in the early 17th century.

The Hôtel de Sens is on your left; walk into the lovely front yard. This is one of the oldest buildings in Paris and one of the three great Parisian medieval mansions (the others being the Hôtel de Cluny – see p48 – and Jacques Coeur's house – see p73). It is a rather odd but wonderful mixture of late-Gothic and Renaissance styles; note the Flamboyant Gothic porch and the weird-looking tower with its machicolated balcony.

Until 1622 Paris was only a bishopric. The archbishop resided in Sens but spent more time in Paris, and thus required a palace of consequence in the capital. The *hôtel* was built in 1475–1519 for Archbishop Tristan de Salazar; his successor, one Antoine du Prat, was so fat that the tables of the palace had to be cut specially so that he could sit down! The most celebrated occupant of the *hôtel* has been Queen Margot. The daughter of Henri II and Catherine de' Medici (1519–1589), and sister of François II, Charles IX and Henri III, she was forced in 1577 to marry the Protestant Henri de Navarre, later Henri IV, although she never actually lived with him. She was known for her ability to collect lovers, a talent she had discovered at age 11; by the time she moved into the Hôtel de Sens, in 1605, she was aged 54 and bald, but this did not diminish her appetites – she was in the habit of having the hair of her blonde pages cut for wigs. The *hôtel* now houses the Bibliothèque Fourney (Fine Arts Library of the City of Paris).

Outside the *hôtel*, carry on down Rue du Figuier until you reach Rue Charlemagne, named in 1844 for Charlemagne (742–814), Emperor of the Francs; on the far left, on the building on the corner of Rue de Fourcy, you can see a scissors-and-knife-grinder sign left over from the city's medieval past. Turn right into Rue Charlemagne and pass on your left Rue du Prévôt, one of Paris's narrowest streets. A little further on, after the Lycée Charlemagne, you come to the Fontaine Charlemagne, dating from Louis-Philippe's reign and showing dolphins supporting a basin with a cast-iron cherub.

Directly across from the fountain is Rue des Jardins-St-Paul, which you now take; it owes its name to the gardens that used to border the walls. Remains of the Philippe-Auguste wall are visible along quite a distance. Follow the sign into the courtyard of Village St-Paul, a rehabilitated group of buildings now housing art galleries, antiques and craft shops. Come out into Rue St-Paul, a lively street, full of galleries and diverse shops. Walk up the street, away from the river, until you reach the rather busy Rue St-Antoine, one of the main roads into the city in Roman times.

Sully and Place Royale
Cross the street at the traffic light on your right. A few metres along is the Hôtel de Sully, built 1624 by Jean Audouet du Cerceau (1585–1649) and bought 10 years later by Maximilien de Béthune (1560–1641), Marquis de Rosny, Duc de Sully, ex-minister to Henri IV. Go through the porch into the courtyard. The *hôtel*'s façade is flanked like that at Carnavalet (see below) with figures representing the seasons. Enter the *hôtel* by the central door; there is a fine ornamental stone staircase and it is worth gazing upwards at the carvings as you pass through the *hôtel* before walking across the garden to the exit door on the far right. You now find yourself in the magnificent Place des Vosges. (If the entrance to the Hôtel de Sully is shut, follow Rue St-Antoine a little further and take first left into the pretty Rue de Birague, which will lead you to the *place*.) Place des Vosges, built in the times of Henri IV and Louis XIII, was called Place Royale until 1800. In the

(1538–1619), the illegitimate daughter of Henri II and an Italian noblewoman, the *hôtel* is one of the oldest buildings in the Marais; it owes its name to Guillaume de Lamoignon (1617–1677), President of the Parliament, who lived there from 1658. From the courtyard you can see the leaning tower on the right and the Corinthian pilasters on the main building, the first example of the 'colossal' style later used in, for example, the Louvre. The *hôtel* now houses the historical library of the City of Paris. Walk in for a look at the stunning painted ceiling of the reading-room.

Leave the *hôtel* and turn left into Rue des Francs-Bourgeois. Stay on the left pavement and go into the Hôtel d'Albret (no 29bis), built in 1550 for the Constable Anne, Duc de Montmorency (1493–1567). Recently renovated, it now houses the Cultural Department of the City of Paris. In the courtyard is a contemporary sculpture by Bernard Pagès (b1940), commemorating the Revolution.

Cross the street and turn right, along Rue Elzévir. Halfway up, on your right, is the Cognacq-Jay Museum, housed in the Hôtel de Donon since January 1991. You must visit this: not only is the building exquisite, the 18th-century collection of paintings, furniture and *objets* is ravishing. It was assembled in the 19th and early 20th centuries by Ernest Cognacq (1839–1928) and his wife Marie-Louise Jay (1838–1925), the founders of the Samaritaine store (see p28). The tour need not take more than half an hour. Each room is exquisitely presented, and there are wonderful works by Jean Antoine Watteau (1684–1721), Fragonard, Jean Baptiste Chardin (1699–1779), Peter Paul Rubens (1577–1640), Jean Baptiste Greuze (1725–1805), Boucher and Maurice Quentin de Latour (1704–1788). A fine collection of boxes by important goldsmiths and silversmiths is in the upper gallery. The *hôtel* itself was built in the late 16th century for Mederic Le Donon, Councillor and Comptroller General of the King's Buildings and husband to Jeanne della Robbia, daughter of the sculptor Girolamo della Robbia (1488–1566).

Coming out of the *hôtel,* carry on up Rue Elzévir until you reach Place de Thorigny. Have a quick look in the Hôtel Libéral-Bruand on your left, built for himself in 1685 by the architect of the Invalides and now housing the Musée de la Serrure (lock museum). Then go straight up Rue de Thorigny until you find at no 5 the Hôtel Salé, built in the 17th century (1656–9) for one Pierre Aubert, a salt-tax collector – hence its name. Renovated in the 1980s, it now houses the Musée Picasso, containing not only a stunning collection (acquired by the state in lieu of death duties) of the works of Pablo Picasso (1881–1973) but also some of his private collection (the Donation Picasso) given to the state by his family and including works by Georges Braque (1882–1963), Henri Rousseau (1844–1910), Paul Cézanne (1839–1906) and others.

The Horses of Apollo
On leaving the museum, take a left into Rue des Coutures-St-Gervais and a left again into Rue Vieille-du-Temple. When you reach Rue des Quatre-Fils, cross over and take a few more steps up to no 87 Rue Vieille-du-Temple to look at the magnificent Horses of Apollo, crowning what were once the stable-doors of Hôtel de Rohan; together with the Hôtel de Soubise, the *hôtel is* now part of the Archives Nationales.

Go back into Rue des Quatre-Fils and stay on the left-hand pavement. At no 11 is an interesting example of contemporary architecture, designed by Stanislas Fiszer and others in 1988. Take a look into the reception hall: its hypermodernity contrasts strongly with the Hôtels de Soubise and de Rohan.

Cross Rue des Quatre-Fils again and follow the right-hand pavement alongside an enormous blank wall, the 19th-century back wall of the Archives warehouse. Soon, on your right, you come to an absolute gem: the Hôtel Guénégaud (entrance at no 60 Rue des Archives on the corner with Rue des Quatre-Fils), designed and built by Mansart in the second half of the 17th century, is one of the architectural perfections of the Marais. The stone staircase on the left is magnificent and the courtyard delightful. It now houses the Musée de la Chasse et de la Nature.

Go south down Rue des Archives. On your left at no 58 are the remains of the remarkable medieval gateway of the Hôtel de Clissons, built for Olivier de Clissons (1336–1407), a Constable of France and companion of Bertrand du Guesclin (c1320–1380), who led the French forces during the Hundred Years' War (1337–1453).

You are now walking along the wall of the Hôtel de Soubise. When you reach its end, turn left into Rue des Francs-Bourgeois and enter the *hôtel*'s majestic courtyard, from the extreme right-hand corner of which you can look onto the gardens of the Hôtel de Rohan (through the gates) and of the Hôtel de Soubise (through the glass doors).

The Hôtel de Soubise was built 1705–9 by Pierre Delamair (1675–1745) for Cardinal Armand de Rohan (1674–1749), son of the Duc de Soubise. Confiscated during the Revolution, it was donated by Napoleon in 1808 to house the Archives Nationales. As a result, the *hôtel* has been preserved, and its splendid decorated interior – by Germain Boffrand (1667–1754), Boucher and Jean Baptiste Van Loo (1684–1745) – has hardly changed at all. Also in the *hôtel* is the Musée de l'Histoire-de-France (Museum of French History), primarily of interest for the 18th-century apartments in which the museum is housed, although it also contains some remarkable items, including the only known contemporary portrait of Joan of Arc (c1412–1431), the diary of Louis XVI and the last known letter from Marie Antoinette (1755–1793).

Standing once more on Rue des Francs-Bourgeois and facing away from the Hôtel de Soubise, you can see on the other side of the street, at no 57, squeezed between two buildings and slightly set back, a red-brick medieval tower, Tour Philippe-Auguste, a piece of the Philippe-Auguste wall.

Rue des Rosiers
Cross the street and take a sharp right into the tiny Rue de l'Abbé-Migne, which leads you into Square des Blancs-Manteaux, so-called because of a 13th-century monastery whose friars wore white robes. On one side of this small garden is the wall of Église Notre-Dame-des-Blancs-Manteaux, built 1685. Leave the garden and turn right, right and right again into Rue des Blancs-Manteaux, where you can find some good cheap-and-cheerful restaurants, including the Gamin de Paris. Then return to Rue Vieille-du-Temple and go left into Rue des Rosiers. This used to be Paris's old Jewish quarter. Unfortunately the street is being brought up to date: fashionable shops have invaded the second half.

Walk on until you reach Rue Pavée, and turn right. Pass the synagogue (no entry), built by Hector Guimard (1867–1942) in 1913, and follow the street down to Rue St-Antoine; from the corner you can see on your right, in the far distance, Tour St-Jacques (see p74) and on your left, closer by, the white upper half of the Bastille Opéra (see p145).

To your left, on the other side of Rue St-Antoine, is the rather curious Église de St-Paul-et-St-Louis, built 1627–41 for the Jesuits and an interesting example of French Baroque architecture; its distinctive cupola is a Parisian landmark.

Métro St-Paul and buses 69 and 76 are almost outside the church.

République and Temple

This section of Paris developed outside the Philippe-Auguste wall but within Charles V's wall, on a side of the city dominated in medieval times by two important institutions: the monastery of St-Martin-des-Champs and the estate of the Knights Templar, who drained the land of the Marais and built themselves a magnificent palace. This walk is an historically rich one through the fringe of the Marais, down small lively streets with intriguing shops and crafts workshops. It starts with Haussmann and Louis XIV, and finishes with the Middle Ages and the Renaissance.

Start: **Métro République; buses 54, 56, 65, 75.**
Finish: **Métro Bastille; buses 20, 29, 69, 76, 86, 87, 91.**
Length: **3km (2 miles).**
Time: **1½–2hr.**
Refreshments: **Plenty of places along this walk; a large welcoming brasserie on Place de la République and smaller friendly cafés in almost every other street, with some especially agreeable ones near the Carré du Temple.**
Which day: **Weekdays are best, as many of the shops and crafts workshops are closed on Sunday; not Monday if you wish to visit the museum.**
To visit:
● **Musée National des Arts et Métiers: daily (not Monday) 10.00–18.00 (late opening Thursday until 21.30).**

The boulevards
Leave the métro by the Place de la République exit. This large square, known until the late 19th century as Place du Château-d'Eau – after a nearby reservoir – was established over one of Louis XIV's fortifications in 1856–65. The statue celebrating the virtues of the Republic was installed in the 1880s and is nearly 10m (33ft) tall. Place du Château-d'Eau was popular with night revellers, and reminders linger on in the large cafés and brasseries around it and in the nearby boulevards, especially the 'elevated' parts of Boulevard du Temple and Boulevard St-Martin. The northern side of the square is occupied by an hôtel and by an army barracks built in the 1850s on the site of a celebrated diorama created by Louis Daguerre (1789–1851), the pioneer of photography.

Leaving the square, walk westward along Boulevard St-Martin. While Place de la République is a characteristically Haussmannian creation, the boulevards belong to Louis XIV's reign. He declared that Paris no longer needed to be a military fortress and could be opened out, with the Charles V and Louis XIII walls being pulled down – although at the same time he prudently built a series of fortified towns in strategic places, with Sébastien de Vauban (1633–1707) as architect. The *cours* established on the sites of the walls were interspersed with a few defensive bastions and became a favourite place for Parisians. These large avenues, with trees on either side, inevitably attracted amusement halls,

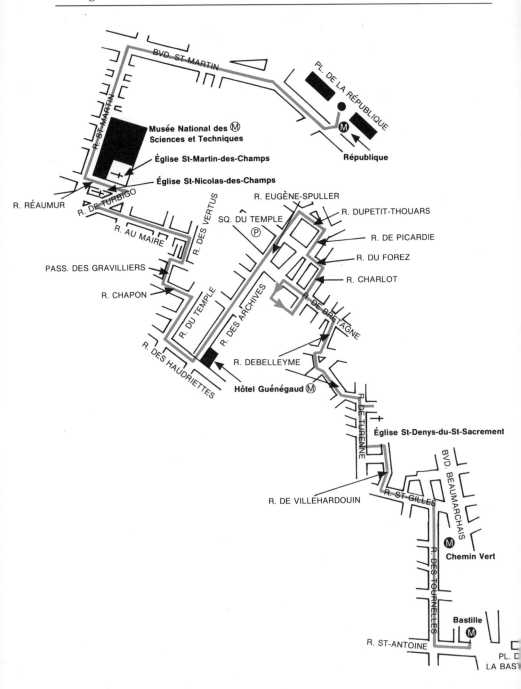

theatres and the like, until there was a sort of ring of entertainment around the city on the boulevards, a tradition that has carried on sporadically until the present.

At no 16 and 20 Boulevard St-Martin are two theatres set up in the 1870s: Théâtre de la Renaissance, run by Sarah Bernhardt (1844–1923) for nearly 10 years, and Théâtre de la Porte-St-Martin, where the famous *Cyrano de Bergerac* by Edmond Rostand (1868–1918) was premiered in 1897. The triumphal arch to Louis XIV was built in 1674 by François Blondel (1618–1686) on the site of an old medieval gateway.

The Conservatoire National des Arts et Métiers
Turn left and walk down the left-hand side of Rue St-Martin, the oldest street in Paris (with Rue St-Jacques), which led out of Lutèce to the north – it later became a Roman road. All the roads leading off Rue St-Martin are ancient and many contain fine houses. Pass Rue Meslay, which bordered Charles V's wall, Rue Notre-Dame-de-Nazareth, named after a convent, and Rue du Vertbois, developed in the 16th century. On this latter corner is the Fontaine du Vertbois, dating from 1712.

A few metres further on you reach the Conservatoire National des Arts et Métiers, on the old site of the medieval Benedictine priory of St-Martin-des-Champs. Set up in the 11th-12th centuries outside the Philippe-Auguste wall, the priory soon exerted an enormous influence on the life of the capital (indeed, of the nation), becoming as famous as St-Germain-des-Prés on the other side of the river. It was abolished in 1790, and nine years later was handed over to the recently created Conservatoire National des Arts et Métiers (National Conservatory of Arts and Crafts – in effect an engineering school). Two magnificent medieval buildings remain: the refectory (now the library) and the church (now part of the Musée des Sciences et Techniques within the Conservatoire complex).

Walk in through the large door, the Cour d'Honneur. The building facing you was part of a reconstruction of the abbey done by Jacques Antoine (1733–1801) in the 18th century and enlarged and modified in the 19th. Follow the 'Bibliothèque' sign to the right to reach the refectory. This is a glorious construction, built in the first part of the 13th century by Pierre de Montreuil (d1267), architect of the Sainte Chapelles of Île de la Cité and St-Germain-en-Laye. Measuring 42m x 11m (138ft x 36ft), it has two naves separated by seven light columns, a double-ribbed vault and ornate keystones.

Leave the Conservatoire, turn left into Rue St-Martin, and left again into Rue Réaumur, walking around the Conservatoire/museum until you reach its entrance on your left, by the apse of the 12th-century Église St-Martin-des-Champs. The museum has been exquisitely reorganized and is now a bustling, exciting place; this church is now one of its main halls. The museum's collection contains over 80,000 items (about 10% are on show) reflecting the development of science and technology from the 16th to the 20th centuries. Among the highlights are early-18th-century automata by Jacques de Vaucanson (1709–1782), the steam engine devised by James Watt (1736–1819), the calculating machine devised by Blaise Pascal (1623–1662), the famous pendulum originally erected in the Panthéon by Jean Bernard Léon Foucault (1819–1868) to demonstrate the Earth's rotation (it hangs from the vault in the church), the aeroplane used by Louis Blériot (1872–1936) for his historic flight (1909) across the English Channel, and the camera invented by the brothers Auguste (1862–1954) and Louis (1864–1948) Lumière.

The Temple
Leave the museum, cross Rue Réaumur, pass the métro station entrance, go right into

Rue de Turbigo and reach Église St-Nicolas-des-Champs a few steps further. The church was originally built in the 11th century for the farmers and servants of the priory. As the city rapidly expanded the church became too small, and it was rebuilt 1420–80 (the façade, the first seven vaulted bays and tower) and greatly enlarged 1560–1615; hence the late-Gothic and Renaissance styles throughout. The humanist Guillaume Budé (1467–1540) and the bestselling 18th-century authoress Madeleine de Scudéry (1608–1671) are buried here. The superb organ is by the Cliquot family.

You can either look around the church (entrance in Rue St-Martin) or cross Rue de Turbigo into the narrow 13th-century Rue au Maire, crossing Rue Beaubourg. The Rue au Maire contains a few old houses. Opposite, at no 3 in another ancient street, Rue Volta, is a half-timbered house supposed to be the oldest house in Paris: dated 1300 by the plaque, it is believed by some to be merely an 18th-century pastiche.

Turn right at the bottom of Rue au Maire into Rue des Vertus, ironically named because prostitutes used to operate there. Reach the 13th-century Rue des Gravilliers, now specializing in wholesale cheap jewellery, and cross it to go down Passage des Gravilliers. You emerge into Rue Chapon; turn left and reach Rue du Temple, into which you turn right. This long street, leading from the Seine to Place de la République, is a 19th-century amalgamation of four medieval streets; this section of it has mostly wholesale rag-trade shops. Pass Rue de Montmorency and the 13th-century Rue Michel-le-Comte. A little further on, in the fine 17th-century Hôtel de St-Aignan at no 71, is the newly installed Musée de l'Art-Juif, where you can see various religious objects, a Bible illustrated by Marc Chagall (1887–1985) and lithographs, drawings, etc., by Chagall, Chaïm Soutine (1893–1943), Max Liebermann (1847–1935) and others.

If you do not wish to go to the museum some 100m (110yd) away, turn left now into Rue des Haudriettes. If you do visit it, retrace your steps in Rue du Temple when you leave the museum and turn right into Rue des Archives. On the corner is the Fontaine des Haudriettes (1705) and facing you is the exquisite Hôtel Guénégaud, built by François Mansart (1598–1666) in the second half of the 17th century and now housing the Musée de la Chasse et de la Nature.

The left-hand side of Rue des Archives has been sadly disfigured. However, there are two fine *hôtels* in the street, at no 70 (18th-century) and no 72 (17th-century), and at no 78 is the fine 17th-century Hôtel Tallard. Pass Rue Portefoin (with more Classical *hôtels*) and reach the wide Rue de Bretagne; cross it into what is now Rue Eugène-Spuller. On your left is Square du Temple, on the site of the palace of the Knights Templar, the last parts of which were razed in 1854.

During the Crusades the Knights Templar, founded in 1128 in Jerusalem, amassed a vast fortune, which they ploughed back into their European estates. When Palestine was lost in 1291 the Templars went back to their various commanderies in Europe; they had their own bank and in many ways were a law unto themselves, creating what was in effect a state within the state. In 1310, concerned about this, Philippe IV compelled the Avignon Pope Clement V (Pope 1305–14) to ban the Order: 54 Templars were burnt alive in 1313 near the Abbaye St-Antoine. What Philip did not keep for himself he gave to the Hospitaliers de St Jean de Jérusalem, later known as the Knights of Malta, who established themselves in several of the commanderies left by the Templars.

On the corner of Rues Eugène-Spuller and Perrée stood the Templar tower, converted into a prison during the Revolution; Louis XVI, Marie Antoinette, the royal children and some of their retinue were incarcerated in it from 10 August 1792. A few months later, on 21 January 1793, the king was guillotined; on 1 August Marie Antoinette was taken to the Conciergerie (see p25), where she stayed until guillotined on 16 October. The Dauphin, 'Louis XVII', almost certainly met his death at the Temple, but the location of his body mystifies historians to this day: was he buried at the Temple or, as many believe, at the St-Marguerite cemetery (see p148)?

Two ancient markets
Cross Rue Perrée to the Carré du Temple, a 19th-century cast-iron structure housing a clothes market in the mornings. On its other side, turn right into Rue Dupetit-Thouars, which has a couple of good cafés. Next, turn right along Rue de Picardie, the eastern limit of the Templars' estate, go left along Rue du Forez (where there is another nice café), and reach Rue Charlot, into which turn right. Claude Charlot, a poor farmer who came to Paris from Languedoc in the early 17th century and amassed a vast fortune, developed most of this area. Two noteworthy *hôtels* are at nos 58 and 57.

Reach Rue de Bretagne again; this portion of it dates to Charlot's days. Cross it slightly to the right, and enter the picturesque covered market of the Enfants Rouges, so-named because the orphans of the nearby hospice were dressed in red. Founded in 1616, the market is almost certainly the oldest in Paris. You can leave it *via* Rue Charlot or Rue des Oiseaux (in which case, turn right, reach the ancient Rue de Beauce, turn right again and reach Rue de Bretagne). Walk eastwards, cross Rue Charlot, and turn right into the curious Rue Debelleyme, an amalgamation of four early-17th-century streets. Cross Rue de Poitou and then Rue Vieille-du-Temple (note the splendid 17th-century *hôtel* at no 110), pass Rue de Thorigny on your right and turn right into Rue de Turenne, over which you cross into Rue St-Claude.

Cagliostro and Ninon de Lenclos
At the far end of Rue St-Claude, at no 1, is the *hôtel* from which the adventurer Giuseppe Balsamo (1743–1795), the self-styled Count Alessandro di Cagliostro, mystified Paris and the court in 1785–6. On the corner of Rues de Turenne and St-Claude is the Neoclassical Église St-Denys-du-St-Sacrement, built by the architect Étienne Godde (1781–1869) in 1826–35. The most remarkable feature of the church is the excellent *Deposition from the Cross* (1844) by Eugène Delacroix (1798–1863).

Leave the church and go left along Rue de Turenne to no 60, the recently renovated Hôtel du Grand-Veneur (1686). Go through the *hôtel* to the right, so that you come out into Rue de Villehardouin, which you follow to reach Rue St-Gilles. Go left, and then turn right into Rue des Tournelles. At no 28 is the splendid Hôtel de Sagonne, which Jules Hardouin-Mansart (1645–1708), Comte de Sagonne, built for himself in 1674–85; he was the architect of many other *hôtels* in the Marais and worked also at the Louvre, Versailles, the Invalides Dôme, Place Vendôme and Place des Victoires. At no 36 the celebrated courtesan Ninon de Lenclos (1616–1706) died. Keep on, crossing Rue du Pas-de-la-Mule (with Place des Vosges to your right) until you reach Rue St-Antoine. The Bastille and your métro are to your left.

Cluny, the Sorbonne and Montagne Ste-Geneviève (Latin Quarter 1)

A semicircular walk in the Latin Quarter – the ancestral home of Paris University and a favourite haunt of its students – taking you from the edge of the Marais, across the Seine, up the Montagne Ste-Geneviève, past the exquisite Cluny Museum (with the stunning Unicorn tapestries), through the Sorbonne and up to Soufflot's astonishing Panthéon; then a gentle walk down the hill, past the beautiful Église St-Étienne-du-Mont, and through some narrow ancient streets to the Institut du Monde-Arabe.

Start: **Métro Pont-Marie; bus 67.**
Finish: **Métro Jussieu, buses 67, 86, 87, 89;** *or* **métro Sully-Morland, buses 67, 86, 87.**
Length: **4km (2½ miles).**
Time: **2hr.**
Refreshments: **Numerous places on the way but nothing of superior quality (except the Tour d'Argent on Quai de la Tournelle) until the last part of the walk. The restaurant at the top of the Institut du Monde-Arabe offers excellent Middle Eastern food and superb views.**
Which day: **Any day except Tuesday; many cafés and restaurants and some colleges shut on Sunday.**
To visit:
● **Musée de Cluny: daily (not Tuesday) 09.45–12.30 and 14.00–17.15.**
● **Panthéon: daily 09.30–18.30 (April to September), 10.00–17.30 (October to March).**

Bismarck, Tsar Alexander I and Wilhelm I
Leave the métro and cross Quai de l'Hôtel-de-Ville. Take Pont Marie to Île St-Louis (see p19); walk down the island's Rue des Deux-Ponts and return to the mainland on the other side of the river by Pont de la Tournelle, with its statue (1928) of St Geneviève by Paul Landowski (1875–1961). This bridge was one of the limits of Philippe-Auguste's wall, and there used to be a small tower (later the Château de la Tournelle, demolished in 1790) on the bank. There are superb views over the apse of Notre-Dame, the Châtelet and the Hôtel de Ville from the two bridges, especially Pont de la Tournelle. Cross Quai de la Tournelle to the Tour d'Argent, one of the best restaurants in Paris. Downstairs is the Petit Musée de la Table, which includes the table where Tsar Alexander II (1818–1881), Wilhelm I (1797–1888) and Prince Otto von Bismarck (1815–1898) had supper together on 7 June 1867 in the salon of the extremely

fashionable Grand Café Anglais. Usually you can see the museum only if you eat in the (expensive) restaurant at the top of the building, from where there is an excellent view.

Exiting, cross Rue du Cardinal-Lemoine and go along Quai de la Tournelle to take the first left, Rue de Poissy (there is an exceptional bakery at no 6). Keep going across the broad Boulevard St-Germain; at no 17 are the remains of the Collège des Bernardins, founded in the 13th century and completely transformed by the monks of Clairvaux in the 14th. The 14th-century cellar and the refectory (visible from the street) are among the most remarkable relics of Gothic architecture in Paris. This was a fire station for 150 years and is now home to the Paris police force. There are plans to transform it into a cultural centre.

Stay on the right-hand pavement of Rue de Poissy and reach Rue St-Victor on the right (do not climb the steps to Rue des Écoles). On this corner stood one of the Philippe-Auguste gates, the Porte St-Victor, so-named for the medieval abbey just outside the city walls (see below). The street leads to Square de la Mutualité, on which are the large Salle de la Mutualité – used for political meetings and concerts – and Église St-Nicolas-du-Chardonnet, a home of the fundamentalist wing of the Catholic Church. The mostly 17th-century church contains works by Charles Le Brun (1619–1690), the decorator of Vaux le Vicomte and Versailles, and by Antoine Coysevox (1640–1720).

Cross the wide avenue beside the church – Rue Monge, opened by Georges Haussmann (1809–1891) – to Rue des Bernardins, a charming old street. At its top, turn right into Rue des Écoles and then almost immediately turn left into Rue de la Montagne-Ste-Geneviève.

The stunning doorway at no 34 Rue de la Montagne-Ste-Geneviève belongs to what used to be the Hôtel d'Albiac, in which the Collège des Trente-Trois was founded in the 17th century; before that the medieval Collège des Lombards occupied the site. Walk through the porch into the courtyard: the Collège des Trente-Trois was on the left and the Collège des Lombards on the right, and you can see remains of both. This street leads to the pleasing little Place de la Montagne-Ste-Geneviève, where there are some agreeable cafés, including Les Pipos. The monumental door you can see is the entrance to what used to be the École Polytechnique, one of France's most prestigious schools (now moved to a greenfield site), and is now the Ministry of Research.

The oldest French teaching establishment

In Roman times the Montagne Ste-Geneviève was densely populated, and there was a Temple to Bacchus (now the Panthéon – p49) at the top of the hill; the Roman presence is still evident in the arenas (see p52) and in the thermae at Cluny. Paris was left relatively untouched by the invasions of the Huns in the 5th century and the Francs in the 6th, but in the 9th century the Normans razed the dwellings on the Left Bank as well as the important abbey situated in the vicinity of the old Roman temple and dedicated to the patron saint of Paris, St Geneviève (*c*422–512), who had saved the city from Atilla in the 5th century. The abbey was rebuilt in the 12th century and grew extremely prosperous; many of its medieval buildings still survive, despite the Revolution.

In the 11th century the arrival of the remarkable Peter Abélard (1079–1142), a theologian and a great favourite with students, signalled the exodus to and second colonization of the Left Bank. Until then education – primarily theology and philosophy – had taken place under the auspices of the Notre-Dame Cloister School on the Île de la Cité (see p23). After a theological dispute Abélard wished to distance himself from the ecclesiastical authorities, and 1000 students followed him. The new university was a great success, with students coming from far and wide, even from abroad. Lessons were held in the open air (almost certainly where Place Maubert now is – see p81) until the 14th century, even though gradually colleges had been built to house homeless students. From its inception – it received its first statutes from Philip II (reigned 1179–1223) in 1200 – the university was jealously independent, relying on patronage for its survival. Tuition was in Latin, a method that lasted until the Revolution (hence the name *Quartier Latin*). Competition arose during the 16th and 17th centuries, when various religious orders were allowed to open new colleges; but these were abolished in 1763, and, although reorganized in 1970, today's university, in terms of structure and statutes, dates back to Napoleon.

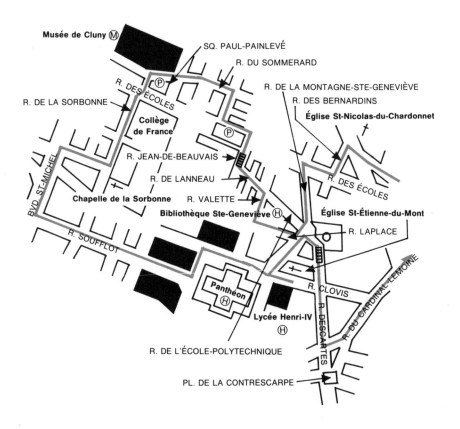

To return to our walk. Turn right from Rue de la Montagne-Ste-Geneviève into the narrow Rue Laplace; the fine door at no 12 belongs to the 16th-century Collège des Grassins. Turn right into Rue Valette, one of the oldest streets on the hill (opened in the 11th century), with houses dating mostly from the 17th and 18th centuries. There are superb views over the Panthéon (left) and the towers of Notre-Dame (right).

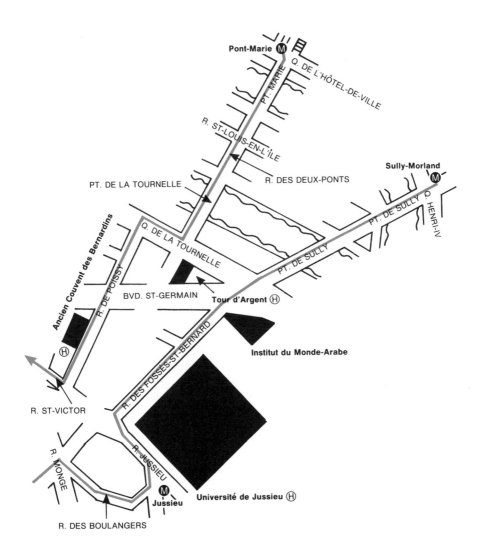

At no 21 was the 14th-century Collège de Fortet, where John Calvin (1509–1564) was a student (the cellar is still extant), and at no 4 is the Collège Ste-Barbe, the oldest teaching establishment in France. Unique in having survived since its inception in 1460, it is now a private institution; among its more famous pupils have been Ignatius de Loyola (1491–1556), founder of the Jesuits (see p139), Gustave Eiffel (1832–1923), Louis Blériot (1872–1936) and the writer Charles Péguy (1873–1914). The building was renovated in the 19th century.

At the point where Rue Valette becomes Rue des Carmes, turn left into Rue de Lanneau, opened in the 12th century. Pass the extremely narrow Rue d'Écosse, where three colleges had their entrance doors, and reach Rue Jean-de-Beauvais; on the left is the ancient Impasse Chartière, once the site of the Collège de Coqueret, renowned for pupils such as Pierre de Ronsard (1524–1585) and Joachim du Bellay (1522–1560), both among the founders of the influential Pléiade group.

Rue Jean-de-Beauvais leads to Place Marcelin-Berthelot, which is dominated by the Collège de France, a unique institution founded by François I and still providing free tuition and public lectures. The teachers, nominated by the government for an open-ended period, usually head their selected fields: among those who have taught here this century have been Roland Barthes (1915–1980), Yves Bonnefoy (b1923), Pierre Boulez (b1925), Georges Duby (1919–1996), Jacques Lacan (1901–1981), Emmanuel Le Roy Ladurie (b1929) and Claude Lévi-Strauss (1908–1996). Most of the buildings were restored in the 19th century. You can enter the courtyard; if you want to see the interior you will have to attend one of the public lectures.

Walk down the steps – the statue is of the physiologist Claude Bernard (1813–1878) – and cross Rue des Écoles to Rue Thénard, passing Rue de Latran on your right; at the bottom of this street is the much altered chapel of the 14th-century ex-Collège de Dormans-Beauvais, now a Romanian Orthodox church and visitable only during services. Turn left into Rue du Sommerard, cross the busy Rue St-Jacques, and continue until you reach the exquisite Musée de Cluny on Place Paul-Painlevé.

The Musée de Cluny
The Hôtel de Cluny was built on the site of Roman baths in the 15th century for the abbot of the powerful Cistercian abbey of Cluny, in whose hands it remained until the Revolution. That it escaped demolition then is a small miracle. Later a rich collector, Alexandre de Sommerard, acquired it to show off his collection of medieval objects, and on his death it was bought by the government as a museum, which now houses an important collection of medieval art: the Unicorn Tapestries are celebrated the world over (the other similar set is at the Cloisters Museum, New York).

Enter the courtyard. The *hôtel* has intricate, attractive stonework, especially the lace-like decoration over the niches (statues missing), doors and windows, and the gargoyles along the eaves. Inside, however, nothing is original except for one chimney and a couple of stairways.

You can visit the remains of the Roman baths on Wednesday afternoons at 15.00 (same entrance as museum); otherwise, you can go down to Boulevard St-Michel (at the bottom of Rue du Sommerard on the right) and view them from the outside.

On leaving the museum, assuming you have decided to skip the baths for now, cross Square Paul-Painlevé and Rue des Écoles to the Sorbonne. This imposing building was erected at the end of the 19th century; before it on the same site were a college founded by Robert de Sorbon (1201–1274) in 1253 and an apparently superb college built by Jacques Lemercier (1585–1684) from 1624. Go left along the university wall and then up a few steps into a rather severe foyer. The right-hand gallery – which has turn-of-the-century frescoes – leads you to the Cour d'Honneur, where you can see the outside of the chapel, built 1635–42 and the only part of Lemercier's building to have escaped reconstruction; its dome is notable. The chapel has been desanctified and is now used for art exhibitions; it is only when one of these is on that you can see the interior. It is a fine example of 17th-century religious architecture – Lemercier was a master. To get in you must leave the university building *via* the gates on your right and turn left.

The Panthéon
Leave the chapel and walk straight on across Place de la Sorbonne (many cafés); there is a good view of the chapel's façade. Reach the crowded Boulevard St-Michel (known to every Parisian student as the 'Boul Mich') and turn left. Stay on the left-hand side, pass Rue Cujas and, opposite the Jardin du Luxembourg (see p61), turn left into Rue Soufflot, named after Jacques Germain Soufflot (1709–1780), the architect of that severe, almost windowless domed building at the bottom of the street, the Panthéon, one of the landmarks of Paris.

Place du Panthéon was and still is an important square; the ancient temple to Bacchus and the medieval abbey have gone, but there are still monuments of great interest. As you come into the *place* there are two Classical buildings, one on each side of the street: on the left the law faculty, built by Soufflot in the late 18th century (but not finished until 1822), and on the right the local town hall (Mairie du Vème arrondissement), built by Jacques Ignace Hittorf (1792–1867) in 1844–6 to mirror the law faculty.

Soufflot had a sense of theatre and staging: he opened the avenue and set up the pavilions so as to show off his church in all its magnificence. On the pediment an inscription reads: '*Aux Grands Hommes la Patrie Reconnaisante*' ('To its great men, a thankful nation'). On the right – on the far side of the town hall – is the dated-looking Hôtel des Grands-Hommes, where André Breton (1896–1966) lived in 1918; it featured in his seminal *Nadja* (1928).

Turn left, pass the law faculty, and reach the Bibliothèque Ste-Geneviève, a huge building erected by Henri Labrouste (1801–1875) in 1844–50 on the site of a 17th-century monastic library created to house the Abbaye Ste-Geneviève's vast collection, and itself built on the site of the medieval Collège de Montaigu, where François Rabelais (*c*1494–*c*1553), Erasmus (1466–1536) and Calvin were students. The collection, open to the public, is renowned: there are more than 2000 medieval manuscripts, many illuminated, several incunabula and upwards of 80,000 rare books, as well as the Jacques Doucet Donation, comprising 19th-century and contemporary literary manuscripts. The enormous reading-room upstairs is impressive.

Leaving the library, cross over to and walk along the wall of the Panthéon. Soufflot's Neoclassical monument, inspired by Greek and Roman examples, had a tremendous influence on its time. Gravely ill, Louis XV had vowed to God that, should he recover, he would build a grandiose new church to replace the decrepit Église Ste-Geneviève. Work began in 1755, but Soufflot encountered serious problems almost straight away, the Romans having extensively excavated the site for the terra cotta, and so in fact the first stone was not laid for 10 years. Soufflot died before he could finish the building, and the last part was done by an assistant of his called Rondelet, who finished just before the Revolution. The Assemblée Constituante decided to convert the new church into a *panthéon* to the great men – *les Grands Hommes* – of the country.

The remarkable nave is adorned with large canvases, giving the illusion of frescoes, by Pierre Puvis de Chavannes (1824–1898) and others. Under the cupola hangs a pendulum, an exact replica of that used by Foucault (1819–1868) in the first public demonstration in 1851 of the rotation of the earth. The crypt, although completely renovated, has an eerie and quite remarkable atmosphere; it contains the tombs of, among others, Soufflot himself, Jean-Jacques Rousseau (1712–1778), Voltaire (1694–1778), Victor Hugo (1802–1885), Émile Zola (1840–1902), Jean Jaurès (1859–1914) and the Resistance fighter Jean Moulin (1899–1943).

On leaving the crypt, climb the stairs to the top of the dome (250 steps), but do not go outside straight away. Instead, step into the inner gallery, underneath the cupola: there is a superb view of the nave, and this is also the best spot from which to view the frescoes by Antoine Gros (1771–1835), one of Napoleon's official painters, depicting the apotheosis of St Geneviève (with many kings of France represented).

Outside, the panorama is sublime. Going clockwise, you can see: the dome of the Hôtel Dieu Hospital (see p24); the dome of the Observatory; Tour Eiffel (beyond Avenue Soufflot); the gilded dome of the Invalides; and the skyscrapers of the Defense (in the far distance). Almost at your feet is the chapel of the Sorbonne, and further away are the roofs of St-Lazare station; on the right Montmartre is easily distinguishable, with Église St-Eustache and the Sainte Chapelle in the foreground. To the right of the Sainte Chapelle are Tour St-Jacques and the Centre Beaubourg, followed by Notre-Dame and St-Germain-l'Auxerrois . . .

A church and an abbey
Leaving the Panthéon, cross Place Ste-Geneviève to the restored Église St-Étienne-du-Mont, a jewel of Renaissance religious architecture in the Flamboyant Gothic style. In fact, it is an interesting hotch-potch of styles, because of the time it took to build (1492–1626). The rare 16th-century stone rood-screen designed by Philibert Delorme (c1510–1570) and the wooden 17th-century pulpit by Germain Pilon (1537–1590) are especially fine. Most of the stained glass is original. The church also contains the reliquary of St Geneviève, purportedly containing a fragment of her coffin.

Outside the church, turn left into Rue Clovis, cross the street and enter the Lycée Henri-IV, probably the most prestigious school in France, which contains bits surviving from the ancient Abbaye Ste-Geneviève, partly destroyed during the Revolution; these include the 15th-century cloister, the tower (all that remains of the 13th-century chapel) and the 14th-century refectory – today the school chapel – as well as the medieval kitchens and the 17th-century library.

On leaving, retrace your steps to Église St-Étienne-du-Mont, then turn right into Rue de la Montagne-Ste-Geneviève and return to the quaint Place de la Montagne-Ste-Geneviève; this time enter the gardens of what used to be the École Polytechnique, founded in 1794 on the site of two previous colleges. The building facing you was erected by the architect Jacques-Ange Gabriel (1698–1782) in the early 18th century, while the others are mostly 19th-century.

Turn right and go up the steps and along Rue Descartes until you reach Rue Clovis: on your left you can see some ruins of Philippe-Auguste's wall. Cross the street and continue on Rue Descartes. The building on your right, now part of the *lycée*, is the 18th-century Hôtel du Duc-d'Orléans. This part of the street contains many cafés and restaurants at the bottom end of the market. The poet Paul Verlaine (1844–1896) died at no 39.

Rue Descartes leads into the charming Place de la Contrescarpe. Turn left and left again down Rue du Cardinal-Lemoine, which, as Rue des Fossés-St-Victor (the old name is still visible), ran along the outside of Philippe-Auguste's wall. Ernest Hemingway (1899–1961) lived at no 74 for a while. At no 75 an *allée* leads to the pleasant garden of the Hôtel des Deux-Écoles, established in a Directoire House. At no

65 was the Collège des Écossais, which was founded in the 17th century by Robert Barclay, an uncle of the famous North American colonist of the same name; it is now a private school run by Dominicans.

The street leads you to Rue Monge, which you cross at a slight angle to the right to enter Rue des Boulangers, opened in the 14th century. In it used to be the Couvent des Filles-Anglaises (the convent of Notre-Dame de Sion), founded for English ladies – though George Sand (1804–1876) was a boarder in 1817–20. The establishment was forced to move out when Rue Monge was laid. Rue des Boulangers is picturesque and contains many old houses, almost all from the 17th and 18th centuries; it leads to Place Jussieu (with the Jussieu métro station nearby).

Facing you now is the abominable Science University building, put up in the late 1960s by Édouard Albert (1910–1968) over a wine market (La Halle aux Vins, which term is still used for the area) that was itself on the site of the great medieval Abbaye St-Victor. Situated just outside the city wall, the abbey was shut down during the Revolution and demolished in 1811 to make way for the wine market.

Go left into Rue Jussieu; then, at the traffic lights, turn right into Rue des Fossés-St-Bernard, which has a couple of good restaurants. At the bottom, on the right, is the remarkable Institut du Monde-Arabe, built by Jean Nouvel (b1945) in the late 1980s. The museum and the library are excellent, as are the view from the cafeteria and restaurant on the top floor and the Middle Eastern food you can eat there!

This is the end of the walk. You can now choose either to cross the river and Île St-Louis to Quai des Célestins and the Sully-Morland métro station – and, if you like, connect with the Îles St-Louis and de la Cité walk (see p19) – or to walk back to métro Jussieu, where you can connect with the next walk.

Arènes, Mouffetard and the Jardin des Plantes (Latin Quarter 2)

This walk is full of surprises, and can make a perfect continuation to the preceding one. It explores the southern limits of the Latin Quarter and of Montagne Ste-Geneviève as well as fringe areas such as the ancient Faubourgs St-Jacques and St-Médard (the latter now known as the *Quartier Mouffetard*). There is an important Roman monument near the beginning (the Arenas), followed by several handsome streets, a temple of high academia (l'École Normale Supérieure), the more popular Rue Mouffetard, the Mosque, a superb 17th-century church (St-Louis de la Salpêtrière), and the Jardin des Plantes with the Musée National d'Histoire-Naturelle.

Start and finish: **Métro Jussieu; buses 67, 86, 87, 89.**
Length: **6.5km (4 miles).**
Time: **2½hr.**
Refreshments: **A broad selection of places, from the cafés on Place Jussieu at the start to those on Rue Mouffetard, halfway, and at the Botanical Gardens at the end. The tearoom of the Mosque takes you to another world. For restaurants explore around Place de la Contrescarpe or further down, in Rue du Pot-de-Fer.**
Which day: **Any day, but the museum is closed on Tuesdays and the Mosque on Fridays.**
To visit:
- **Musée National d'Histoire-Naturelle: daily (not Tuesday). Grande Galerie 10.00–18.00 (Thursday to 22.00). Other galleries 10.00–17.00.**

Roman Arenas
Exit Jussieu métro onto the leafy Place Jussieu. The enommous building facing you is the windswept Science University, built over the ancient wine market (La Halle aux Vins – see p51). With your back to it, cross the square and turn left into Rue Linné, and then some way along, turn right into Rue des Arènes.

The writer Jean Paulhan (1884–1968) lived in the neo-Gothic house at no 20 (plaque), opposite which is the entrance to the Roman Arenas – the Arènes de Lutèce – the oldest monument in Paris. Knowing what is original is rather difficult; the Arenas were heavily restored on being rediscovered at the end of the last century, having been largely forgotten for 12 centuries or so. They functioned as both a circus and a theatre, probably for no more than about 80 years (*c*200–*c*285). Later, when the Barbarians invaded Gaul in the 3rd and 4th centuries, the inhabitants of the small island of Lutèce used the stones from the steps to build a defensive wall. What little was left of the ancient monument was gradually overlain by earth, eventually to a depth of up to 18m (60ft); most of it was covered by the garden of the nearby English convent of Notre-Dame de Sion (Couvent des Filles-Anglaises). The remains were found again when Rue Monge was created, and were restored in the 1880s.

Go up the steps and into what is now really a public garden. Turn right and walk along the wall, from which you can overlook the circus, then up to a pleasant sitting area before going down the windy fake-stone steps to the circus itself. Where once there were lions and bulls there are now *boules* players and rather a lot of schoolchildren.

Walk across and exit into Rue de Navarre, turning right. Cross Rue Monge and climb the 35 steps of Rue Rollin, directly facing you. Rue Rollin is a delightful example of a typical residential Parisian street that has not been too spoilt. There are a few ancient houses, especially no 4 (17th-century), where Jacques Henri Bernardin de St Pierre (1737–1814) wrote his phenomenally successful *Paul et Virginie* (1788), no 7 (17th-century), and no 14 (porch and door surrounds), where René Descartes (1596–1650) stayed during his Parisian sojourns in 1646, 1647 and 1648 – he generally lived in Holland, since his works were banned in France.

Turn left in Rue du Cardinal-Lemoine – an attractive café, L'Époque, is at no 81 – and reach Place de la Contrescarpe, now alas much changed. You are only a stone's throw from the Panthéon, on the southern side of Montagne Ste-Geneviève (see p49). The *place* was created in 1852, but there has been an important crossroads here since medieval times. Note the painted sign, '*Au Nègre Joyeux*', above one of the shops in the square. Cross the square to Rue Blainville, which leads you to Rue de l'Estrapade.

The Pilgrim Route

Quite a few of France's prestigious Grandes Écoles are to be found in the area you are now entering. Rue de l'Estrapade, an ancient track that ran along the outside of the city wall, contains old houses, especially no 3 (built 1681) – where Denis Diderot (1713–1784) lived – no 5 and no 7. Walk to the traffic lights and cross Rue d'Ulm – note the view of the Panthéon on the right – to Rue des Fossés-St-Jacques, which has many old houses (mostly 18th-century), a couple of pleasant cafés, especially the Café de la Nouvelle Mairie, and, at no 4, an old-fashioned cheese shop, the Ferme Ste-Suzanne, with its turn-of-the-century window and painted sign. Reach Rue St-Jacques and then turn left.

You are now at the top of the hill. To your right is a great vista over the city, with Notre-Dame's towers in the distance; close by on your right, at no 172, stood the Porte St-Jacques, marking the beginning of the Faubourg St-Jacques, a medieval village just outside the city wall. Turn left down Rue St-Jacques. Starting at the river and cutting the city in half, this was the ancient road south out of the city. In medieval times it was the great pilgrimage way to Santiago de Compostela, and before the Revolution up to 10 religious institutions were established along it, including the Abbaye de Port-Royal (see p63). There are many 18th-century houses in the street, and also interesting food shops including, at no 202, an old-fashioned *crémier glacier*. Pass Rue Royer-Collard, opened in the 16th century; further along on the right, at no 212, you see a plaque indicating that here lived Jean de Meung (c1250–1305), one of the two authors of *Roman de la Rose*, probably the most important epic poem of medieval France. The house's vaulted cellars were used as a hiding-place during the Revolution. Opposite this house is Rue Pierre-et-Marie-Curie, which leads to the École Nationale Supérieure de Chimie.

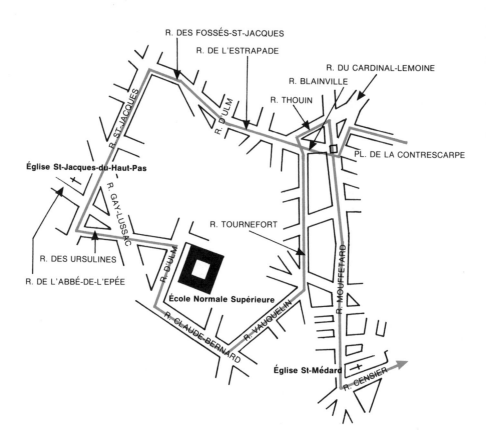

The Grandes Écoles

Keeping to Rue St-Jacques, cross the wide Rue Gay-Lussac, opened by Georges Haussmann (1809–1891) in 1859. On your right is the 17th-century Église St-Jacques-du-Haut-Pas, recently renovated, and next to it used to be the first of many hospices where the Santiago pilgrims could partake of both physical and spiritual sustenance; it is now an institute for the Deaf and Dumb, founded in the 18th century by Charles Michel (1712–1789), l'Abbé de l'Épée.

Cross Rue de l'Abbé-de-l'Épée and turn left into Rue des Ursulines, opened in 1799 over the convent of that name. Cross Rue Gay-Lussac once more, this time to go down Rue Louis-Thuillier; at the bottom turn right into Rue d'Ulm. This street is best known as the home of the great École Normale Supérieure ('Normale Sup'), the most prestigious of the Grandes Écoles. Founded during the Revolution, it has nurtured many illustrious students: Victor Cousin (1792–1867), Louis Pasteur (1822–1895), Hippolyte

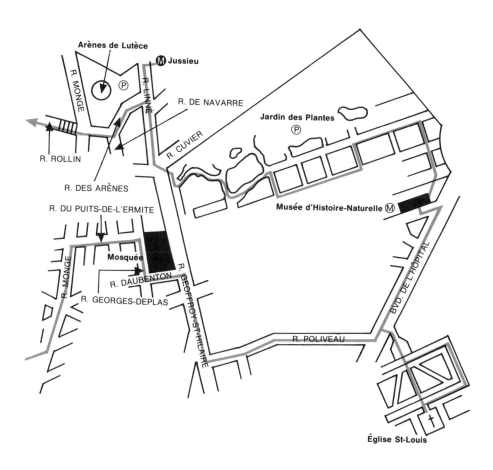

Arènes de Lutèce
R. MONGE
Jussieu
R. LINNÉ
R. DE NAVARRE
Jardin des Plantes
R. CUVIER
R. ROLLIN
R. DES ARÈNES
R. DU PUITS-DE-L'ERMITE
Musée d'Histoire-Naturelle
R. MONGE
Mosquée
R. DAUBENTON
R. GEORGES-DEPLAS
R. GEOFFROY-ST-HILAIRE
BVD. DE L'HÔPITAL
R. POLIVEAU
Église St-Louis

Taine (1828–1893), Henri Bergson (1859–1941), Romain Rolland (1866–1944), Charles Péguy (1873–1914), Jean Giraudoux (1882–1944), Pierre Henri Simon (1903–1972) and Jean-Paul Sartre (1905–1980), to name but a few.

Go in and walk across the foyer to emerge in the restful gardens; if you sit long enough on one of the benches you may find yourself in the middle of one of the intellectual discussions favoured by the students here. The buildings date from the 19th century.

Leave the school and go left. The plaque on the wall a few metres down indicates the site of the laboratory where Pasteur isolated several important vaccines, including the rabies vaccine. Turn left into the busy Haussmannian Rue Claude-Bernard; take the second left, into Rue Vauquelin, built in 1860 over the estates of two religious institutions closed at the Revolution. At no 10 are some of the buildings of the École de

Physique et de Chimie Industrielle, where Marie (1867–1934) and Pierre (1859–1906) Curie isolated radium (plaque).

This street leads you to Place Lucien-Herr, from which you walk up the village-like Rue Tournefort. There are numerous old houses: at no 25 lived Prosper Mérimée (1803–1870), author of *Carmen* (1846), and at no 16 are a very fine coach door and almost all that remains of the convent of the Communauté Ste-Aure. On the way you pass (on the right) the old Rue du Pot-de-Fer, now full of restaurants. The tower of Église-St-Étienne-du-Mont is visible in the distance and, as you go up the hill, the dome of the Panthéon rears into view.

At the top, cross Rue Blainville and turn right down Rue Thouin until you reach the famous Rue Mouffetard at Place de la Contrescarpe. Turn right, cross the *place*, and walk down Rue Mouffetard, which was a Roman way. In the mornings the street's bottom end is given over to a fruit and vegetable market; the much changed upper section is filling up with fashion shops. Once again there are quite a few old houses; at no 61 is the Fontaine du Pot-de-Fer (1624).

At the bottom of the street, on the left, is Église St-Médard; opposite the church, above a butcher, is a turn-of-the-century mural showing pigs, boars, pheasants and so on. The church took over 300 years to complete: the façade and the nave are 15th-century, the choir and side-chapels 16th (Renaissance style), the sides 17th, and the apse chapel and most of the redecoration 18th; another chapel (*la chapelle des catéchismes*) was added at the turn of this century, and the whole was recently renovated. Despite this hotch-potch, it is a fine parish church with a surprising feeling of depth; the organ case is by Germain Pilon (1537–1590).

Leaving the church, go left along Rue Censier, which runs by the church wall, until you reach Rue Monge, into which you turn left. Cross the street and take second right into Rue du Puits-de-l'Ermite; various 17th-century sculptors, including Antoine Coysevox (1640–1720), lived in this street. Go along it to Place du Puits-de-l'Ermite, which has concrete ping-pong tables in the middle; on the far side is the Mosque. Built in the 1920s and heavily inspired by the Alhambra in Granada, the Mosque can be visited daily (not Fridays) 10.00–12.00 and 14.00–17.30; the gardens are a joy. Walk around the building; on the corner with Rue Geoffroy-St-Hilaire is the entrance to the tearoom (recommended) and the baths.

The Salpêtrière and Église St-Louis
Turn right into Rue Geoffroy-St-Hilaire (outside the Mosque tearoom) and continue until you reach the 13th-century Rue Poliveau, on your left, now with modern residential blocks along it. Walk down to the bottom and cross Boulevard de l'Hôpital, go under the elevated métro, and enter the imposing gates of Hôpital de la Salpêtrière.

In the 1630s it was decided to build on the empty space here an annexe, the Salpêtrière (saltpetre-works) to the Arsenal on the other side of the river (on Quai des Célestins). However, within 30 years Louis XIV fixed on this as the perfect site for a large hospice to confine some of Paris's 50,000 tramps; one building would be for children, one for men and one, the Salpêtrière, for women. There was also a jail where husbands and fathers could imprison their wives and daughters; this was where Manon Lescaut – the heroine of the famous 1731 novel of that name by Abbé Prevost (1697–1763), adapted as operas by Auber in 1856, Massenet in 1884 and Puccini in 1893 – was incarcerated by her husband. Libéral Bruand (1635–1697) started building in 1660 and

Louis Le Vau (1612–1670) completed the project. It was an enormous place, the largest Parisian *hôpital:* at one time over 8000 people lived here. Some of the original Salpêtrière buildings have been demolished, and new ones have been added. The one facing you is classic 17th-century, in the style of the Invalides.

Walk along the *allée* and across a *passage* to the remarkable Église St-Louis, built by Bruand. The vast interior has a remarkable sobriety. Built on a Greek-cross plan, with four equal naves around the central choir to separate the social classes, it is now often used for concerts and exhibitions.

Leave by the west wing, turn right and go around the church to walk through the shady gardens and so exit where you came in.

The botanical gardens
Cross Boulevard de l'Hôpital again; it was opened in the late 18th century as part of the Boulevards du Midi (southern boulevards) planned by Louis XIV a century earlier. Here there are many cafés because of the proximity of the Austerlitz railway station, towards which you should now head. Opposite the station, the boulevard meets Rue Buffon, on the other side of which you will see a small gate, the entrance to the wonderful Jardin des Plantes (botanical gardens), containing not only gardens and a small zoo but also a museum and a school.

The original garden was created in the early 17th century as a herb-garden for the instruction of students of the university. The first director was a Gui de la Brosse (d1641); his most famous successor has been the Comte de Buffon (1707–1788), whose reign lasted nearly 50 years. Many celebrated scientists have taught here, including Louis Daubenton (1716–1789), both Bernard (*c*1699–1777) and Antoine (1748–1836) Jussieu, the Chevalier de Lamarck (1744–1829), the Comte de Lacépède (1756–1825), Louis Vauquelin (1763–1829), Étienne Geoffroy St-Hilaire (1772–1844) and Joseph Gay-Lussac (1778–1850).

The Musée National d'Histoire Naturelle has been partly renovated, with great success. The *Grande Galerie de l'Evolution* contains a fascinating array of exhibits, including the skeleton of a whale, and is arranged over three floors. There are other galleries devoted to botany and geology elsewhere in the park.

From the *Galerie de l'Evolution* walk across to the main gates by the riverside. There is a fine view down to the zoology gallery. The statue is of Lamarck, a pre-Darwin pioneer of evolution theory. Walk over to Allée Cuvier, turn left down it (the entrance to the zoo is along to the right) and then take second left into Allée Jussieu.

The garden of the École de Botanique on the right contains a wide collection of rare plants and shrubs. Go through it to the top, turn right, and walk straight over to the wonderful alpine gardens; there is a path to your left that takes you round among the plants, shrubs, rockeries, small waterfalls and so on. Outside the alpine gardens, turn right towards the 19th-century greenhouse; before you reach it, turn right again and follow a crescent-shaped path down to an amphitheatre. From here take a left and walk up a funny hill to a maze at the top, then down the other side and over to the gates.

Leave the gardens at the junction of Rues Linné, Cuvier, Lacépède and Geoffroy-St-Hilaire. Just to the right is the handsome Fontaine Cuvier, built in 1840. Finally, go up Rue Linné to the Jussieu métro station.

St-Michel, Luxembourg, Val-de-Grâce and Gobelins

In this unusual walk, one of the most popular stretches of Boulevard St-Michel is followed by reminders of the literary Paris of the 1920s-30s and of the Revolution. We also visit two remarkable religious monuments, the Abbaye de Port-Royal and Val-de-Grâce, before reaching the fascinating Manufacture des Gobelins. But the walk's pivotal point is, of course, the Jardin du Luxembourg.

Start: **Métro St-Michel; buses 21, 27, 38, 85, 96.**
Finish: **Métro Les Gobelins; buses 27, 47, 83.**
Length: **5.5km (3½ miles).**
Time: **2¼hr.**
Refreshments: **Several places, some quite interesting, in the first half of the walk, but little thereafter.**
Which day: **Tuesday, Wednesday or Thursday to visit the Gobelins; otherwise, any day.**
To visit:
• **Manufacture des Gobelins: Tuesday, Wednesday and Thursday, 14.00 and 14.45 (guided tour).**

L'École de Médecine and le Couvent des Cordeliers
Leave St-Michel métro *via* the Boulevard St-Michel exit. This is the heart of the Latin Quarter; the late-19th-century boulevard, though much changed, still pulsates with life – shops, cafés and brasseries, cinemas and people. Walk up the left-hand side of the boulevard – with the Sainte Chapelle spire on the Île de la Cité behind you – and cross Boulevard St-Germain. On your left at the corner of the two boulevards are the remains of the ancient Roman baths (see p48) with, backing onto the baths, the Hôtel de Cluny, now housing a handsome collection of medieval art (see p48). The entrance to both is in Rue du Sommerard, on your left.

Now cross Boulevard St-Michel to Rue de l'École-de-Médecine, constructed over an ancient Gallo-Roman track. Sarah Bernhardt (1844–1923) was born at no 5 (on your left, just after Rue Racine); the building is part of the Sorbonne, and now houses the Institut des Langues Modernes. In termtime you can take a look at the small amphitheatre, built in 1691–5. The premises were erected for the Confrérie des Barbiers-Chirurgiens – in those days barbers carried out many surgical operations. The *confrérie* became the School of Surgery in 1775 and moved further down the street. Opposite the Institut is the Patisserie Viennoise, where you can enjoy superb coffee, hot chocolate and cakes.

Further along, at no 15, almost opposite Rue Hautefeuille (one of the Left Bank's oldest streets; note the delightful 16th-century turret halfway down), are the gates to the

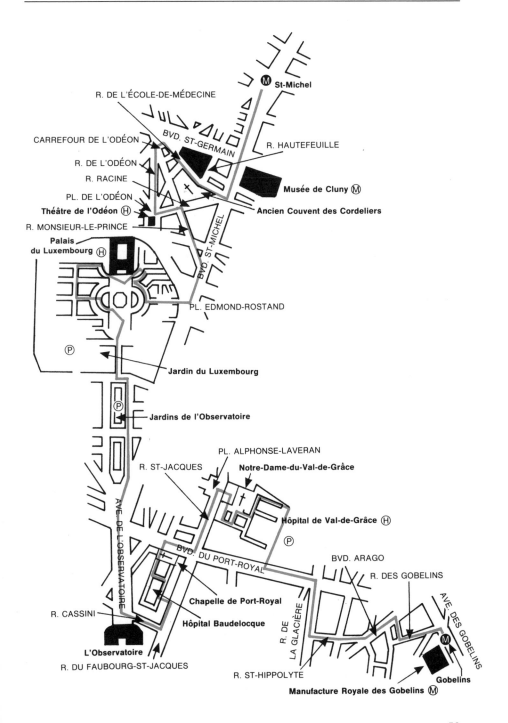

modern half of the École de Médecine (University of Medicine). The buildings themselves are dull, but it is worth going in to see the medieval refectory of the Couvent des Cordeliers.

The Cordeliers – they attached a *corde* (rope) to their robes – were one of the great medieval orders, part of the Franciscans. Their 15th-century monastery, backing onto Philippe-Auguste's wall, quickly grew prosperous. At the Revolution it was taken over by a leading Revolutionary group, the Club des Cordeliers, founded by Camille Desmoulins (1760–1794) and including among its members Georges Danton (1759–1794) and Jean Paul Marat (1743–1793). Most of the monastery was razed very early in the 19th century; l'École Pratique de Médecine erected the present buildings in 1872–1900. The sublime refectory, opened to the public in 1989 (bicentenary of the Revolution), can be seen when there is an exhibition on in it. A simple barn-style building built at the end of the 15th century, a little before the Hôtels de Sens and de Cluny (see p34 and p48), it has stone walls, and central wooden pillars supporting a wooden vault.

Leave the building and carry on down the street before crossing to the more ancient part of l'École de Médecine. You can walk in through the Cour d'Honneur of this large Neoclassical building – erected 1769–86 and enlarged in the 19th century at the same time as the École Pratique – and wander in the corridors, which evoke a kind of 19th-century opulence. At the end of the school, by the Carrefour de l'Odéon, stood the house where Marat was murdered in his bath by Charlotte Corday (1768–1793).

Sylvia Beach and Adrienne Monnier

At the *carrefour*, pass Danton's statue, stay on the left-hand side and turn left at the traffic lights into Rue de l'Odéon, the first Parisian street to have pavements and gutters (from 1779); most of the houses date from 1780. There is, by design, a fine vista from here over the Théâtre de l'Odéon at the bottom of the street – in accordance with the Classical principle of creating perspectives to attract attention to specific monuments. Rue de l'Odéon was a literary temple in the 1920s. At no 7 Adrienne Monnier (1892–1955) had her shop Amis du Livre, where André Gide (1869–1951), Paul Valéry (1871–1945) and many other representatives of the French literary scene met. At no 12, opposite, used to be the celebrated Shakespeare & Co., run by Adrienne's friend Sylvia Beach (1887–1962), where the likes of Ernest Hemingway (1899–1961) and Gertrude Stein (1874–1946) would congregate. Beach was a remarkable woman: not only did she give financial help to impoverished authors, including Hemingway, she was responsible for publishing books such as *Ulysses* (1922) by James Joyce (1882–1941) – that first edition of only 1000 sold very badly, but copies are now worth a small fortune. The first translator of Joyce into French, Valery Larbaud (1881–1957), was another aficionado of the two bookshops. Gustave Flaubert (1821–1880) lived at no 20 and Camille Desmoulins (1760–1794) at no 22 (plaque).

As you reach Place de l'Odéon (the good fish restaurant, La Méditérannée, is on the right) you see the back of the theatre: walk round the building to see its front façade, which faces the Jardin du Luxembourg. Le Théâtre-Français, as it was originally called, was built in 1782 by two Neoclassical architects, Marie-Joseph Peyre (1730–1785) and Charles de Wailly (1730–1798). It was much restored by Jean François Chalgrin (1739–1811) after suffering a fire in 1799. Now the Théâtre de l'Europe, it specializes in foreign-language productions.

Turn left into Rue Racine, opened at the same time as Rue de l'Odéon – George Sand (1804–1876) lived at no 3 for a while – and stroll along to Rue Monsieur-le-Prince, once the track that ran outside the city's fortified wall. Turn right. At no 39 is the great Polidor restaurant. Cross Rue de Vaugirard, down which, to the left, there is a fine vista over the Chapelle de la Sorbonne. At no 54 Rue Monsieur-le-Prince, Blaise Pascal (1623–1662) wrote his *Lettres Provinciales* (1656–7) and *Pensées* (1669).

At the top of the hill you come to Boulevard St-Michel; keep going a little further until you reach Place Edmond-Rostand, with its 19th-century fountain. On your left, on the other side of the boulevard, Rue Soufflot beautifully frames a view of the Panthéon (see p49).

The Jardin du Luxembourg
The Jardin du Luxembourg, known locally as the 'Luco', was created in 1613 for Marie de' Medici (1573–1642) on grounds belonging to a Carthusian charterhouse which had been built on the site of an ancient medieval fortress, the Château Vauvert. This fortress occupied quite a bit of land, and had a reputation so sinister – rather like Bluebeard's Castle – that to this day the expression *aller au diable Vauvert* signifies a dangerous journey. In the 13th century Louis IX gave the estate to the Carthusians, a very strict order founded by St Bruno (*c*1030–1101).

The gardens were greatly enlarged following the abolition of the charterhouse at the Revolution; Chalgrin was appointed to re-landscape them, and it is his work that we admire today. The many statues, mostly 19th-century, are almost all identified. Go through the main gates, take the central *allée*, pass the music kiosk and walk down the steps. The Palais du Luxembourg now houses the Senate and can be visited only by appointment; what you are seeing is the back of it, the main entrance being in Rue de Vaugirard (see p69). After the assassination of her husband, Henri IV, in 1610 the isolated Italian-born Marie wanted a palace in the image of her cherished Palazzo Pitti. Salomon de Brosse (1565–1626), her architect, erected a fine building that owed more to 17th-century Classicism than to the Renaissance, but little of it is now left, except for the Cour d'Honneur and some of the ornate bosses inside. The building was modified in the 19th century by Chalgrin and by Alexandre de Gisors (1762–1835). It stayed more or less in the hands of the Bourbons until the Revolution, when it served as a prison. It became the Senate in 1801 and then, during the Restoration (1815–48), the Chambre des Pairs (House of Lords); it became the Senate once more in 1852, at the birth of the Second Empire.

Turn right at the bottom of the steps and head for the beautiful Fontaine Médicis, erected by de Brosse in the Italian Rocaille style; the statues were added in the 19th century, when the fountain was moved to its present site.

Retracing your steps a little, walk over to the palace, now fully restored and quite impressive. The façade you are looking at was done in the 19th century by de Gisors. Walk beside the Senate wall and then turn right along it – you can see the towers of St-Sulpice in the distance – and pass another fountain ('offered to Delacroix by his admirers') before you come to the Orangerie, open to the public when exhibitions are on. On the other side is a children's playground with, next to it, a *jeu de boules* and a large area where people play chess.

Turn left at the bottom of the Orangerie, pass the chess players and the tennis court, and turn left into an *allée* that will take you to the Grand Bassin (pond). (Had you turned right here you would have found yourself in Rue de Fleurus, where Gertrude Stein lived with Alice B. Toklas [1877–1967].) The octagonal Grand Bassin is today a favourite place for children to try out their model boats.

With the palace at your back, walk across the gardens to come out in Rue Auguste-Comte. Facing you in the distance is the 17th-century Observatoire.

L'Observatoire

Walk down the tranquil Jardins de l'Observatoire – a grand name to describe a fenced-off lawn. These *jardins* were designed by Chalgrin over the estate of the Carthusians.

Avenue de l'Observatoire, which goes on either side of the gardens and then extends beyond Boulevard du Montparnasse, was opened in 1798. You are surrounded by academic institutions. First is the Institut des Hautes Études d'Outremer, now occupied by the Institut International d'Administration Publique; then comes the École de Pharmacie (built 1876–85); and next is the rather ugly red-brick building of the École d'Archéologie, built by Paul Bigot (1870–1942) in 1927 in a complete reaction against Modernism.

At the end of the gardens is a splendid fountain, erected by Gabriel Davioud (1823–1881) in 1875; the horses are by the sculptor Emmanuel Fremiet (1824–1910), who specialized in monumental animals (many of his sculptures adorn the *parvis* of the Musée d'Orsay – see p88), and the group showing the four parts of the world is by Jean Baptiste Carpeaux (1827–1875), the brilliant author/sculptor responsible for *Groupe de la Danse* (1866) at the Garnier Opéra (see p116). On the other side of the fountain, in an island in the middle of the avenue, is a celebrated statue by François Rude (1784–1855) of Marshal Ney (1769–1815), who was shot near here.

The very busy intersection of Boulevard St-Michel, Boulevard du Montparnasse and many other streets was created by Georges Haussmann (1809–1891). Turn right briefly in Boulevard du Montparnasse; on the corner is La Closerie des Lilas, the café *par excellence* of the literati: Charles Baudelaire (1821–1867), Paul Verlaine (1844–1896) and Charles Cros (1842–1888) were followed a generation later by André Gide and Alfred Jarry (1873–1907), then by Guillaume Apollinaire (1880–1918) and Francis Carco (1886–1958), then by the Americans, including Hemingway and F. Scott Fitzgerald (1896–1940), and finally by Jean-Paul Sartre (1905–1980) and Simone de Beauvoir (1908–1986). The décor is great; it is an agreeable place to sit and read the papers. The café got its name because, before the boulevard was developed, there was an outdoor dancing-place here planted with 1000 lilac trees (see also p151).

Continue down Avenue de l'Observatoire all the way to the Observatory (visitable only by appointment). The building was designed by Claude Perrault (1613–1688) and completed in 1672. The Paris meridian splits it exactly in half. Jean Dominique Cassini (1625–1712) was the first astronomer in charge of it; his illustrious successors have included Joseph de Lalande (1732–1807), Pierre Simon de Laplace (1749–1827) and Dominique Arago (1786–1853).

Artists' villas and Port-Royal

Now turn left into Rue Cassini, where you can see three interesting villas (nos 3bis, 5 and 7) erected at a time when Art Nouveau was waning, Art Deco was just about to burgeon and Modernism was not such a long way off. They were designed in 1903–6 by the now rather forgotten Bordeaux-born architect, Louis Süe (1875–1968), for various now certainly forgotten artists. The villas are all completely different in style, with a bit of Gothic, a bit of ornamentation *à l'*Art Nouveau, but, above all, something very individual and pleasing.

At the bottom of the street, turn left into Rue du Faubourg-St-Jacques, between two large hospitals; the one on the right, l'Hôpital Cochin, is among Paris's leading teaching hospitals. About 100m (110yd) along, just after a rather drab grey 1960s building, turn left through some small gates into what is a now a maternity hospital (Hôpital Baudelocque). Follow the *allée* to the right and then turn left, following the signs saying 'Chapel', until you reach the cloisters of the ancient Abbaye de Port-Royal.

This abbey was built in the early 17th century for the nuns of Port-Royal-des-Champs, near Paris, where the doctrines of the Dutch theologian Cornelius Jansen (1585–1638) flourished. The Jansenists – who had attracted many influential people to their cause, including Saint-Cyran (1581–1643), Pascal and Antoine Arnauld (1612–1694), whose sister, Marie-Angélique Arnauld (1591–1661), was the abbess – soon got into a serious theological battle with the Jesuits and a no less serious political battle with Cardinal Richelieu (1585–1642); they lost both, and the Abbaye de Port-Royal-des-Champs was razed on the orders of Louis XIV. The Parisian nuns were sent to other convents and the Parisian abbey was transferred to another order. It became a prison during the Revolution and a maternity hospital in 1814.

Exit the cloisters by the northwest corner, through the double glass doors and into the corridor. You can visit the Salle Capitulaire and the fine chapel, both of which were parts of the original abbey.

Leaving the building, you find yourself on Boulevard de Port-Royal. If the doors are locked – opening times are a little erratic – retrace your steps through the building and then walk all the way round it to the boulevard.

Val-de-Grâce
Cross the boulevard outside the hospital, turn right and then left into Rue St-Jacques and walk down to the half-moon-shaped Place Alphonse-Laveran, which opens onto the ancient abbey of Val-de-Grâce, one of the finest 17th-century monastic ensembles and strongly evocative of the Grand Siècle. The abbey has been almost completely preserved, thanks to its having been converted into a military hospital in 1795, at an early stage of the Revolution.

It was essentially the work of the unfortunate Anne of Austria (1601–1666), daughter of Philip III of Spain (reigned 1598–1621) and queen to Louis XIII, whom she married at age 14: the king would have little to do with her, beyond the necessary, until she gave birth to a son, the future Louis XIV, when she was 36 years old. In order to thank God for this blessing, she had the abbey, already her personal sanctuary, much enlarged and beautified. The chapel was erected 1645–65 by four architects: François Mansart (1598–1666), Jacques Lemercier (1585–1684), Pierre Le Muet (1591–1669) and a certain Gabriel Le Duc, who installed the handsome dome, the third highest in Paris.

The Val-de-Grâce is almost always empty, and the presence of the army adds to the slightly uncanny atmosphere. Architecturally inspired by St Peter and St Gesu at Rome, it is a fine example of Classicism, though there are some Baroque influences. The cupola shows the celebrated fresco, the *Séjour des Bienheureux*, with more than 200 figures, by Pierre Mignard (1612–1695), completely restored in 1984. The marble floor is excellent, there are marble medallions in the Siennese tradition, and the canopy is impressive. Anne had her own oratory in the scholastic chapel. Access to the fine but severe cloisters is *via* the St-Louis chapel on the right of the altar.

Leaving the church, go left and left again through a small *passage* into the old abbey, most of whose buildings date from the mid-17th century. The *passage* leads you to a small courtyard from which you can step into the gardens, flanked to the east by the modern military hospital. On the right is the Anne d'Autriche Pavillon, where Anne had her apartments. The southern façade of the ancient abbey is noteworthy.

The Gobelins

Leave the gardens and the Val-de-Grâce by the hospital gates on the left. Walk leftwards about 100m (110yd) along Boulevard de Port-Royal, then cross it into Rue de la Glacière. Take first left into Rue St-Hippolyte, where tanners and dyers lived in the 19th century. The Bièvre river ran nearby (where Boulevard Arago now is), and accordingly this was one of the industrial centres of the 19th and early 20th century; the Bièvre was finally completely covered up in 1912. At the end of the street, cross Boulevard Arago to Rue des Gobelins, a small street that has retained some of its character. No 19 dates from the early 16th century while most of the other houses are late-18th- and early-19th-century. At no 17 you can enter the yard to see an intriguing house, the so-called Château de la Reine Blanche, built in 1520 over a more ancient house where Blanche de Bourgogne (1296–1325), the adulterous queen of Charles IV, had a *château*; the present *hôtel* was the home of the Gobelins family, a family of skilled dyers and cloth merchants.

Reach Avenue des Gobelins and turn right. The Manufacture Royale des Gobelins is along to the right. It was created as such by Colbert in 1666 after a colourful past (the Gobelin family had been working here since the mid-15th century) and ever since has specialized in high-quality tapestry (*tapisserie de Haute Lice*). Most of the original 17th-century buildings were burnt during the Commune (there are some remains, mostly at the back), and the façade on the avenue dates from 1914.

The walk ends here – your métro station is almost outside the *manufacture* – but you might like to carry on up the avenue, away from the métro, to Place d'Italie, where you will find cafés, cinemas and métro and bus connections. You will pass on your left the cinema La Fauvette, once the Théâtre des Gobelins; its façade was decorated by Auguste Rodin (1840–1917).

St-Germain-des-Prés

A pleasant circular walk in St-Germain-des-Prés, along attractive, narrow streets among shops and art galleries, historical cafés and literary and other landmarks. This is one of the most popular parts of Paris, and you will enjoy sitting at the terrace of Les Deux Magots or the Café Flore. As well as the Musée Delacroix there are two important churches, St-Germain-des-Prés and St-Sulpice. Also on the way is Pierre Chareau's extraordinary Maison du Verre.

Start and finish: **Métro Odéon; buses 58, 63, 70, 86, 87, 96.**
Length: **3.5km (2¼ miles).**
Time: **1¾hr.**
Refreshments: **Cafés and eating-places abound.**
Which day: **Any day; Sunday is a little quieter, since the art galleries and antiques shops are shut.**
To visit:
• **Musée Delacroix: daily (not Tuesday) 09.45–12.30 and 14.00–17.15.**

Porte Buci
Leave the métro *via* the Carrefour de l'Odéon exit onto Boulevard St-Germain, opened by Georges Haussmann (1809–1891).

Cross the boulevard to Cour du Commerce-St-André, a cobbled alleyway with gates. Now only half as long as it was before the creation of the boulevard, the *cour* ran along Philippe-Auguste's wall, and until the 17th century was a place for *boules*-players. Most of the houses were built in the 1770s. Jean Paul Marat (1743–1793) had the print-shop for his newspaper *L'Ami du peuple* at no 8. At no 9 Joseph Ignace Guillotin (1738–1814) conducted the first trials (using sheep) of his new head-cutting machine in 1792. On the right is Cour de Rohan, with three very picturesque courtyards: one was established over the Philippe-Auguste wall and another contains a fine 17th-century *hôtel* and a stone mounting-block. Much of Cour du Commerce-St-André is occupied by the (renovated) Café Procope, one of the great literary cafés of the 18th century, favoured by the *Encyclopédistes* and the first establishment in Paris where you could drink coffee.

Reach Rue St-André-des-Arts and turn left. The crossroads you almost immediately come to, Carrefour de Buci, has always been an important landmark in Parisian life. Two of the fortified wall's gates were nearby. At the *carrefour* is the five-storey Montholon apartment block, dating from the 1770s and a kind of prototype for future generations of apartment blocks in the city: Classical domestic architecture, with an arcaded ground floor and above it four almost equal square floors.

Turn left into Rue de l'Ancienne-Comédie, named for the Comédie-Française, which was at no 14 in the ancient Jeu de Paume-de-l'Étoile. Passing the Café Procope on your left, return to Boulevard St-Germain and turn right. This portion of the boulevard,

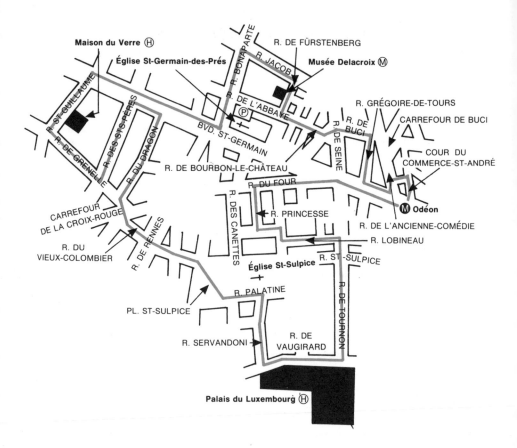

between the Odéon and St-Germain-des-Prés, contains several fashion shops and cafés, including the ever-popular Rhumerie, and you might want to come back later to explore it. The cafés stay open late in the evenings, and there are restaurants of all kinds in the side-streets.

The abbey palace
Take the first right into Rue Grégoire-de-Tours. At the bottom is Carrefour de Buci again; this time turn left into the busy Rue de Buci, with its very lively market, good patissiers and other food stores. Cross Rue de Seine and go slightly to the right into the short Rue de Bourbon-le-Château, where there are late-18th-century houses.

You are now in a warren of small narrow streets opened on the old grounds of the Abbaye St-Germain-des-Prés. The peaceful abbey, a stone's throw from the university, ruled over this area for centuries. It was really a state within the state, with its own laws and judicial system, its own prison and the right to levy taxes, and it was under the direct authority of the Pope rather than the Bishop of Paris. As it was outside the city wall it had its own fortified wall and gates. The original 6th-century building was a reputedly superb

Merovingian Basilica. Germain (*c*496–*c*576), then Bishop of Paris and later a saint, had asked Childebert I of the Francs (reigned 511–558) to build a church to house St Vincent's cloak, which the king had retrieved from Saragossa. So rich was the basilica that it proved tempting rather too often, and eventually it was destroyed during the Norman invasions of the 9th century. Rebuilt 200 years later, it slowly grew to become one of the richest Parisian abbeys; Pierre de Montreuil (d1267) was responsible for several further buildings. During the Revolution the abbey was used as a gunpowder store. One day in August 1794 there was a terrific explosion and most of the building went up in smoke.

Cross Rue de l'Echaudé, originally a track that ran along the abbey wall, and reach Rue de l'Abbaye, opened in 1800 after the destruction of the abbey. The large red brick-and-stone building on your left (at nos 3, 5 and 7) is what is left of the 16th-century abbey palace built by the then abbot, Cardinal de Bourbon (1523–1590), Henri IV's uncle; the abbey's high revenues attracted many influential people to the post of abbot. The palace was sold in 1797, was an artists' colony for a while, and is now a medical centre. Go up a few steps to the gates and peep in.

Behind you is Rue de Fürstenberg, leading to one of the most delightful *squares* in Paris: small and with an odd provincial charm. The left-hand side used to be the stables, etc., of the abbey palace.

At no 6, in the corner, Eugène Delacroix (1798–1863) had his studio, now a museum and very evocative of the life of one of the greatest artists of the 19th century. The apartment where he lived from 1857 has not been changed, and there is always an interesting selection of paintings (some on loan from the Louvre).

Leaving the museum, walk down Rue de Fürstenberg – note the narrow crescent-shaped Rue Cardinale on your right – and turn left into the classy Rue Jacob; this section is renowned for its antiques shops. There are many fine houses hidden away in the courtyards: you must push doors to appreciate fully the character of the area. Richard Wagner (1813–1883) lived briefly in an apartment at no 14. Nathalie Barney, the US hostess of a famous literary salon at the turn of the century and the 'Amazon' of several novels by Colette (1873–1954), lived at no 20. Jean Racine (1639–1699) lodged in his uncle's fine *hôtel* at no 7.

At the traffic lights, go left into Rue Bonaparte – where August Comte (1798–1857), the founder of Positivism, lived at no 36 – and along to Place St-Germain-des-Prés, the centre of late-1940s and early-1950s nightlife and a kind of big club for the Existentialists and others such as Simone de Beauvoir (1908–1986), Juliette Greco (b1927), Raymond Queneau (1903–1976), Jean-Paul Sartre (1905–1980) and Boris Vian (1920–1959). Most of the cafés, bars and clubs, like the famous Tabou, were in nearby streets such as Rue St-Benoît and Rue Dauphine.

Église St-Germain-des-Prés
The *place* was created in 1866, in the Second Empire, on the site of the old church square. In the small garden at the side of the church is a bust by Pablo Picasso (1881–1973) of the writer Guillaume Apollinaire (1880–1918). Facing the church is the interesting jewellery shop Arthus Bertrand, with a fine façade, and next to it is that most elegant of Parisian cafés, Les Deux Magots. The church itself is about 65m (71yd) long and is in a mixture of styles: the main body is Romanesque but the chancel is Gothic; the façade is 17th-century, the bell-tower belongs to the original 11th-century church, and

the choir and ambulatory are 12th-century. The latter was restored in the 1950s and is stunning; it opens onto nine chapels. Most of the decoration, including the nave frescoes by Jean Hyppolite Flandrin (1809–1864), is 19th century.

On leaving the church, go left to Boulevard St-Germain and turn right. Next to Les Deux Magots is the other temple of St-Germain life, the Café Flore, and on the other side is the great Brasserie Lipp, with its *fin-de-siècle* decor. Stay on the right-hand side, where there are a few art galleries. Further along, the small garden on the right – Square Tarass-Chevtchenko – backs onto the Ukrainian Byzantine Catholic church of St-Vladimir-le-Grand (*c*956–1015); the entrance is in Rue des Sts-Pères. The church, which has a fine iconostasis, was built by Robert de Cotte (1656–1735) in the 1730s, being then known as the Chapelle St-Pierre.

Cross the boulevard at the next set of traffic lights and go left along Rue St-Guillaume, now split in half. The Institut des Sciences Politiques is at no 27, but the real focus of interest is no 31, where there is a spectacular little house in the courtyard: the Maison du Verre, built by Pierre Chareau (1883–1950). One entire wall is made of glass and metal, and the whole is typical of what Modernism was trying to achieve in the 1930s. The house can be visited by appointment.

Turn left at the end into Rue de Grenelle – antiques and fashion shops and, at no 25, the Hôtel de Benulle – and left again into Rue des Sts-Pères. The most interesting *hôtels* in this agreeably quaint street are de Meilleraie and de Cavoie (nos 56 and 52), both of which were built in 1640.

Reaching Boulevard St-Germain again, turn right; note the fine windows of the Sonya Rykiel shop – nos 175, 173 and 169 date from the 18th century. Turn right again into the narrow Rue du Dragon. There are several art galleries and restaurants. Almost all the houses in this delightful street are 17th- or 18th-century; Victor Hugo (1802–1885) lived at no 30 in 1821 while writing his famous *Odes et Ballades* (1826). The narrow Rue Bernard-Palissy, which you pass on the left, seems to have remained unchanged since the 18th century.

Reach Carrefour de la Croix-Rouge, so-named since the 15th century. The massive metal statue on your right, near Rue du Cherche-Midi, is by César (1921–1998). Cross Rue du Four into Rue du Vieux-Colombier, where you can see one of the spires of Église St-Sulpice. Go along the street, cross Rue de Rennes and reach Place St-Sulpice, now dominated by the church.

St-Sulpice

Place St-Sulpice was designed in the second half of the 18th century by the Florentine architect Giovanni Servandoni (1695–1766); it was completed in 1833, and the handsome fountain by Lodovico Visconti (1791–1853), with sculptures of four famous preachers – Jean Baptiste Massillon (1663–1742), François Fénelon (1651–1715), Esprit Fléchier (1632–1710) and Jacques Bossuet (1627–1704) – was installed in 1844. Until recently almost every shop on the northern side of this *place* was a religious shop, selling clerical wear, etc.

The church itself has a long history. It was essentially the work of Louis Le Vau (1612–1670) and Daniel Gittard (1625–1686). The first stone was laid in 1646, but funds ran out in 1670, and work did not resume until 40 years later, when the nave, the roof and the façade (by Servandoni) were completed. However, there was a problem about the towers. Servandoni's plan was rejected, and an architect called MacLaurin was given the job, but the two towers he built were not liked. Jean François Chalgrin (1739–1811), then an up-and-coming architect, tendered a new plan, which was accepted: in 1777–88 the northern tower (that on the right) was demolished and a new one erected. But then came the Revolution, and Chalgrin never had the opportunity to replace the south tower. The church thus has two towers of different heights and shapes: one is round, the other square.

St-Sulpice is enormous – at 110m (360ft) long it is among the largest churches in Paris. The majestic interior cannot fail to impress. The organ (1781) is by François Henri Clicquot (1732–1790) with a case by Chalgrin. A little marvel is the Chapelle des Sts-Anges (first on the right as you come in), with superb frescoes by Delacroix. Most of the decoration is by other 19th-century artists. There are eight chapels on either side, plus the larger Chapelle de l'Assomption beyond the choir and the ambulatory, and beyond that the smaller Chapelle de la Vierge, containing another artistic treasure, a superb sculpture of the Virgin by Jean Baptiste Pigalle (1714–1785).

Leave the church by the southern exit (on the right just before the chancel) and find yourself in Rue Palatine. Facing you is Rue Servandoni, a pleasant medieval street with mostly 17th- and 18th-century houses. At the top, on the other side of the railings in Rue de Vaugirard, are the Jardin and Palais du Luxembourg (see p61). Turn left along Rue de Vaugirard, pass Rue Garancière and, just opposite the entrance to the *palais,* turn left into the handsome Rue de Tournon.

This street, opened in the early 16th century on land belonging to the Abbaye St-Germain-des-Prés, contains many fine houses. There is a good façade at no 29. The poet Clément Marot (c1497–1544) lived in a house at no 27 (plaque); Giacomo Casanova (1725–1798) lived for a time in the present no 27. The Scottish-born hero of the US War of Independence, Paul Jones (1747–1792), lived and died at no 19. The fine Hôtel de Brancas, at no 6, now houses the Institut Français d'Architecture. Alphonse de Lamartine (1790–1869) lived in the 17th-century Hôtel de Palaiseay at no 4. Alphonse Daudet (1840–1897) and Léon Gambetta (1838–1882) both lived at no 7. Finally, the superb early 17th-century Hôtel de Châtillon, where Honoré de Balzac (1799–1850) lived for three years, is at no 2.

The Marché St-Germain

At the end of Rue de Tournon, cross Rue St-Sulpice into Rue de Seine and turn immediately left into Rue Lobineau, which leads to Marché St-Germain, now renovated and containing boutiques on the ground floor and a small auditorium upstairs. Only a few arches are left of the original market, built in 1813–18 on the remains of the ancient St Germain Fair, which had been there since the late 15th century.

At the end of the street turn right into Rue Mabillon and then first left into Rue Guisarde – where there are restaurants of varying calibre – and right again into Rue Princesse. Both the latter streets were opened in the 17th century, and the most private of Parisian clubs, Castel, is in Rue Princesse. Turn right into Rue du Four and right again at the boulevard; along a little way is Odéon métro station, where this walk ends.

You can connect this walk with the previous walk, which will take you to the Luxembourg Gardens, Port-Royal, Val-de-Grâce and beyond. Cross the boulevard, continue eastward, pass Rue Danton, take the second turning left into Rue Hautefeuille, and cross Place St-André-des-Arts to Place St-Michel.

Beaubourg and Châtelet

A pleasant walk with the Musée National d'art Moderne (Centre Georges-Pompidou) as a highlight. The museum is in Beaubourg, one of the oldest parts of Paris. The medieval village of Beau Bourg became part of the city when Philippe-Auguste built his wall. The village was not known for the social quality of its inhabitants: brigands, cutpurses and prostitutes frequented the area until the 1970s, when the museum was opened and the area was cleaned up. The walk goes from the vestiges of the medieval monastery of St-Martin-des-Champs *via* ancient streets, one of the few medieval houses still extant in Paris, several fine 17th- and 18th-century *hôtels*, the churches of St-Merri and St-Gervais, the Hôtel de Ville (town hall) and Place du Châtelet, on the river.

Start: **Métro Arts-et-Métiers; buses 20, 75.**
Finish: **Métro Châtelet; buses 38, 47, 69, 72, 75, 76, 81.**
Length: **5.5km (3½ miles).**
Time: **1½hr.**
Refreshments: **Trendy bars around the museum as well as some old-fashioned and interesting restaurants, the better ones being at the end of the walk. The cafeteria at the top of the Pompidou Centre offers ravishing views.**
Which day: **Any day except Tuesday; though always rather full, the museum gets quieter in late afternoon and early evening.**
To visit:
● **Musée National d'Art Moderne: daily (not Tuesday). 11.00–21.00 (Thursdays until 23.00)**

St-Martin-des-Champs
Exit Arts-et-Métiers métro station onto Rue Réaumur. The church nearby is that of the 12th-century monastery of St-Martin-des-Champs (see p41). With the church behind you, walk eastwards along Rue Réaumur and turn right into the narrow Rue Volta. At no 3 on the right is what purports to be the oldest house in Paris: opinions are divided as to whether it is a 14th-century building, as the plaque claims, or whether it is merely an 18th-century pastiche.

Take Rue au Maire to the right until you reach Rue Beaubourg. Take a left and then first right into Rue des Gravilliers. In Rue Beaubourg you will have had your first sight of the multicoloured pipes on the service side of the Musée National d'Art Moderne building, which some Parisians irreverently call the Oil Refinery. Continue along Rue des Gravilliers – passing the impressive *hôtel* with mascaron and pleasing courtyard at no 70 and the old houses at nos 69 and 71 – until you reach the traffic lights, where you turn left into Rue St-Martin, one of the two oldest streets in Paris, the other being Rue St-Jacques.

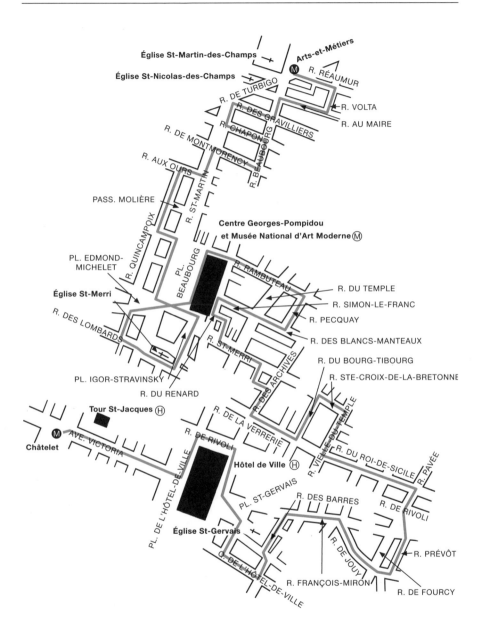

Go left along Rue Chapon – more fine old houses – then right into Rue Beaubourg, with the towers of Notre-Dame in the middle distance, and right again into Rue de Montmorency, where at no 51 is the much restored house of Nicolas Flamel (*c*1330–1418), dating from 1407 and thus either the oldest or the second-oldest house in Paris, depending on one's opinion of the house in Rue Volta! Flamel was an esteemed lawyer, calligrapher and writer as well as something of an alchemist and a favourite with students.

Turn left into Rue St-Martin (there is a handsome house at no 201) and right almost immediately into Rue aux Ours. Cross the street to Rue Quincampoix, which contains many fine houses, especially in the bottom section. The unfortunate protagonist of *Justine* (1791) by the Marquis de Sade (1740–1814) lived in this street. The top half has changed greatly over the last 15 years because of its proximity to the Centre, but has not yet become trendy; there are a few art galleries.

Walk down to no 82, where you will find the delightful Passage Molière, opened in 1791 alongside the reborn Théâtre Molière, erected during the Revolution. If the *passage* is shut (it often is on Sundays), continue down Rue Quincampoix, turn left into Rue Rambuteau and then first right into Rue St-Martin; otherwise use the *passage* to reach Rue St-Martin, and turn right.

The National Museum of Modern Art

You are now at the Centre Georges-Pompidou, named for the French president who initiated the project; it is often called the Centre Beaubourg. The centre was extensively renovated and reorganized in the late 1990s and re-opened in 2000. It houses not only the museum, on the top floors, but also a vast public library plus various exhibition rooms, workshops, etc. The caféteria/restaurant on the top floor is especially recommended on a clear day: the view from its terrace is stunning. In fact, this may be the best place to visit first: take the escalators for a slow ascent over the city (no ticket required).

The Centre Beaubourg, built in the 1970s by two young architects, Richard Rogers (b1933) from the UK and Renzo Piano (b1937) from Italy, is a great building, and remarkably versatile. It is one of the city's largest museums – the collection of 20th-century art is one of the largest in the world – and the contents cannot sensibly be described here. There are superb works by nearly all the giants of the century as well as by lesser known artists. The library on the mezzanine is also well worth a visit.

Around the esplanade are many cafés, the Cavalier Bleu at the corner of Rues St-Martin and Rambuteau being among the best.

St-Merri

Leave the museum and go left down Rue St-Martin and left again into Rue St-Merri; you are effectively going round the museum. At the corner of the building, a little way up, there was previously a clock that gave a second-by-second countdown to AD2000. Turn right into Place Igor-Stravinsky, where there is an amusing fountain dedicated to the composer, with sculptures in painted fibreglass by Niki de St Phalle (1930–2002) and in metal by Jean Tinguely (1925–1991). The *place* backs onto the north wall of the handsome Église St-Merri. At the northwest side of the *place* is the entrance to the IRCAM (Institut de Recherche et de Coordination Musicale et Acoustique), the ultracontemporary music-research institute previously run by Pierre Boulez (b1925).

Cross the square, go around the church into Rue des Juges-Conseils and turn right into Rue de la Verrerie, one side of which is occupied by the church. Rue de la Verrerie, one of the oldest streets in the city, was one of the most important streets of ancient Paris, being the main east-west axis (a role now fulfilled by Rue de Rivoli). Enter the church by the side door at no 76, which is also the vicarage. Église St-Merri was built in 1520–60, during the early Renaissance, the heyday of Flamboyant Gothic, on the site of a much older church that had become too small; it was transformed into a Baroque edifice a couple of centuries later, when Gothic art was out of fashion. Most of the decoration dates from its restoration in the 18th-19th centuries; during the Revolution it was a temple of commerce. The organ case is by Germain Pilon (1537–1590); Camille Saint-Saëns (1835–1921) was organist here for many years.

Leave the church *via* the main door and glance back: the façade is of interest, although all the statues are 19th-century. Now turn left, and then right into Rue des Lombards; the name acknowledges the wealthy Italian merchants and financiers who lived here in the Middle Ages. Giovanni Boccaccio (1313–1375) was born in this street.

Turn immediately right into Rue Quincampoix; this narrow section contains many fine 17th- and 18th-century houses. Keeping to Rue Quincampoix, cross Place Edmond-Michelet, completely changed since the erection of the Centre Beaubourg, and then Rue Aubry-le-Boucher. At no 65 Rue Quincampoix stood the house where the Scottish financier John Law (1671–1729) established his famous bank during the Regency. Turn right into Rue Rambuteau, cross Rue St-Martin, and walk along the north end of Place Georges-Pompidou. Cross Rue Beaubourg and continue down a lively section of Rue Rambuteau. Cross Rue du Temple and turn right into Rue Pecquay, where there are old houses and art galleries, and emerge into Rue des Blancs-Manteaux; turn right. Cross Rue du Temple again to the picturesque, ancient Rue Simon-le-Franc, which was already in existence by the time of Louis IX.

At the end, go left down Rue du Renard (a continuation of Rue Beaubourg) and turn left into Rue Pierre-au-Lard; the celebrated café de la Gare, run by one of the great men of French theatre, Romain Bouteille (b1937) – his pupils have included Patrick Dewaere (1947–1982), Miou-Miou (b1950) and Gérard Depardieu (b1948) – is here. The street bends sharply towards Rue St-Merri, in which you turn left. At no 12 is the recently renovated Hôtel le Rebours, a superb 16th- and 17th-century building with a lovely courtyard and fine stone stairs with a wrought-iron banister; it now houses the Galerie Maeght, itself a wonderful space.

Walk on and turn left into Rue du Temple (notice the turret at no 24), cross the street and turn right into Rue du Plâtre and right again into Rue des Archives. Over the street, at no 22/24, is the entrance to Paris's only surviving medieval cloister: the Cloître des Billettes, dating from 1415, a vestige of the Carmes-Billettes monastery. The church dates from the 18th century and has been a Lutheran temple since 1812. At no 40 is the elegant house of the Coeur family: Jacques Coeur (c1395–1456) was one of the wealthiest merchants in medieval France and a financial adviser to Charles VII.

Yet further down, go left into Rue de la Verrerie and along to Rue du Bourg-Tibourg, a typical local street, into which turn left; there are quite a few reasonable restaurants in the street. At the top of the street turn right into Rue Ste-Croix-de-la-Bretonnerie, where there are many trendy bars; the bistro-type restaurant Le Gavroche on the left is fun. Next turn right into Rue Vieille-du-Temple and then left into Rue du Roi-de-Sicile (a peaceful continuation of Rue de la Verrerie). The street takes its name from Charles d'Anjou (1225–1285), brother of Louis IX and King of Naples and Sicily, whose 13th-century *hôtel* stood at no 2, on the corner with Rue Pavée. The estate was split in the 17th century, and here stood the Hôtel de la Force, later a prison where, during the Revolution, over 170 people were put to death, including the Princesse de Lamballe (1749–1792), confidante to Marie Antoinette (1755–1793).

Turn right into Rue Pavée. Cross Rue de Rivoli to the very narrow Rue du Prévôt, on the other side of St-Paul métro station. Turn right at the bottom and cross Rue de Fourcy to Rue de Jouy, where at no 7 is the rather severe Hôtel des Ducs-d'Aumont, designed by Louis Le Vau (1612–1670). Terribly damaged after the Revolution, it was restored by the city of Paris and now houses the Tribunal Administratif.

Turn left at the top of Rue de Jouy into Rue François-Miron, an old section of Rue St-Antoine. Turn left again, some way along, into the charming pedestrian Rue des Barres, where there is a fine half-timbered house at no 12   and a wonderful view over the apse of Église St-Gervais. Walk down to Quai de l'Hôtel-de-Ville, a restful spot with cafés and restaurants; the Brasserie du Pont-Louis-Philippe is on the corner.

St-Gervais
Walk along the *quai*: there are good views over the Îles St Louis and de la Cité as well as good cafés, shops and restaurants. Turn right into Rue de Brosse, where Voltaire (1694–1778) lived when he was 39; the street leads to Église St-Gervais and to the square of the same name. The church is interesting; built, like so many in Paris, on the site of a more ancient church, it was a long time in construction. It was started in the late 15th century by Martin Chambiges (d1532) in Flamboyant Gothic and completed during the 17th century; the most evident contrast is between the body of the church and the 1620 early-Baroque façade by Clément Métezeau (1581–1652), where for the first time in Paris one can see the three Classical orders: Doric at the bottom, Ionic in the middle and Corinthian at the top. The church was vandalized during the Revolution and restored during the 19th century, from which time most of the interior decoration dates. Three members of the Couperin family – they lived next to the church and were the organists of the church for more than a century – were buried here.

Capital Punishment
Leave the church and walk across Place St-Gervais towards the back of the 19th-century Hôtel de Ville, where you turn right into Rue de Lobau (a continuation of Rue des Archives). Reach Rue de Rivoli; the great department store, Bazar de l'Hôtel-de-Ville, is on the other side. Turn left, walk along the *hôtel de ville* (town hall) and reach Place de l'Hôtel-de-Ville, in which you turn left.

The original Renaissance building, itself built on the site of the medieval town hall set up by the important Merchant Prévost, Étienne Marcel (*c*1316–1358), was burnt down during the Commune and replaced by the present building, with Théodore Ballu (1817–1885) and Édouard Deperthes (1833–1898) as architects. You are not usually allowed in, although there are sometimes interesting exhibitions in the vast Salle des Fêtes (St-Gervais side), which was decorated by leading artists of the Third Republic.

Place de l'Hôtel-de-Ville was once Place de la Grève (river bank), and from 1310 to 1830 public executions took place here. They were so popular that people paid huge sums to hire window- and roof-spaces on the houses around the square. The square was relaid in 1982; the fountains are by the sculptor/designer François Xavier Lalanne.

Now take Avenue Victoria from the centre of the *place* down to Place du Châtelet. On the way you pass Tour St-Jacques, set in a small public garden (Square St-Jacques). This tower is all that remains of the church of St-Jacques-la-Boucherie, demolished during the Revolution, one of the starting points for the great pilgrimage to Santiago de Compostela. Although this walk ends at the Châtelet métro station, on Place du Châtelet, the next one, the Les Halles walk, makes an ideal continuation.

Les Halles

The great food market of Les Halles has long gone, but the *quartier* has retained its old vitality. Although the cafés, restaurants and shops no longer possess the atmospheric seediness traditionally associated with the area, there are still echoes of it, as in the busy Rue Montorgueil and in Rue des Petits-Carreaux. Among the interesting monuments are the extraordinary Bourse du Commerce and the colossal Église St-Eustache. The area around Rue Pierre-Lescot and the Halles is especially buoyant in the evenings, with many places being open well into the small hours. Much of that area is closed to traffic, so it is particularly attractive for a stroll.

Start and finish: **Métro Châtelet; buses 38, 47, 69, 72, 75, 76, 81.**
Length: **4.5km (2¾ miles).**
Time: **2hr.**
Refreshments: **A vast array of places. New cafés and restaurants seem to spring up daily, especially around the Halles, but there are also a few hardy perennials, as noted in the main text.**
Which day: **Any day, although the *quartier* is a little too quiet on Sundays and fills up with hordes of shoppers on Saturday afternoons.**

Prison, morgue and divas
Leave the métro station by the Place du Châtelet exit. The *place* was created in the reign of Napoleon I over the site of a medieval fortress which had later become a prison and morgue. The *place* was greatly enlarged by Georges Haussmann (1809–1891) at the same time as he created the wide Boulevard de Sébastopol which, with Boulevard du Palais in the Île de la Cité and Boulevard St-Michel on the Left Bank, makes up the city's central north–south axis. As its east–west axis is formed by Rue de Rivoli and the greatly enlarged Rue St-Antoine, Place du Châtelet is at, as it were, the Ground Zero of Paris's traffic.

The fountain was built in 1806 and the two theatres by Gabriel Davioud (1823–1881) in the 1860s: the Théâtre de la Ville, to the east, specializes in ballet and avant-garde theatre, while the Théâtre du Châtelet now concentrates on music and opera; Jean-Jacques Beinex filmed the famous opening sequence of the cult film *Diva* (1981) in the latter theatre while it was in the process of restoration.

Walk towards the Théâtre du Châtelet in Avenue Victoria; on the right are many plant and flower merchants. Before the theatres were built and the square enlarged, there were many narrow, insalubrious streets here; in one of them, now occupied by the stage of the Châtelet Théâtre, the romantic poet Gérard de Nerval (1808–1855) hanged himself from a lamp-post. Turn left at the bottom and immediately right into the picturesque Rue St-Germain-l'Auxerrois (9th-century), one of the oldest streets in Paris; it leads to the parish church of the same name 200m (220yd) further on (see p91). At the end, turn right into Rue des Bourdonnais, today unfortunately split by Rue de Rivoli;

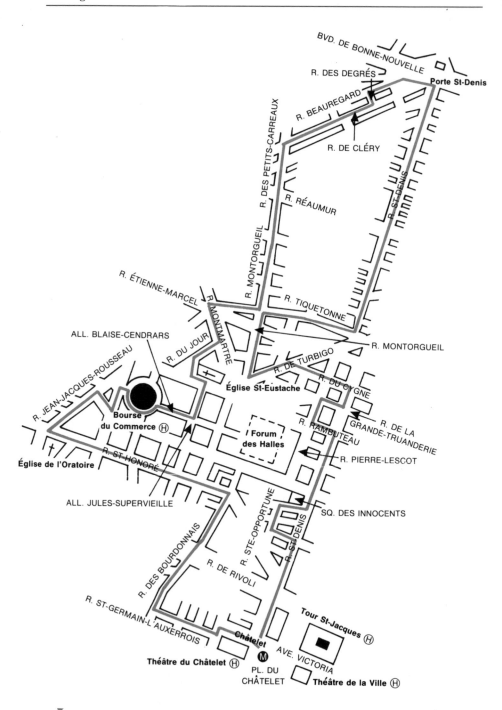

the houses at nos 26 and 24 are 17th-century. Cross Rue de Rivoli carefully – people drive a little fast – and continue down Rue des Bourdonnais. You can catch a glimpse of the new Halles development nearby. There is a handsome door on the 17th-century *hôtel* at no 34 and there is another fine *hôtel* at no 39. In the 14th century two witches were burnt in the small Impasse des Bourdonnais, on the left.

Turn left into Rue St-Honoré, another ancient way, which linked the Louvre, the Palais-Cardinal (later Palais-Royal) and the royal residence at St-Germain-en-Laye.

Playwright, barber and pharmacist
This section of Rue St-Honoré is extremely lively (especially by day), and contains several old houses, mostly from the 17th and 18th centuries. Cross Rue du Pont-Neuf – which offers a nice perspective over Église St-Eustache to the right – and Rue des Prouvaires, where Cyrano de Bergerac (1619–1655) was born, where the excellent À La Tour de Monthléry restaurant can be found, and where there are two fine *hôtels*, at nos 1 and 3. There is a fine wrought-iron 17th-century balcony on the corner with Rue des Prouvaires, at no 54 Rue St-Honoré, interesting mascarons at no 56/58, and at no 93 a peculiar house with a Directoire sign, 'Au Bourdon d'Or', at the first-floor level. Just before this, Village St-Honoré, at no 91, leads to various antiques shops. The 'À la Renommée des Herbes Cuites' sign at the first-floor level of no 95 shows where Louis XIV's barber used to reside.

Rue de l'Arbre-Sec, on the left, has the fine Fontaine du Trahoir (1776) by Jacques Germain Soufflot (1709–1780), the architect of the Panthéon. The handsome pharmacy at no 115 Rue St-Honoré is the oldest establishment of its kind in the capital (1715). Almost directly opposite, at no 96, on the corner with Rue Sauval, is a plaque indicating that Molière (1622–1673) was born in a house that stood here – a claim that is almost certainly true, although a similar plaque on one of the houses in nearby Rue du Pont-Neuf makes the same claim (but gets his birthdate wrong!).

Cross Rue du Louvre. The first Porte St-Honoré (there were three altogether – see p100), one of the gates of the Philippe-Auguste wall, stood in the vicinity of no 145. A little further along is the Protestant Église de l'Oratoire, sited since Napoleonic times in the ancient chapel of the Congrégation de l'Oratoire, built 1620–30 by Jacques Lemercier (1585–1684) and later a Royal Chapel. Unfortunately the church is often closed; the best time to go is when there is a service on.

Commerce and astrology
Reach Rue Jean-Jacques-Rousseau and turn right. Pass the charming 19th-century Galerie Véro-Dodat on the left and get to Rue du Louvre and Place des Deux Écus, which cross towards the Bourse du Commerce and the Halles esplanade.

The Bourse du Commerce, designed by François Joseph Bélanger (1745–1818), was built in 1765–8 on the site of the Hôtel de La Reine (see below) as a *halle au blé* (corn market). This vast circular building is not without its elegance; walk around it to appreciate it fully. The entrance was modified during the 19th century and is a little severe. The interior is a superb space; the steel structure of the roof dates from 1811 and most of the decoration (recently renovated) is 19th-century. The building became the Bourse in 1889, and is now the City of Paris Trade Centre.

The Hôtel de la Reine was built by Philibert Delorme (c1510–1570) for Catherine de' Medici (1519–1589), and was soon deemed to be, after the Louvre Palace, the most sumptuous house in Paris. Catherine was devoted to astrology and other arcane sciences. Her astrologer, the celebrated Cosimo Ruggieri (d1615), predicted that she would die 'near St-Germain', whereupon which she resolved never again to set foot in St-Germain-en-Laye and, more pertinently in our context, determined to leave the royal Tuileries Palace (situated in the parish of St-Germain-l'Auxerrois). The site where she wanted to build her new house was already occupied, by the *couvent* of the Filles Pénitentes ou Repenties – an odd institution, in that applicants had to provide proof of their dissolute lives, and a favourite haunt of kings and aristocrats. The *couvent* was moved to Rue St-Denis, the building was pulled down and Catherine's *hôtel* was built. Incidentally, she died at distant Blois, in 1589; however, as a sop to astrology fans, the priest who gave her the last rites was one Julien de St-Germain.

Some 200 years later the *hôtel* was pulled down to make way for the corn market. As you leave the Bourse, turn left and follow the building around Rue de Viarmes – named for the merchant's prevost who initiated the corn market – you will find the sole remnant of the old *hôtel*: Ruggieri's astrological column. Built by Jean Bullant (c1520–1578), this observatory is nearly 30m (99ft) high, with 147 steps leading to its top.

St-Eustache

You are now at the western side of the Jardin des Halles. The area around the Halles consisted mostly of fields until the 12th century, when Louis le Gros (Louis VI) installed a market there; the market was developed by Philippe-Auguste, who roofed it and enclosed it within his fortified wall. It remained a market until the 1960s, when pressure for space caused its removal outside Paris. The wondrous cast-iron structure by the 19th-century architect Victor Baltard (1805–1874) was demolished, with at least one of its 10 different pavilions being shipped entire to the USA. The site remains, however, dedicated to shopping and entertainment, with the vast underground Forum des Halles and its many shops, restaurants, cafés, cinemas, etc., soon due for a complete refit. Expect complications.

Take Allée Blaise-Cendrars, facing you, and 100m (110yd) along it turn left towards St-Eustache into Allée Jules-Supervieille. This leads to a large piazza in the shape of a shell – a tiny Siennese echo – with an intriguing statue by Henry de Miler, *Head and Hand*, listening to the sea from the shell.

Église St-Eustache took over 100 years (1532–1637) to build, and is in a Renaissance Gothic style; it is the largest Parisian church after Notre-Dame, by which it was influenced, and, despite its size, is graceful. It shows heavy borrowings from Gothic techniques: there are flying buttresses, semicircular vaulted doorways and windows. The façade was added in the 18th century and was never finished – the left-hand clock tower is missing. The church contains many delights, especially in the side-chapels and in the chapels of the ambulatory; they include the tomb of Jean Baptise Colbert (1619–1683) by Antoine Coysevox (1640–1720), the *Emmaus Pilgrims* (school of Rubens), the extraordinary *Virgin's Ecstasy* by Rutilio Manetti (1571–1639), the stunning *Virgin* by Jean Baptiste Pigalle (1714–1785) and finally, in the left-hand side-chapel, an equally extraordinary contemporary sculpture by Raymond Mason (b1922), *Le Déménagement des Halles*.

Leave the church. A little further on is the celebrated restaurant Au Pied de Cochon. Turn right into the narrow and much altered Rue du Jour, which has 17th- and 18th-century houses and a couple of popular clothes shops. At the bottom of the street, turn left into Rue Montmartre.

Court of Miracles

You are entering an area where food is king: there are butchers, wholesalers, delicatessens, vegetable stalls . . . This is the oldest section of Rue Montmartre, which dates back at least to the 13th century, when it led – as of course it still does – to Montmartre. At no 15, Le Cochon à l'Oreille is an agreeable little bar with turn-of-the-century décor. At no 30 was Philippe-Auguste's Porte Montmartre.

Cross the broad 19th-century Rue Étienne-Marcel to Rue Tiquetonne. Some 50m (55yd) along, turn left into Rue Montorgueil, now forming a pedestrian precinct with Rue des Petits-Carreaux (its continuation on the other side of the intersection with Rues St-Sauveur and Léopold-Bellan). These two picturesque streets have retained a strong *quartier* spirit, with busy shops and interesting houses (mostly 18th- and 19th-century); the old 'Rocher de Cancale' sign on the house at the corner with Rue Grénéta is worth noting. Keep going along Rue des Petits-Carreaux and cross the wide Rue Réaumur. Rue du Nil, on the right, used to lead to the notorious Court of Miracles, made world-famous by Victor Hugo (1802–1885), who featured it in his *Notre-Dame de Paris* (1831). Built in the shadow of the city wall, this muddy yard with its dingy shacks was home to brigands, prostitutes and beggars. Deserted by day, it became extremely rowdy at night, when they all came back from their expeditions in the city. It was razed in the 17th century, but the memory lingers . . .

Take the third turning to the right, Rue de Cléry, and find yourself entering the Sentier, a distinctively different area, dominated by the rag trade. Rue de Cléry itself was established in the 1630s over the Charles V wall when Louis XIII extended the city wall to the west, demolishing this part of the old wall in the process. The street is home to several small clothing businesses catering for, mostly, the bottom end of the market. Most of the houses are 18th- and 19th-century. Pierre Corneille (1606–1684) lived in this street for 16 years, and Mme de Pompadour (1721–1764) was born and brought up in a house near no 29, on the left of Rue des Petits-Carreaux. At the crossroads with Rue Poissonnière is the handsome building that used to be the Hôtel de Noisy, erected in 1740.

Just after no 87, on the left, is Rue des Degrés, a few steps leading to Rue Beauregard, which you should follow downhill towards Louis XIV's triumphal arch, built by François Blondel (1618–1686) in 1672.

Turn right into Boulevard St-Denis and then into Rue St-Denis, once renowned as the handsomest street in Paris. It was probably laid out in the 8th or 9th century, leading to the basilica of St-Denis, where the kings of France are buried, but became important in the 12th century, taking over from the nearby Rue St-Martin as the main route north out of the city while also being the kings' official entrance into the city. It has lost its old magnificence: many of the fine 17th- and 18th-century *hôtels* have been demolished or obscured by 19th-century development. This top section is home to more clothing wholesalers and is a red-light district; there are also old-fashioned cafés and shops. Many *passages* lead off towards Boulevard de Sébastopol (on the left) and Rue du Caire (on the right); although they are more fully explored on p169, it is worth popping your nose into a few of them now. Several lead to ancient *hôtels;* for example, the one at no 226 leads to the Hôtel St-Chaumon (1631).

Trendy city

Cross Rue Réaumur and keep on down Rue St-Denis past the 16th-century houses at nos 176 and 174 and the mascaron at no 142. When you reach Rue Tiquetonne, turn right; on its corner with Rue de Turbigo you can see, at no 13, a magnificent 18th-century house with a mascaron. On reaching Rue Montorgueil, turn left into it and keep going across Rue Étienne Marcel. At no 38 Rue Montorgueil is the exquisite restaurant À l'Escargot, established 1832.

At the bottom of the street turn sharply left into Rue de Turbigo and stay on the left, passing a few interesting shops selling clothes and designer furniture. At the first traffic lights, cross over to Rue Mondétour and then go immediately left along Rue du Cygne to Rue Pierre-Lescot; if you detour briefly left to the top of this pleasant pedestrian street you can see, on the other side of Rue Étienne Marcel, Tour Jean-Sans-Peur, all that remains of the 15th-century *hôtel* of the dukes of Burgundy, then almost more powerful than the kings of France.

Return to Rue du Cygne and continue along it to Rue St-Denis, in which turn right; a ceramic sign on the corner depicts a swan. Facing you is Église St-Leu-St-Gilles, a medieval church adapted several times over the centuries; the façade is 14th-century and the roof 18th-century. Take first right into Rue de la Grande-Truanderie and turn left into Rue Pierre-Lescot.

The innocents and the recluses

Go left into Rue Rambuteau and then right into Rue St-Denis, which you follow all the way down to Square des Innocents. Café Coste, a temple of 1980s design by Philippe-Patrick Starck (b1949), is on the corner; the eastern entrance to the Halles shopping mall is to the right. This area has changed beyond recognition since the Halles development: modern and not entirely successful buildings have sadly damaged the view. In the middle of the *square* is a fine Renaissance fountain designed by Pierre Lescot (c1510–1578), later the architect of the Louvre, and with bas-reliefs (now in the Louvre) by Jean Goujon (c1510–1568), whose work is found also at Carnavalet and Église St-Germain-l'Auxerrois.

The *square* was built over a small section of the ancient Cimetière des Innocents, opened in the 10th century and until the 18th century the only cemetery in Paris. It was operated on simple principles: a big hole was dug and bodies were piled in on top of each other until it was full, when another hole would be dug. Its church possessed, in the 15th century, *reclusoirs* – small stone huts, built on the side of the church, into which women would, out of mystic fervour, voluntarily shut themselves for years if not decades, their only contact with the outside world being *via* a slit in the church wall.

By the 18th century the stench of the cemetery had become unbearable – the novel *Perfume* (1985) by Patrick Süskind (b1949) uses this area as a background – and the local population petitioned the king for the cemetery to be transferred. This was eventually done, and over a period of more than 15 months in 1785–6 the bones of two million corpses were moved from here to what is now known as the Catacombs (see p154); at the same time, the church was demolished.

Cross the square diagonally and go into Rue Ste-Opportune (the *passage* under the arch). Rue de la Ferronnerie, which you cross, was the continuation of Rue St-Honoré before Haussmann's urban transformation disrupted the street. It was somewhere along here, probably near no 11, that Henri IV was assassinated in 1610 by the monk François Ravaillac (1578–1610).

Turn left into Rue des Lombards and right into Rue St-Denis. Keep straight on down Rue St-Denis until you reach Place du Châtelet, where the walk ends.

Maubert to Orsay

This almost linear walk between the river and Boulevard St-Germain links three *quartiers*: the Latin Quarter, St-Germain-des-Prés and Faubourg St-Germain. It visits medieval Paris, the birthplace of the University, Classical Paris, three stunning churches, the Musée d'Orsay (more fully discussed in the next walk) and numerous small streets with shops, cafés, restaurants and art galleries.

Start: **Métro Maubert-Mutualité, buses 24, 27, 47, 63, 86, 87.**
Finish: **Musée-d'Orsay (RER line C) *or* métro Solférino; buses 24, 27, 73, 84, 94.**
Length: **4km (2½ miles).**
Time: **2hr.**
Refreshments: **A profusion of places, especially around Rue St-Séverin and Rue de la Huchette, and along the streets near St-Germain-des-Prés. Then a void until the end of the walk, at Musée d'Orsay, where there are a couple of cafés and the museum cafeteria.**
Which day: **Any day except Monday, when the museum is closed. Saturdays are extremely busy, especially in the first part of the walk, near Place St-Michel.**
To visit:
● **Musée d'Orsay: Thursday 10.00–21.45, Sunday 09.00–18.00, other days (not Monday) 10.00–18.00.**

The birthplace of the University
Exit Maubert-Mutualité station onto Place Maubert; there is a good view over the Panthéon and the houses of Montagne Ste-Geneviève. The original Place Maubert, a little further north, was an early meeting-place for students after Peter Abélard (1079–1142) had left Notre-Dame Cloister School and really invented the Rive Gauche. (He was later famously castrated on the orders of the uncle of the girl he had fallen in love with and seduced, Heloïse [*c*1100–1164].) A little further on from here stood the College de Constantinople, established 1206, the first such student college (see pp45–6 for a further discussion of Abélard and the colleges).

Walk eastward across the *place*, go along the left of the boulevard, and turn left into Rue de Bièvre, which, like almost all the streets in the area, has recently been done up – they were quite seedy well into the 1970s. President François Mitterand (1916–1996) has his private apartment here, and there are 17th- and 18th-century houses at nos 28, 24, 8 and 7. The Bièvre River ran from Versailles and across Paris to the Seine. Now covered over, in the 19th century it was extremely important as an axis of industrial activity, especially further south near Place d'Italie and the Butte aux Cailles (see p155). The name is the old French word for 'beaver', and dates back to Roman times.

Reach Quai de Montebello – where you can enjoy one of the finest views over Notre-Dame and the Île St-Louis – and turn left, pass the 14th-century Rue Maître-

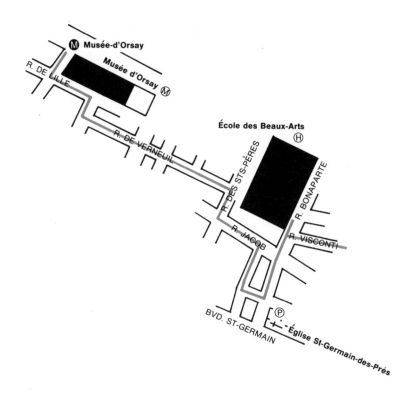

Albert and then go left along Rue des Grands-Degrés to the picturesque Rue de la Bûcherie, opened in 1202. A *bûche* is a log: until the 16th century, wood for fuel and for building – most medieval houses were half-timbered – was floated down the Bièvre to a small port, the *port aux bûches*, near here.

The houses at no 7 and 9 Rue de la Bûcherie are 17th-century, but the most interesting is at nos 13–15, on the angle with Rue de l'Hôtel-Colbert (which itself contains some fine 17th-century *hôtels*). Dating from the end of the 15th century, it used to be the École de Médecine; from the street you can see the cupola of the 18th-century amphitheatre. When the original medical university was set up in the 14th century the would-be doctors, like many of their fellow students, took their lessons in the open air. This situation obtained until this building was erected; it was enlarged during the 16th and 17th centuries. During the First Empire the school was moved to a larger location (see p60).

Shakespeare & Co. and Église St-Julien-le-Pauvre
Cross Rue du Fouarre – another spot where students took lessons in the open air, sitting on bales of straw (*fouarre* means 'straw' in Old French) – into the recently created Square Viviani. This is what is left of the garden of the Église St-Julien-lePauvre, and contains what may be the oldest tree in Paris, a false acacia planted in 1601. On the other side of the garden, at no 27 in what is still Rue de la Bûcherie, is the English-language bookshop, Shakespeare & Co. (see p60).

Books are piled from floor to ceiling, and you can explore all the crannies of this amazing place to get a feel for it. Upstairs is still part of the shop, but doubles as a hostel for impoverished US students. (Note that the original 1920s Shakespeare & Co. was in Rue de l'Odéon – see p60.)

Outside the shop, turn right into Rue St-Julien-le-Pauvre (a couple of nice tearooms) and walk up to the fine Église St-Julien-le-Pauvre. One of the first sanctuaries on the Left Bank, it was erected in the 6th century, destroyed by the Normans, and rebuilt by the Benedictines in 1170–1280. It became one of the preferred churches of the university: among those said to have prayed here were St Thomas Aquinas (1225–1274), Dante Alighieri (1265–1321), François Villon (b1431) and François Rabelais (c1494–c1553). The present building demonstrates the transition from Romanesque to Gothic: in the 17th century, when the church was falling into disrepair, it was shortened and received a new façade. During the Revolution it was used as a barn.

Inside, all is simplicity: a simple nave, four bays and a 17th-century vault – the side-vault is original. Now Greek Orthodox, the church has a remarkable iconostasis (i.e., screen with icons separating chancel from nave).

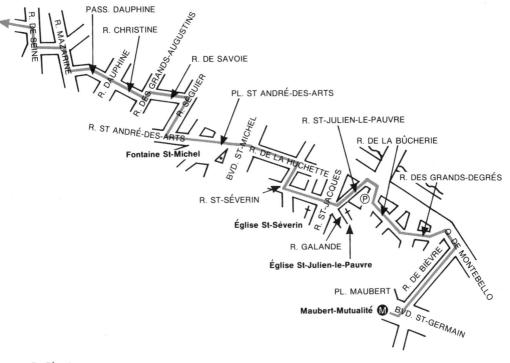

St-Séverin

Leave the church, turn left and reach Rue Galande; facing you is a bizarre-shaped dark-green house. This is one of the oldest streets in Paris; it was the start of the old Roman way to Lyon and Rome. Turn right and cross Rue du Petit-Pont to another extremely ancient street, Rue St-Séverin – indeed, all the streets around here are ancient. You are entering the pedestrian Quartier St-Séverin-La Huchette, now given over to restaurants and shops of dubious quality. Walk along the Église St-Séverin wall and enter the church itself *via* the entrance on Rue des Prêtes-St-Séverin.

This is one of Paris's older and finer churches. Built in the 13th century (from which period date the tower and the first three bays of the nave) on the site of an older sanctuary, it was enlarged in the 15th century, hence the predominant Flamboyant Gothic style. It was further redecorated and altered in the 17th century, when medieval architecture was out of favour. The painting on the columns, as in the side-chapels, is 19th-century, when the medieval was back in fashion. The double-sided ambulatory, with its fine fan-vault so typical of the Flamboyant style, is remarkable. A door leads to a side-chapel built by Jules Hardouin-Mansart (1645–1708) in 1673. Many of the stained-glass windows are 15th-century, restored in the 19th.

Outside, the first part of the façade is 13th-century Gothic while the upper level is late 15th-century, a scheme repeated on the bell-tower. Take a look at the southern wall, which is in good condition, with gargoyles and all.

17th-century streets
Retrace your steps to Rue St-Séverin, turn left and then immediately right down Rue Xavier-Privas, almost all of whose houses are 17th-century. At the bottom, turn left into Rue de la Huchette, which has been so-named for 800 years. Here there are more restaurants as well as some handsome houses, as at nos 16 and 21. At Place St-Michel, cross Boulevard St-Michel to the fountain, which shows St Michael killing the Dragon; designed by Gabriel Davioud (1823–1881) in 1860, it is now a meeting-place for the young. The many cafés on the *place* attract throngs.

Cross to Place St-André-des-Arts and into Rue St-André-des-Arts, up which walk briefly – passing a fine 17th-century *hôtel* (1640) at no 27 – before turning right into Rue Séguier, which contains several good houses, almost all 17th- or 18th-century, such as Hôtel Séguier at no 16 and Hôtel d'Aguesseau at no 18 (the latter rebuilt in the 18th century after the original had burnt down accidentally). The poet, traveller and painter Henri Michaux (1899–1984) lived at no 8 and Albert Camus (1913–1960) at no 18.

Almost at the bottom – the river is a few steps away – turn left into Rue de Savoie, another fine 17th-century street; Blaise Cendrars (1887–1961) lived in a very small flat at no 4, returning there periodically from his tireless travels, and Pablo Picasso (1881–1973) had a studio in the street.

Rue de Savoie leads to Rue des Grands-Augustins; cross it into Rue Christine, opened in Henri IV's reign, following the creation of the nearby Pont Neuf; the repertory cinema Action Christine shows good US classics. Reach Rue Dauphine, where there is a fine view over Pont Neuf to your right. Like Rue Christine, Rue Dauphine was opened across the gardens of the Couvent des Grands-Augustins early in the 17th century. Cross over, go through the gates into Passage Dauphine, and emerge in Rue Mazarine (explored on p106). Turn right and, some way along, go left into Rue Jacques-Callot; on the corner is a plaque indicating that here stood the Jeu de Paume de la Bouteille, where the first Paris Opéra was created in 1671. At the far end of the street, on the corner with Rue de Seine, is the great Café La Palette. Turn right into Rue de Seine; note the 17th-century turrets and medallions on no 41. George Sand (1804–1876) lived at no 31 – today Akademia Raymond Duncan – after she had separated from her husband at age 27; she scandalized the neighbourhood by dressing like a man.

A few metres further on, turn left into the narrow Rue Visconti, opened in 1540 across the Pré-aux-Clercs ('clerics' meadow') of the nearby Abbaye St-Germain-des-Prés (see p66) and named after the 19th-century architect Lodovico Visconti (1791–1853). This street was occupied from the start by Huguenots, perhaps because of its remoteness from the city centre. In 1718–30 one of the best loved actresses of 18th century France, Adrienne Lecouvreur (1692–1730), lived at no 16; Francesco Cilea (1866–1950) used Lecouvreur's short life for his opera *Adriana Lecouvreur* (1904). Honoré de Balzac (1799–1850) had his print-shop at no 17 – he dreamt of making his fortune as a printer-publisher – and in the same house, 10 years later, in 1836–41, Eugène Delacroix (1798–1863) had his studio. Jean Racine (1639–1699) died at no 24.

The Beaux-Arts
Rue Visconti leads to Rue Bonaparte, in which turn right. At no 14, on your left a little way down, is the entrance to the École des Beaux-Arts, established from 1820 in what was left of the 17th-century Couvent des Petits-Augustins and the 18th-century Hôtel Chimay, with new buildings being added during the 19th century. If there is an exhibition on, do go in (there is no access to the building otherwise); the chapel, built 1617–19 by Philibert Delorme (*c*1510–1570), is a masterpiece of Classical architecture, showing one of the first appearances of the three Classical orders in Paris.

Among the many illustrious people who have lived in Rue des Beaux-Arts, opposite the school, have been Charles de Montalembert (1810–1870) at no 3, Gérard de Nerval (1808–1855) at no 5 and Oscar Wilde (1854–1900), who died at no 13, then the Hôtel d'Alsace; Jorge Luis Borges (1899–1986) liked to stay at that *hôtel* during his Parisian sojourns. Retrace your steps to Rue Bonaparte and keep going until you reach Place St-Germain-des-Prés; turn right into Rue Guillaume-Apollinaire and right again into Rue St-Benoît, where you will find some pleasant, lively restaurants.

Turn left into Rue Jacob, where there are interesting *hôtels* at nos 52 and 56. At the bottom, turn right into Rue des Sts-Pères; before the Revolution Mme de Récamier (1777–1849) lived in the *hôtel* at no 13. Then take the first turning to the left, Rue de Verneuil, effectively to leave St Germain-des-Prés for Faubourg St-Germain (see next walk). This residential street was developed in the 17th century, like most of that *faubourg*. At the first house on the left lived and died the singer Serge Gainsbourg (1928–1991), who came to symbolize an entire generation in the 1960s-80s. The second street you pass, Rue de Beaune, is full of art galleries and antiques shops, and is worth a detour. Back on Rue de Verneuil, the last *hôtel* on the left (no 36) was d'Artagnan's house – Dumas's hero was based on a real musketeer. At no 53 is the new Centre National des Lettres (with a good café), installed in part of the 18th-century Hôtel d'Avejean.

Continue along the street to Rue Poitiers, at the end. Facing you at no 12 is the 18th-century Hôtel de Poulry, now the club for the old boys of the École Polytechnique. Turn right, then left at the bottom into Rue de Lille; on the other side is the southern wall of the old Orsay railway station, now the Musée d'Orsay, where the walk ends. Turn left to reach the museum piazza and RER station Musée-d'Orsay; or, to reach métro Solférino, continue along Rue de Lille and turn left up Rue de Solférino.

You can connect this walk with the Faubourg St-Germain walk (see p86), missing out the first bit, which is on the other side of the river.

Faubourg St-Germain

This walk starts by the Jardin des Tuileries and takes you across it and the river to the grand Musée d'Orsay – home of the finest Impressionist collection in the world – and then for a pleasant wander through narrow streets lined with handsome 17th- and 18th-century *hôtels* until you reach another fine museum: the Musée Rodin.

Start: **Métro Tuileries; buses 72, 73.**
Finish: **Métro Varenne.**
Length: **4.5km (2¾ miles).**
Time: **2hr.**
Refreshments: **A few cafés along the way, and the Musée d'Orsay caféteria is good.**
Which day: **Any day except Monday, when the museums are shut, and Sunday, when several of the fine *hôtels*, now occupied by embassies and ministries, are closed. The Musée d'Orsay is quiet early on Sunday mornings and on Thursday evenings.**
To visit:
● **Musée d'Orsay: Thursday 10.00–21.45, Sunday 09.00–18.00, other days (not Monday) 10.00–18.00.**
● **Musée Rodin: daily (not Monday) 10.00–18.00.**

Jardin des Tuileries
Leave the métro station and walk westward (in the direction of the traffic) under the arcades of the 19th-century Rue de Rivoli, one of the city's grand avenues, passing Rue d'Alger on your right. At no 206 Rue de Rivoli Leo Tolstoy (1828–1910) lived for a while, and at no 226 is the oldest Anglo-American bookshop in Paris, Galignani. Reach Rue de Castiglione, with the Colonne Vendôme in the near distance.

At the traffic lights, cross Rue de Rivoli to the Jardin des Tuileries (more fully discussed on p95); walk down the steps and follow the cemented *allée* across the gardens. As you walk towards the river you will see, on either side of the alley, sculptures and/or installations by Alberto Giacometti (1901–1966), Carl André (b1935), David Smith (1906–1965), Max Ernst (1891–1976) and others including Giuseppe Penone (b1947).

When you reach the Grande Allée, which bisects the gardens, you come across one of the best perspectives in all Paris: on your left the small Arc du Carrousel frames the glass Pyramid, by Pei Ieoh Ming (b1917), and is itself framed by the Louvre; while on your right you see the Grand Bassin, the Obélisque de Louqsor on Place de la Concorde, and the Arc de Triomphe at the top of the Champs-Élysées.

Keep going the way you were, and take the underpass that leads to a new footbridge across the river to the Musée d'Orsay, the walls of which you can see to your left. There are also excellent views to be enjoyed on both sides – to the left, of Notre-

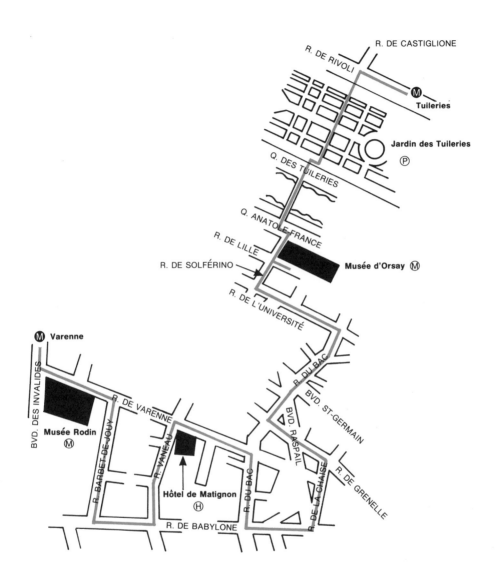

Dame, the Sainte Chapelle and Tour St-Jacques, and, to the right, of Pont Alexandre-III and the Grand and Petit Palais.

Your arrival on the south side of the river marks your entry into the Noble Faubourg St-Germain, as it used to be called. The area was developed relatively late, from the early 17th century. This followed a well-known Parisian pattern. The Church was the first to 'colonize' the green pastures, and several orders settled, including the Dominicans and the Carmelites. Then two factors changed the physiognomy of the *quartier*. First, in 1681 a new bridge was built, Pont Royal, linking the Faubourg St-Germain (the village beyond the Abbaye St-Germain-des-Prés) to the royal palace of the Tuileries and Louvre; second, on Louis XIV's death in 1715, the Prince Regent – Philippe, Duc d'Orléans (1674–1723) – moved the court back from Versailles to Paris, while he himself settled at the Tuileries. These two factors helped create a development boom on the other side of the river. The aristocracy, abandoning the Marais, needed great houses near the palace, and some 200 splendid *hôtels* were erected between 1690 and the Revolution, when most were demolished; about 50 still stand, however, now usually occupied by government offices and foreign embassies. Architecturally, even though nearly a century may separate the various remaining *hôtels*, the houses are essentially Classical or Neoclassical.

The Musée d'Orsay

Reach Quai Anatole-France, turn left and cross to the museum. On the *parvis* are several statues by Emmanuel Fremiet (1824–1910), mostly done for the 1877 Exposition Universelle.

The museum, opened in 1986 and among the finest in the world, is in a building converted from a railway station built 1898–1900 by the architect Victor Laloux (1850–1937). It is remarkable to think that this rather pompous *fin-de-siècle* building, determined to hide its industrial architecture under a façade of stone and stucco, was built during the heyday of Art Nouveau. However, the superb metal-and-glass vault has been preserved, and this gives the museum an added aura. The conversion was the work of several architects including the brilliant Italian Gae Aulenti (b1927), who was mostly responsible for the interior.

The collection is one of the world's largest devoted to the second half of the 19th century. Symbolism and Impressionism, Art Nouveau and Neoclassicism, Realism and Art Deco and other styles are all together under the same massive roof; both the bookshop and the cafeteria are excellent. It is beyond the scope of this book to provide a guide to the collection: free orientation maps in several languages are available at the entrance. Every conceivable artist, designer and craftsman of the period is represented. A comprehensive tour takes several hours.

An ancient ferry

Leave the museum and turn left briefly into Rue de Lille to have a peek at the Palais de la Légion d'Honneur, formerly the Hôtel de Salm, erected 1782–9 by Pierre Rousseau (c1750–c1810), partly burnt down during the Commune, and restored in 1874–8. A little further on, at no 78, is the magnificent Hôtel de Beauharnais, one of the finest in the *faubourg*, built for himself by Germain Boffrand (1667–1754) in 1714. The house became the property of Eugène de Beauharnais (1781–1824), son of the Empress Joséphine (1763–1814), in 1803, and the German embassy in 1961. Next door, at no 80, is another *hôtel* built by Boffrand.

Return to Rue de Solférino and turn left into Rue de l'Université, opened across the Pré-aux-Clercs (see p85) in the 17th century, though most of the houses are 18th-century. Alphonse de Lamartine (1790–1869) lived at no 82 in 1837–53, there is a fine mascaron at no 78, the writer Alphonse Daudet (1840–1897) died at no 51 (plaque), and no 33 is an interesting 18th-century *hôtel* . . . but the jewel of the street is the Hôtel Pozzo di Borgo (sometime called Hôtel de Soyecourt), built in 1707 and decorated by Claude Nicolas Ledoux (1736–1806).

Plate 10: The famous café *Les Deux Magots, haunt of artists and writers, in St-Germain* (see the *St-Germain-des-Prés walk, page 67*).

Plate 11: The Centre Georges-Pompidou, 'the Beaubourg', one of 20th-century Paris's major landmarks (see the Beaubourg and Châtelet walk, page 72).

Plate 12: Foies gras *and other luxury groceries advertised on a turn-of-the-century glass panel in the* Rue Montmartre *(see the* Les Halles *walk, page 79).*

Plate 13: *The modern Forum des Halles which replaced the 19th-century Les Halles market buildings (see the Les Halles walk, page 78).*

Plate 14: *The Arc du Carrousel through which can be seen the Obélisque de Louqsor and the Arc de Triomphe (see the Louvre and Champs-Élysées walk, page 94).*

Plate 15: Model boats for hire in the Jardin des Tuileries (see the Louvre and Champs Élysées walk, page 95).

Plate 16: The impressive Louvre and its 20th-century pyramidal entrance (see the Louvre and Champs-Élysées walk, page 93).

Turn right into Rue du Bac; had you gone left you would have reached the famous Pont Royal, which opened the sector to the developers. Rue du Bac is a longish street and one of the liveliest in this otherwise rather severe *quartier*; there are art galleries and shops of all kinds. It was opened in the mid-1500s as a dirt track along which stones extracted for the construction of the Palais des Tuileries were carried from the Vaugirard quarries, 2km (1¼ miles) south, to the river to be ferried (*bac* = ferry) to the other side; the ferry ran where Pont Royal now is.

At no 40 are a fine *hôtel* and the cobbled Impasse de Valmy, leading to a secluded Empire *hôtel*, now government property. Many of the houses in the area are like this, with a porch opening onto a courtyard and gardens that cannot always be seen from the street. At no 46 is the superb Hôtel de Jacques-Samuel-Bernard, built by Boffrand in 1741–4. To your left, 100m (110yd) down the small Rue de Gribeauval, are Place St-Thomas-d'Aquin and the church of that name, built 1682–1769 to plans by Pierre Bullet (*c*1639–1716). The church was originally the chapel of a Dominican *couvent*, abolished at the Revolution.

The Fontaine des Quatre-Saisons
Cross both Boulevard St-Germain and Boulevard Raspail, which intersect here, and continue briefly on Rue du Bac before turning left into Rue de Grenelle, where there are more 17th- and 18th-century houses. On your right is the superb and rather mad Fontaine des Quatre-Saisons, erected 1736–9 by the sculptor Edmé Bouchardon (1698–1762) to provide fresh water for the local population. Next to this is the intriguing Musée Maillol, containing an important exhibition of the artist's work as well as temporary exhibitions.

Continue, cross Boulevard Raspail again, carry on in Rue de Grenelle and then turn right into the narrow Rue de la Chaise; though this is a 16th-century street, the houses are essentially 18th-century, the finest being at no 7 (1763). It leads you to a busy intersection known as Sèvres-Babylone, by the Place Le Corbusier. Facing you, on the corner of Boulevard Raspail and Rue d'Assas, is the large Hôtel Lutetia where you will find a reliable restaurant/brasserie.

Cross Boulevard Raspail to Rue de Babylone, on the right-hand side of the triangular Square Boucicault, named for the founder of the Bon Marché, Aristide Boucicault (1810–1877), and established on the site of the leprosy hospital of Abbaye St-Germain-des-Prés. The Bon Marché, now facing you, is Paris's oldest department store; it was designed by Louis-Charles Boileau (1837–1910), aided by Gustave Eiffel (1832–1923) for the metal frame. Its Rue du Bac store houses the Grande épicerie, probably the finest food hall in Paris.

Pass the store and turn right into Rue du Bac once more. On your left is the Couvent des Soeurs-de-Vincent-de-Paul, where the Virgin Mary is said to have appeared to Sister Catherine Labouré (1806–1876) in 1830. Further on is the Séminaire des Missions Étrangères, with its chapel dating from 1691 and late 17th-century garden.

Further along on the left, at nos 118–20, are the twin 17th-century *hôtels* of Clermont-Tonnerre, where Chateaubriand (1768–1848) lived the last 10 years of his life; the view is best from the small public garden on the other side of the street. Just beyond no 108 is the restful Square de La Rouchefoucauld, actually an *allée* bordered by pleasing apartment blocks. Two further interesting *hôtels* on Rue du Bac, Hôtel de Ste-Aldegonde at no 102 and Hôtel de Ségur at no 97, date from the early 18th century.

Turn left into Rue de Varenne, which is full of stunning houses: there are two interesting *hôtels* at nos 41–43; at no 47 is the superb Hôtel de Boisgelin, built in 1732 and now the Italian Embassy; at no 50 is the fine Hôtel de Gallifet, also now part of the Italian Embassy; at no 51 is the Cité de Varenne, a calm *allée* typical of the area; at no 53 lived Edith Wharton (1862–1937), one of the first US writers to move to Paris; the porch at no 56 is exquisite (1719); at no 57 is the Hôtel de Matignon, built in the 1720s, the most magnificent house in the *faubourg* and now the Prime Minister's residence; at no 58 is the Hôtel de Feuquière; and at no 60 is the Hôtel du Prat, built in 1720. The street continues with more splendid houses, as we shall later see; but now turn left along the tranquil Rue Vaneau. André Gide (1869–1951) lived and died at no 9bis, but the most interesting house is the Hôtel de Chanaleilles (1770), where the writer Antoine de St-Exupéry (1900–1944), author of *The Little Prince* (1943), lived in the 1930s; to get the full benefit of its fine late-18th-century façade you have to detour into Rue de Chanaleilles, to your right.

Musée Rodin
Reach Rue de Babylone and turn right. The highlight of the street is La Pagode, the curious Chinoiserie at no 57bis, built by Alexandre Marcel in 1905 and now housing an excellent cinema. The restaurant Le Pied de Fouet is at no 45.

Go back a little and then up the quiet Rue Barbet-de-Jouy, opened in 1838, to rejoin Rue de Varenne. At no 69 is the fine Hôtel de Clermont (1711–14); at no 72 is the Grand Hôtel de Castries (1700); at no 73 is the Hôtel de Broglie (1735); at no 75 is the Hôtel de Châtillon (1704); and finally, at no 77, is the splendid Hôtel de Biron, now holding the wonderful Musée Rodin, and one of the few houses in this area that you can actually enter. It was built by Jacques-Ange Gabriel (1698–1782) and Jean Aubert (d1741) in 1728–31. It had a rather complex history before being a *couvent* in 1820–1904, and then the state granted Auguste Rodin (1840–1917) the lease for life. It was converted into a museum in 1919 and has just been entirely restored.

The collection focuses on the work of this great French sculptor and contains several treasures; some are on show in the gardens. As well as Rodin's sculptures and drawings there are works he collected by artists including Van Gogh and Auguste Renoir; but most memorable is the extraordinary power of Rodin's own works, such as *La Porte de l'Enfer, Les Bourgeois de Calais, Le Baiser* and *L'Age d'Airain*.

Leave the museum after a walk in the gardens. Turn left into Rue de Varenne; métro station Varenne is near the point where you reach Boulevard des Invalides.

Louvre and Champs-Élysées

A classic walk from the lovely old Église St-Germain-l'Auxerrois through the Louvre, across the Jardin des Tuileries and Place de la Concorde, and finally into the Champs-Élysées and up to Place Charles-de-Gaulle (usually still called Place de l'Étoile by Parisians). On the way are three superb museums as well as the smart shops and cafés of the Champs.

Start: **Métro Louvre, buses 69, 72.**
Finish: **Métro Charles-de-Gaulle-Étoile, many bus lines.**
Length: **5km (3 miles).**
Time: **1½hr.**
Refreshments: **Many cafés; the most interesting place in terms of food is probably the restaurant in the Louvre.**
Which day: **Any day except Tuesday (when the Musée du Louvre is shut), preferably in the late afternoon; the best time to visit the Musée du Louvre is late on a Wednesday afternoon, when it is much quieter than usual.**
To visit:
- **Musée du Louvre: Monday and Wednesday 09.00–21.30, other days (not Tuesday) 09.00–17.30.**
- **Musée de l'Orangerie: Has just reopened after a complete refit. Open daily (except on Tuesdays) 09.00–19.00.**
- **Musée du Jeu de Paume: temporary exhibitions only.**

A royal parish
Even the Louvre métro station is fun, as if you were already in the museum. On leaving it, cross Rue de Rivoli into Place du Louvre and walk towards Église St-Germain-l'Auxerrois. Georges Haussmann (1809–1891) was the man responsible for giving Place du Louvre the appearance it has today, pulling down most of the houses that bordered Rue des Poulies, between the Louvre and the church. At the same time were built the motley-styled *mairie* (town hall) to the left of the church and the belfry between the church and the *mairie*.

The present church is the third on this site since the 6th century. What we have now, after the modifications of the ages, is this: a 12th-century clock tower, 13th-century choir and central portal, 14th-century porch, nave and transept, and 16th-century side-chapels and lateral porches. Its parish, always fairly rich, became even more so when Charles V and the royal family installed themselves at the Palais du Louvre. Many of the artists who worked on the *palais* in the 17th and 18th centuries are buried here, including Louis Le Vau (1612–1670), Jacques Lemercier (1585–1684), Antoine Coysevox (1640–1720), François Boucher (1703–1770), Jean Baptiste Chardin (1699–1779), Jacques Germain Soufflot (1709–1780) and Jacques-Ange Gabriel (1698–1782). The church was much disfigured during the 18th century and was damaged in rioting in 1831; it was

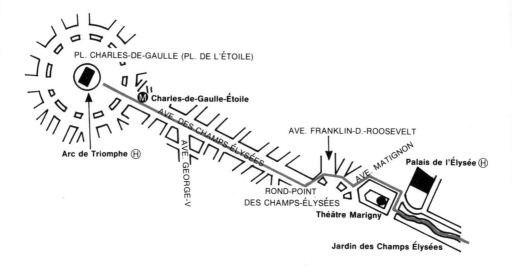

PL. CHARLES-DE-GAULLE (PL. DE L'ÉTOILE)

Ⓜ Charles-de-Gaulle-Étoile

AVE. DES CHAMPS-ÉLYSÉES

AVE. FRANKLIN-D.-ROOSEVELT

AVE. MATIGNON

Arc de Triomphe Ⓗ

AVE. GEORGE-V

Palais de l'Élysée Ⓗ

ROND-POINT
DES CHAMPS-ÉLYSÉES

Théâtre Marigny

Jardin des Champs Élysées

restored in the late 1830s by Victor Baltard (1805–1874), the architect of Les Halles, and Eugène Viollet-Le-Duc (1814–1879), the great 19th-century restorer. It has recently been renovated.

The wall paintings are 19th-century, and many of the stained-glass windows are after cartoons by Viollet-Le-Duc. There is a bells concert daily between 14.00 and 14.30; the best place to listen is outside on one of the benches.

The Louvre

On leaving the church, cross Place du Louvre to the Palais du Louvre, the world's largest building – bigger even than St Peter's in Rome.

The Louvre has a tortuous history. Philippe-Auguste was responsible for the first Louvre. With the 9th-century Norman invasion of Paris *via* the river in mind, he determined, when building his fortified wall around the city, to set a fortress at the weak river link; this fortress, the first Louvre, was little over one-quarter the size of the present Cour Carrée, and had a dungeon in its middle courtyard, moats and battlements. Charles V greatly modified it, turning it into what was almost a pretty *château*, before, in the heyday of the French Renaissance, François I, responsible for Fontainebleau (see pp179ff), decided he must have something similarly splendid and genteel as his Parisian palace. After a few attempts to modify the old Louvre, he simply demolished it and started afresh. (Some remains of it were unearthed during the restoration of the Cour Carrée and are now on view.) Pierre Lescot (*c*1510–1578) was pulled from his work at Carnavalet (see p35) and told to build the finest and largest *château* in the world. In the event, it took 300 years – until the First Empire – to finish, involving architects as diverse as Jacques Lemercier (1585–1684), Louis Le Vau (1612–1670), Claude Perrault (1613–1688) and Jacques Germain Soufflot (1709–1780). Work stopped when Louis XIV moved the court to Versailles, and building did not resume until the 1770s, with Soufflot as architect; it was interrupted by the Revolution, and finally the building was completed in 1810. Le Vau's and Perrault's plans were respected (they themselves had tried to find a dynamic that would fit Lescot's great project) – hence the remarkable apparent unity of the whole.

Facing you is probably the *palais*'s most impressive exterior façade: the famous colonnade, begun in the second half of the 17th century on plans by Le Vau and Perrault, but not completed until the First Empire. Go through into the Cour Carrée (square courtyard). Now that the *palais* and *cour* have been restored to their former glory, you can appreciate the astonishing harmony of the place – doubly astonishing when we remember the timescale over which it was built. The west wing and a little of the south wing are all that remains of Lescot's and Goujon's tremendous achievement. Jean Goujon (*c*1510–1568) was a superb artist, and his figures adorning the façade have great grace and elegance. The middle pavilion (Pavillon de l'Horloge or Pavillon Sully) was done by Jacques Lemercier in the 1620s; the rest is mostly from the 1670s, done by Le Vau, Perrault and Le Brun.

The recently restored Cour Carrée is a very pleasant place to be, so you might sit for a while by the *bassin* to take in its quiet elegance.

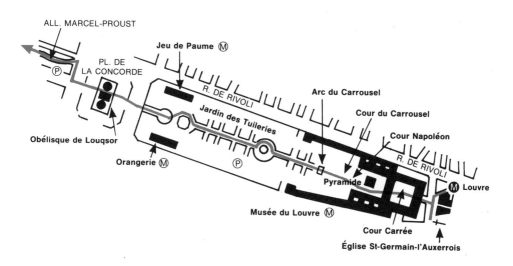

A modern pyramid
Leave the *cour via* the Pavillon de l'Horloge for the grandiose Cour Napoleon, dominated by the remarkable Pyramide by the Chinese-US architect Pei Ieoh Ming (b1917). The buildings surrounding the Cour Napoleon and the Cour du Carrousel (Louis XIV had an equestrian carousel there) form the Grand Louvre, and most were built during the Second Empire (1850s) by Hector Martin Lefuel (1810–1880) to plans by Lodovico Visconti (1791–1853), though much of the wing bordering Rue de Rivoli dates from the First Empire. Many streets and houses were obliterated; Haussmann, responsible for the urbanization side of the project, declared later that it was with the Louvre that he had learned how to raze houses!

The celebrated Grande Galerie or Galerie du Bord-de-l'Eau, initiated by Catherine de' Medici (1519–1589) to link the two royal castles of the Louvre and the Tuileries –

and where the imposing Italian Renaissance collection is now housed – is hidden from you by the Pavillon Denon. (A wonderful view of the *galerie* can be gained from Pont des Arts – see p107.)

The Musée du Louvre is the largest in the world with nearly 60,000m^2 (15 acres) of exhibition space out of a total area of 160,000m^2 (nearly 40 acres). The Pyramide, with its underground foyer and corridors (all opened in 1989), links the various elements of this huge museum, thus saving walks of up to 2km (1¼ miles) to get from one part of it to another.

Since the 1980s the museum has been undergoing extensive restoration and renovation work. It is therefore not possible to give much guidance here as works of art are constantly being shuffled around. The collections are organised in three wings leading off from the Pyramide. The best thing is to go down into the Pyramide, to the central information desk where you can obtain excellent location maps as well as catalogues outlining the collections. There is a good signposting system and it is easy to find your way around. There is a large underground shopping mall with boutiques, cafés and restaurants leading from the central hall to underneath the Place du Carrousel and eventually to the entrance to the métro.

The collections of the Louvre cover all ages and fields of artistic endeavour. The *Mona Lisa is* here, of course, but so also are:

- a collection of Italian artists almost as good as at the Uffizi; it includes works by Piero della Francesca (*c*1420–1492), Paolo Uccello (1397–1475), Andrea Mantegna (*c*1431–1506) and others
- a collection of French artists from the 14th to the 17th century, including Georges de La Tour (1593–1652), Nicolas Poussin (1594–1665), and others
- a Flemish and Dutch collection, with works by Jan Vermeer (1632–1675), Rembrandt van Rijn (1606–1669) and others
- a remarkable department of antiquities, containing Egyptian, Oriental, Etruscan, Greek and Roman pieces
- a furniture collection, notably including some superb pieces by André Charles Boulle (or Buhl; 1642–1732), inlaid with leather, precious metals, tortoiseshell, etc.
- a silverware collection
- a china collection, including pieces by Bernard Palissy (*c*1509–1589) and others

plus objets d'art of all descriptions – everywhere you look there is more and more and more . . . Target just a couple of areas for now and plan to come back later.

Venice in Paris
From the Pyramide, walk on to the Arc du Carrousel, built by Charles Percier (1764–1838) and Pierre Fontaine (1762–1853) in 1806 to celebrate Napoleon's victories. The famous horses of St Mark in Venice used to decorate it. Napoleon had the embarrassing habit of acquiring works of art during his travels, and he thought the horses – in turn appropriated by the Venetians 200 years earlier from a Corinthian temple – would look rather good in Paris. They were returned to Venice in 1815. However, you can see the quadriga (chariot and four horses) by Baron Bosio (1769–1845), which has recently been restored and regilded.

Standing beneath the Arc, you can look along a world-famous perspective, all the way up the Champs-Élysées to the Arc de Triomphe, with the Obélisque de Louqsor neatly in the centre; on a clear day you can also see La Grande Arche de la Défense (see p192) in the far background. The Arc du Carrousel also served as the Emperor's gateway into the Château des Tuileries, originally built by Catherine de' Medici (1519–1589) so that she could be independent from the royal residence (although not *too* isolated from it: a *passage* ran to Galerie du Bord-de-l'Eau). The *château*, which used to link the northwest and southwest tips of the present Louvre building, so that the assemblage formed an imperfect rectangle, was completely destroyed during the Commune in 1871.

The Tuileries

Continue your walk into the Jardin des Tuileries, one of the best examples of *jardins à la française* in Paris. The gardens have been extensively replanted and restored. They were originally designed by Pierre Le Nôtre at the behest of Catherine de' Medici, who wanted it for her new *château*. However, decades later, André Le Nôtre (1613–1700), Pierre's grandson and probably the greatest of all French gardeners, was commissioned by Jean Baptiste Colbert (1619–1683) to replace it. He greatly increased the size of the garden, created the two long terraces on either side – Terrasse du Bord-de-l'Eau along the river and Terrasse des Feuillants along the Rue de Rivoli – and opened up an *allée* in the countryside to the west so as to establish a grand perspective: that *allée* is today's Avenue des Champs-Élysées. From very early on, largely thanks to the efforts of Charles Perrault (1628–1703), the famous fairy-tale writer and brother to the architect, the gardens were open to the public.

Walk up the gardens in the central *allée* from the Bassin Rond to the Bassin Octogonal on the west; both ponds were created by André Le Nôtre. The gardens are peppered with various statues and installations.

Nymphéas

The Bassin Octogonal is flanked by the Musée de l'Orangerie on the Terrasse du Bord-de-l'Eau, to your left, and the Musée du Jeu de Paume on the other side. Both buildings are Second-Empire. The Jeu de Paume was originally a real-tennis court, but was converted to house the Impressionist collection that has since gone to the Musée d'Orsay; it has recently been completely renovated, and now hosts exhibitions of contemporary art. In the terraced garden near the Jeu de Paume, you will find statues by Auguste Rodin (1840–1917), Jean Dubuffet (1901–1985) and a rather astonishing set of six bronzes entitled *The Welcoming Hands* by Louise Bourgeois (b1911).

The Orangerie is special: if you have not been too drained by the Musée du Louvre, you should certainly explore this (however, note that the museum is being renovated and should not reopen before late 2004). It is in two parts: the startling *Nymphéas*, by Claude Monet (1840–1926), and the celebrated Walter-Guillaume Collection, donated to the Louvre in 1977. The *Nymphéas* were painted during WWI in Monet's cherished Giverny, and were offered by the artist to the nation upon the signing of the armistice; these enormous canvases hang in two large oval rooms on the Orangerie's ground floor. The Walter-Guillaume Collection, on the first floor, is not large, but each of its 144 works is a jewel. Paul Guillaume (1893–1934), an art merchant, supported the artists he loved; he was one of the few to back Amedeo Modigliani (1884–1920), Chaïm Soutine (1893–1943) and Maurice Utrillo (1883–1985) in their early days. Artists whose works are on display here include these three as well as Paul Cézanne (1839–1906), Pablo Picasso (1881–1973), Henri Matisse (1869–1954) and Henri Rousseau (1844–1910).

Les chevaux de Marly
Come out of the Orangerie and leave the gardens through the main gates. Notice the fine sculptures of winged horses, the Chevaux Ailés, at the top of the gate-pillars. They are copies of originals done by Antoine Coysevox (1640–1720); those originals, which used to adorn the 'watering-trough' at Louis XIV's *château* of Marly (destroyed during the Revolution), were brought here in the mid-18th century and are now in the Louvre.

Cross Place de la Concorde, designed by Jacques-Ange Gabriel (1698–1782) in the 18th century as a Place Royale for Louis XV. Gabriel was also responsible for the two large buildings on the right, the Hôtel de la Marine (Ministry of the Navy) on the right, and the Hôtel Crillon. (For a fuller history of the *place* see p114.) Cross the *place* by the pedestrian crossing to the central island, with its handsome fountains – inspired by, if not imitated from, a fountain at St Peter's, Rome – and the Obélisque, given to Louis-Philippe by Mohammed 'Ali (*c*1769–1849), viceroy of Egypt, in 1831.

Use the pedestrian crossing again to get to the far side of the *place*. At the entrance to the Champs-Élysées is a second pair of horses also known as the Chevaux de Marly, this one by Guillaume Coustou (1677–1746). Official ceremonies are held between here and the Arc de Triomphe.

'In search of time past'
Leave Avenue des Champs-Élysées and enter the Jardin des Champs-Élysées, also designed by André Le Nôtre but greatly altered since. The garden's hour of glory was really the Second Empire, when new Parisian centres of pleasure kept popping up. Many of the garden's ornaments, statues and fountains were installed then, as were cafés, theatres, a 'panorama' similar to that of Passage des Panoramas (see p172), and so on.

Go right, past the Théâtre des Ambassadeurs, into Allée Marcel-Proust. Proust (1871–1922), author of *À la recherche du temps perdu*, used to play in the gardens, and it was here that he experienced a violent childhood passion for the pretty blonde Marie de Bernardarki, the Gilberte of his great novel.

Pass the Espace Pierre-Cardin, the centre of Avant-Garde happenings in the early 1970s, and the delightful Pavillon Gabriel. On the other side of the gardens, to your right, are the gardens of various residences – the US Embassy, the British Embassy, and finally the Palais de l'Élysée, the official residence of the French President. All their entrances are in Rue du Faubourg-St-Honoré (see p98).

The oldest puppet theatre in Paris
Staying in the gardens, reach Place Clemenceau and cross Avenue de Marigny; on your left is a wonderful vista over Pont Alexandre-III and the gilded Dôme of the Invalides. Also on the left, but closer by, are the two exhibition halls dating from the 1900 Exposition Universelle, the Petit Palais on the left and the Grand Palais on the right (see p124). This side of the gardens, known as the Carré Marigny, is dedicated to children's games, and it is here that you will find Paris's oldest puppet theatre, the Théâtre de Marionettes des Champs Élysées, opened 1818. The Théâtre Marigny, on your left as you look up Avenue de Marigny, was designed by Charles Garnier (1825–1898). The fine Restaurant Laurent, nearby, has been around for over 150 years.

Reach the Rond-Point des Champs-Élysées, designed by André Le Nôtre as the culmination of his garden and now a rather busy intersection. Walk anticlockwise around the roundabout, crossing Avenue Matignon, Rue Jean-Mermoz and Avenue

Franklin-D.-Roosevelt, all lined with smart apartment blocks and shops, as is the Rond-Point; you are now in one of the *quartiers chics*, the 8th arrondissement.

The Avenue

Now walk up Avenue des Champs-Élysées. Like the gardens, it became a place for elegant people in the Second Empire, a time when much of the Champs-Élysées started being seriously built up. Today the avenue is becoming progressively pleasanter as the *contre allées* (side-alleys) are slowly being given back to pedestrians and new trees are being planted.

This is a good place for an evening stroll: the cinemas often do not shut before 02.00, the cafés and shops stay open late, there is a music hall – the Lido – and there are nightclubs in the side-streets. Over the past 10 years or so at least seven shopping malls have opened between the Rond-Point and the Arc de Triomphe, the best – and also one of the earliest – being the Arcade du Lido at no 78.

The unknown soldier

Walk up to Place Charles-de-Gaulle (Place de l'Étoile) at the top of the hill. In the 18th century several metres were lopped from the hilltop so that the gradient would be equal on both sides. Only in the 1850s did the *place* start to look like it does today, although there were only five avenues; seven more were later added according to a rigorous geometric design, and in the same period Jacques Ignace Hittorf (1792–1867), one of the great architects of the time, built the 12 *hôtels* surrounding the *place*. The whole design focused on the Arc de Triomphe, inaugurated by Napoleon in 1806 to celebrate the victories of the French armies; when the Arc was at last finished, 30 years later, it was decided to inscribe on its walls the names of all the generals and battles of the Empire – 660 generals and 128 battles. The flame and the brass plaque indicate the tomb of an unknown French soldier killed in WWI. The tomb was built in 1921 and the flame, revived every evening, has not stopped burning since. The Arc, the largest of its type, is 50m (164ft) high and 45m (148ft) wide.

Do not attempt to cross the *place*: there is a pedestrian subway from the Champs (signposted near métro station) to the central island. This subway also leads you to the ticket office, should you wish to climb to the top of the Arc, whence there are lovely views over Haussmann's Paris and further down to the Louvre and city centre.

The same subway takes you to Charles-de-Gaulle-Étoile métro station or to your bus-stop – there is one at the top of each of the avenues. Alternatively, you can connect this walk with the short Étoile to Trocadéro walk (p175) or the slightly longer Ternes and Parc Monceau walk (p125).

Faubourg St-Honoré

A long walk, mainly along Rue du Faubourg St-Honoré and Rue St-Honoré, across some of the city's smarter *quartiers*. The shops are the main focus of this walk: there are many art galleries, and most of the names that have made Paris one of the world's leading capitals of fashion are featured. Also on the way are a couple of churches, including the important Église St-Roch.

Start: **Métro George-V; bus 73.**
Finish: **Métro Madeleine; buses 24, 42, 52, 84, 94.**
Length: **4.25km (2⅔ miles).**
Time: **2hr.**
Refreshments: **This is an expensive area, but there are still a few old-fashioned cafés dotted about, including a couple of reasonable restaurants serving decent food at decent prices in Rue de La Sourdière.**
Which day: **Any day except Sunday, when the area is dead.**

Église St-Philippe-du-Roule
Leave the métro and find yourself on the Champs-Élysées with a good view over the Arc de Triomphe (see p97). With the Arc at your back, walk a little way down the left-hand side of the avenue and turn left into Rue Washington, a typical residential street of the area, mostly developed in the early 19th century. At no 20 is the charming Cité Odiot: walk through the porch and emerge in the private *allée*. The door is shut at weekends, but otherwise you can go round and come out again in Rue Washington.

Go along to the wide Avenue Friedland, with Place de Charles-de-Gaulle and the Arc on your left. Just on the other side of the avenue stood the celebrated 18th-century Folie Beaujon. Turn right into Rue du Faubourg-St-Honoré, this section of which is dominated by antiques shops, art galleries and antiquarian bookshops; nos 155, 157 and 159 are 18th-century. Cross Rue de Berri, opened, like most streets in this area, at the end of the 18th century. At nos 139–41 Rue du Faubourg-St-Honoré was the entrance to the Comte d'Artois's grand stables, demolished during the Empire. Nos 137 and 135 are handsome 19th-century *hôtels*. Cross the elegant Avenue Franklin-D.-Roosevelt and Place Chassaigne-Goyon to Église St-Philippe-du-Roule.

The medieval Village du Roule was chiefly celebrated for its goose market. The village was in two distinct parts: the Haut Roule, near what is today Place des Ternes (see p126), and the Bas Roule, around where the church now stands. Nothing is left of the village except vestiges of the *hôtels* and *folies* that flourished nearby in the 18th century. Rue du Faubourg-St-Honoré (once Chaussée du Roule) led from the city to the village. While the village was on the north side of the track, the large ribbon-shaped tract of land between the *chaussée* and the Champs-Élysées was occupied by the royal nurseries, seedsmen and so on for the gardens of the Louvre and Tuileries. The land was eventually given to the Comte d'Artois, the future Charles X, who decided to develop it with the architect François Joseph Bélanger (1745–1818) as a 'Nouvelle Amérique': the streets were to be named after heroes of the War of Independence. In the end nothing was built, but the names remain – Rue Washington, Rue La Fayette, Place Franklin.

Église St-Philippe-du-Roule was built to the plan of a basilica (three naves) by Jean François Chalgrin (1739–1811) in 1774–84 on the site of the ancient parish church of the Bas Roule, and was enlarged first in the 1840s and then again by Victor Baltard (1805–1874) in 1860. Beyond the ribbed vault and coffered ceiling is an interesting half-dome (*cul-de-four*). The building as a whole was rather novel in the 18th century, and influenced subsequent religious edifices such as Notre-Dame-de-Lorette and even the Madeleine (see p115). The frescoes – by the great 19th-century religious artist Théodore Chassériau (1819–1856) – include a fine *Descente de la Croix*.

Continue along the elegant street and cross Rue La Boétie, which again has many art galleries; this part of St-Honoré is reminiscent of London's Bond Street and Cork Street. Rue La Boétie was built over the old track that followed the 6km (3¾ mile) Grand Égout (great sewer). Pablo Picasso (1881–1973), tired of slumming it in Montmartre, lived at no 29 in 1918–39; his first wife, Olga Khoklova, occupied a separate floor.

Returning to Rue du Faubourg-St-Honoré, you find more galleries and bookshops, including two great French art dealers: Picard and Blaizot. Cross Rue de Penthièvre. There are three noteworthy *hôtels*, at nos 120, 118 and 85. Cross the elegant Avenue Matignon. At no 114 was the Porte du Roule, the limit of Louis XIII's wall. At no 110 is the celebrated Hôtel Bristol, with an excellent restaurant. The art gallery Colnaghi is at no 108. Pass Rue du Cirque and reach Place Beauvau, where since 1861 the Ministry of the Interior has been housed in the very much enlarged Hôtel Beauvau (1770). Just before it is Rue de Miromesnil, opened in 1776; Chateaubriand (1768–1848) lived at no 31. On the other side is Avenue de Marigny, which borders the gardens of the Palais d'Élysée down to Place Clemenceau. Pass Rue des Saussaies, which has a good *bistro à vin*, Le Griffonier, at no 8.

The Palais d'Élysée
On the other side is the Palais de l'Élysée, the residence of the President of the French Republic; you cannot go in, but you can look into the courtyard from the pavement. The *palais* was built at the beginning of the 18th century for Louis Henri de la Tour d'Auvergne, Comte d'Evreux, on his death passing to Mme de Pompadour (1721–1764), who enlarged it with the help of François Boucher (1703–1770), Jean Baptiste Van Loo (1684–1745) and others. Then the financier Nicolas Beaujon (1718–1786), one of the wealthiest men of the 18th century, purchased it and embellished it; poor Beaujon, ill, impotent and living on a diet of spinach, liked nothing better than being pushed around in his wheelchair by bevies of pretty girls from the aristocracy. He sold the *hôtel* to Louis XVI, who gave it in turn to the 'Princess' Amélie de Bourbon-Conti (1756–1825). Its history during the Revolution and the First Empire is too complicated to unravel, although certainly Napoleon signed his second abdication there, on his way to St Helena. At the Restoration the 'Princess' was given her *hôtel* back, and she swapped it with Louis XVIII for Hôtel Matignon (see p90). During the reigns of Charles X and Louis-Philippe and the Second Empire, it was used mainly as a residence for foreign dignitaries: Victoria (1819–1901) and Tsar Alexander II (1818–1881) stayed here. Finally, with the advent of the Third Republic the *palais* became the President's official residence.

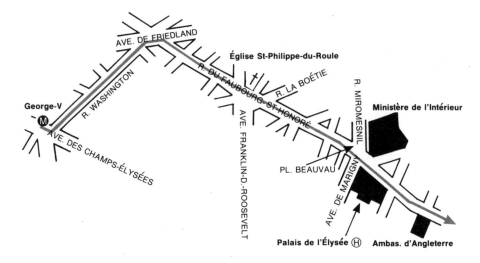

This section of the *faubourg* is mostly diplomatic. At no 41 is the fine *hôtel* built by Lodovico Visconti (1791–1853) in the 1830s and now the private residence of the US Ambassador. Next door at no 39 is the even finer *hôtel* built in 1723 for the Duc de Chârost. Napoleon's sister, Pauline Borghese (1780–1825) – who also occupied the Petit Trianon (see p186) – reigned within these walls throughout the Empire. After Waterloo she sold the *hôtel* to the Duke of Wellington (1769–1852), and it has been home to the British Embassy ever since. Here Hector Berlioz (1803–1869) married the UK actress Harriet Smithson (1800–1854), whom all Paris came to applaud in her performances of Ophelia and Juliet, both with Edmund Kean (c1789–1833).

On the other side of the street the world of fashion, in the shape of the Gianni Versace shop, intrudes on the world of diplomacy. The 18th-century Hôtel Chevalier at no 35 is part of the British Embassy.

Once you have crossed Rue d'Anjou on your left – at no 8 the Marquis de Lafayette (1757–1834) spent the last seven years of his life – you are in the third section of the *faubourg*: that of fashionable boutiques and the ultra-chic Parisian department store, Colette. Most of the great names of Haute Couture are here: Ted Lapidus, Yves Saint Laurent, Balmain, Givenchy, Lagerfeld, Lanvin and Hermès, to name a few. Reach the sumptuous Rue Royale, where you can see the Madeleine on your left.

After you cross Rue Royale the street-name becomes Rue St-Honoré and the atmosphere changes: you are going deeper into both the heart and the history of the city. Before the Revolution this section of the street led to six *couvents* and a church; now only the church, l'Église d'Assomption, remains. There was another city gate here, one of the three Portes St-Honoré, this one from the Louis XIII wall, built in 1632 and demolished exactly 100 years later. On your left, at no 398, a plaque indicates that Maximilien de Robespierre (1758–1794) lived there for three years.

Further along, Rue Richepance, on your left, is situated over the Couvent de la Conception. At Place Maurice-Barrès is l'Église d'Assomption, now a church for the Polish community; it was built in the 1670s as the chapel of the Couvent des Dames-de-l'Assomption, of which it is the only surviving part. It is an interesting building, a circle topped by a seemingly over-large dome; inside, there are a couple of good pictures including Van Loo's *Adoration of the Magi.*

Pass Rue Cambon, opened 1719, and carry on along Rue St-Honoré past a series of fine 17th-century houses on the left. At no 374 was the Royaume de la Rue-St-Honoré (plaque), run by Marie-Thérèse Geoffrin (1699–1777), probably the most fashionable literary salon of the later 18th century. Between nos 364 and 360 was the first Capuchin convent, and on the other side of the street, a little to the left, was the Capuchin monastery established by Catherine de' Medici (1519–1589).

Turn left at no 362 into Cour Vendôme and reach Place Vendôme, one of the Places Royales (see p14). Turn right, walk past the IBM building and turn right again to return

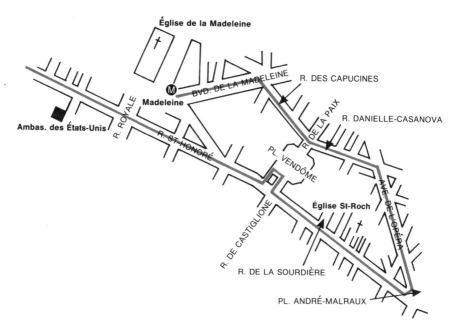

to Rue St-Honoré. Cross Rue de Castiglione, on your right, established over the site of the late-17th-century Couvent des Feuillants (part of the Cistercian order) in 1804. This *couvent* housed one of the most famous Revolutionary Clubs, the Club des Feuillants, of which Lafayette was a member for a while; all that remains of the *couvent* is the building at nos 235–29, built in 1782.

Further along there are more handsome houses, especially at nos 334 – where Pierre de Marivaux (1688–1763) resided for a while – and 211, once the stunning 17th-century Hôtel de Noailles, now the Hôtels St-James and d'Albany, where Lafayette lived on his return from the USA.

Église St-Roch

Cross Rue du Marché-St-Honoré, which led to the Couvent des Jacobins, and the narrow picturesque Rue de La Sourdière, where there are good restaurants, and so reach

Église St-Roch, Paris's most fashionable church in the 18th century. Its relatively narrow façade, built by Robert de Cotte (1656–1735) in the 1730s, is deceptive: this is one of the largest churches in Paris, being, at over 120m (130yd) long, almost as long as Notre-Dame. It took just over a century to complete: from the 1650s to the 1760s.

It is an oddly fascinating building. Added to the original Jesuit plan are three further chapels which give quite a different tonality to the whole. The first and largest, the astonishing elliptical Chapelle de La Vierge – with ambulatory and a great painted dome bearing an *Assumption* by Jean-Baptiste Pierre (1714–1789) – was designed by Jules Hardouin-Mansart (1645–1708). The Chapelle de la Communion is circular; the rectangular Chapelle du Calvaire was added in 1754 but was greatly modified in the 19th century.

The church is full of 17th-, 18th- and 19th-century works of religious art, some originating from the *couvents* decimated during the Revolution. Among the interesting examples of 18th-century funereal art are two busts by Antoine Coysevox (1640–1720) and a mausoleum by Guillaume Coustou (1677–1746) for the unsavoury Cardinal Guillaume Dubois (1656–1723), Philippe d'Orléans's *éminence grise*. As might be expected of a fashionable church, many illustrious people are buried here, including Pierre Corneille (1606–1684), Pierre Mignard (1612–1695), André Le Nôtre (1613–1700), Denis Diderot (1713–1784), René Du Guay-Trouin (1673–1736) and the 'Princess' de Conti. The organ, made by members of the Clicquot family, is renowned.

Walk down the steps of the church to Rue St-Honoré and carry on eastward, passing many old houses, mostly 18th-century. Cross Rue des Pyramides and reach Place André-Malraux (previously Place du Théâtre-Français); opposite are the Théâtre Français and, to the left of that, the entrance to the Palais-Royal (see p170).

At no 161 Rue St-Honoré, where the street joins the *place*, the second Porte St-Honoré, that of the medieval Charles V's wall, stood from 1380 to 1636. There were many attempts to force a way into Paris through here. Joan of Arc (*c*1412–1431) and her lieutenant, Gilles de Rais (1404–1440), with 12,000 men, unsuccessfully tried to force the gates and penetrate the city, which was at the time occupied by the English. And it was here, too, that Henri IV tried to get into the capital which refused to acknowledge his right to the crown.

Turn left in the majestic Avenue de l'Opéra (the Opéra is visible in the distance), opened by Georges Haussmann (1809–1891) to link the Opéra and the Louvre. More, perhaps, than any of his other projects, the opening of this avenue, which involved the destruction of many houses, created an artificial frontier within the city.

Walking on the left, pass Rue des Pyramides and Rue St-Roch and turn left into Rue Danielle-Casanova, a continuation of Rue des Petits-Champs. This street contains many old houses, mostly 18th-century, including the fine Hôtel de Coigny at no 15. At no 10 is an excellent Anglo-American newsagent-bookshop, Brentano's. Stendhal (1783–1842) died at no 22. On the top floor of that house the Dada painter Francis Picabia (1879–1953) had his studio for a while. On your left is a small section of Rue du Marché-St-Honoré, leading to the *place* of that name, where stood the celebrated Dominican Couvent des Jacobins, celebrated not so much for its monastic as for its republican activities: once the *couvent* itself had been closed down, part of the building was rented by the Société des Amis de la Constitution; with Robespierre as a leader, the Club des Jacobins, as it became known, was soon extremely influential, with 1200 clubs in the provinces. It now houses a spectacular development by Ricardo Boffil.

Cross Rue de la Paix, opened 1806 over part of the second Couvent des Capucines – look left for another perspective over Place Vendôme – and continue into Rue des Capucines, opened in 1700; many of its houses are 18th-century. Reach the *boulevard* created in Louis XIV's days; to your right it is called Boulevard des Capucines and to your left it is Boulevard de la Madeleine. This segment hummed during the 19th century: cafés, ballrooms, amusement halls. Straight across, at 34 Boulevard des Capucines, is the Olympia, one of the last music-halls of Paris, now essentially a rock venue. Turn left into Boulevard de la Madeleine. In a house at no 17 lived Alphonsine Plessis, the model for *La Dame aux Camélias* (1848) by Alexandre Dumas fils (1824–1895) and *La Traviata* (1853) by Giuseppe Verdi (1813–1901); she is buried in Cimetière Montmartre. Facing you is Église de la Madeleine (see p115).

Your walk ends at Place de la Madeleine, but you can connect it with the shortish Assemblée Nationale, Concorde and Opéra walk (p112): either go two stops on the métro to Assemblée-Nationale or take a 10–minute walk; just before you reach the *place*, turn left into Rue Richepance, cross Rue St-Honoré, go along Rue St-Florentin and cross both Place de la Concorde and then Pont de la Concorde before turning left into Boulevard St-Germain to reach the Assemblée-Nationale métro station.

Odéon, Bourse and Palais-Royal

A lovely walk that takes you from the heart of the Latin Quarter past the Institut de France, over the river by the charming pedestrian Pont des Arts, through the Louvre and some quaint streets, and past the Bourse des Valeurs and the Bibliotheque Nationale to the superb Palais-Royal. But not all is history: there are also art galleries, antiques shops and designer boutiques.

Start: **Métro Odéon; buses 63, 86, 87, 96.**
Finish: **Métro Palais-Royal; buses 21, 27, 39, 48, 67, 81, 95.**
Length: **3.5km (2¼ miles).**
Time: **1¾hr.**
Refreshments: **Many cafes, bars and tearooms on the way.**
Which day: **Any day, but weekdays are best.**
To visit:
• **Bibliothèque Nationale: temporary exhibitions only.**
• **La Bourse: weekdays 11.00 and 12.30.**

The Procope and the Comédie Française
Leave the métro and cross Boulevard St-Gennain to Rue de l'Ancienne-Comédie, which, as Rue des Fossés-St-Germain, used to run along the Philippe-Auguste wall. It took its present name in 1770 when the Comédie-Française left no 14, the premises it had occupied for over a century. The dome at the bottom of the street is that of the Institut de France.

Pass the Pub St-Gennain, one of the first 'English pubs' in Paris – it opened over 30 years ago – and the celebrated Café Procope at no 13, now completely tarted up, so that little remains to remind us that it was once one of the great literary cafes of the city. Founded in 1686 by a Sicilian, Francesco Procopio dei Coltelli, it was the first place in Paris where one could drink real coffee. It became very successful, thanks to all the artistes from the theatre opposite and the *boules* players who used the *terrain* just behind the café in what is now Cour du Commerce-St-Andre (see p65). *L'Encyclopédie,* that apotheosis of the Age of Enlightenment, was born out of a casual conversation at the Procope between Denis Diderot (1713–1784) and Jean le Rond D'Alembert (1717–1783), and thereafter the *Encyclopédistes,* among them also Voltaire (1694–1778) and Jean-Jacques Rousseau (1712–1778), used to meet there. A few years later it was the turn of the local revolutionaries, including Georges Danton (1759–1794), Jean Paul Marat (1743–1793), Camille Desmoulins (1760–1794) and Philippe Fabre d'Eglantine (1750–1794). When Romanticism flourished in the 1830s it was the turn of Alfred de Musset (1810–1857), George Sand (1804–1876) and Honor6 de Balzac (1799–1850). At the end of the 19th century Paul Verlaine (1844–1896), Anatole France (1844–1924) and Joris Karl Huysmans (1848–1907) kept up the tradition. Quite a place.

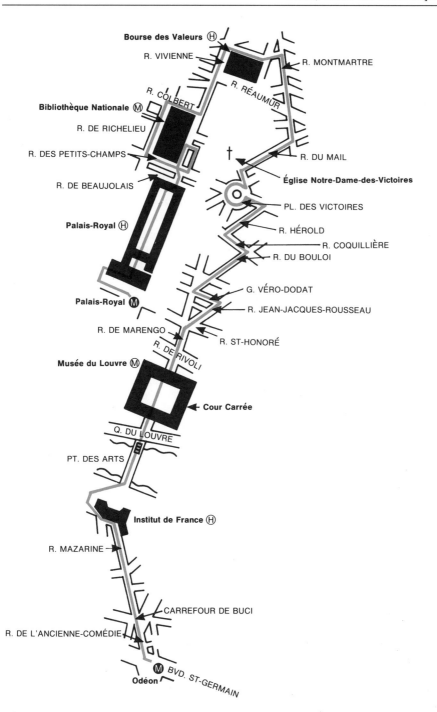

Bourse des Valeurs Ⓗ

R. VIVIENNE

R. MONTMARTRE

R. COLBERT

R. RÉAUMUR

Bibliothèque Nationale Ⓜ

R. DE RICHELIEU

R. DES PETITS-CHAMPS

R. DU MAIL

Église Notre-Dame-des-Victoires

R. DE BEAUJOLAIS

PL. DES VICTOIRES

Palais-Royal Ⓗ

R. HÉROLD

R. COQUILLIÈRE

R. DU BOULOI

G. VÉRO-DODAT

Palais-Royal Ⓜ

R. JEAN-JACQUES-ROUSSEAU

R. DE MARENGO

R. ST-HONORÉ

R. DE RIVOLI

Musée du Louvre Ⓜ

Cour Carrée

Q. DU LOUVRE

PT. DES ARTS

Institut de France Ⓗ

R. MAZARINE

CARREFOUR DE BUCI

R. DE L'ANCIENNE-COMÉDIE

Ⓜ

Odéon

BVD. ST-GERMAIN

At no 14, as noted, was the theatre of the Comédie-Francaise, whose first presentation, on 18 April 1689, was *Médecin malgré lui* by Molière (1622–1673) and *Phèdre* by Jean Racine (1639–1699). Marat lived at no 16 during 1790.

You are approaching the Carrefour de Buci, which has been a busy place since Henri IV's reign, when two of the main Left Bank gates into the city were nearby; today the Rue de Buci market draws many shoppers.

Continue into Rue Mazarine, named in 1687, a few years after the death of Cardinal Mazarin (1602–1661). Like Rue de l'Ancienne-Comédie, of which it is a continuation, it was once a path along the fortified city wall; today it has nice old bookshops and houses, many dating from the 17th century. At no 19 Robert Desnos (1900–1945), one of the leading Surrealist poets and also a medium – the other members of the group drew on his talents in their automatic-writing experiments – lived 1934–44, before being deported to Germany. At no 30 is the fine Hôtel des Pompes, in effect Paris's first fire station; Louis XIV gave 30 water pumps to the city under the direction of François Dumouriez du Périer (1650–1723), renowned for having fathered 32 children.

Pass Rue Guénéguaud on the right, with a lovely perspective down to the Seine; there are two good cafés on the corner, the Balto and the Bistro Mazarin. This section of Rue Mazarine contains many art galleries, a feature of this district. Jean François Champolhon (1790–1832) was living at no 28 when, in 1822, he discovered the key to Egyptian hieroglyphics, and the same house was the home of the artist Horace Vernet (1789–1863), famous for his Napoleonic battle scenes.

L'Institut de France

At the bottom of the street is the small Square Piemé – whose fountain was created in 1830 by a son of Jean Honoré Fragonard (1732–1806) – and, on the other side of Rue de Seine, Square Honoré-Champion, with recent statues of Charles de Montesquieu (1689–1755) and Voltaire. Facing you is the back wall of the Institut. Go through the small arch on the right into Place de l'Institut and keep walking along the wall to the gates, through which you can admire the *cour* and façade. Unfortunately, you cannot enter this wonderful building unless you have booked for a guided tour (write to the Secrétariat of the Institut) – certainly worth considering if you are to be in the city for a while.

When Mazarin, Prime Minister and virtual ruler of France for 18 years, died in 1661, he ordered that part of his vast fortune should be used to build an ensemble comprising a college (officially the Colège Mazarin but generally called the Collège des Quatre-Nations) and a library that was to open to the public twice a week – the first French public library. Designed by Louis Le Vau (1612–1670) – who originally planned it for the axis of the Louvre – and completed by others, the building was erected in 1663–84 (and thoroughly restored in the 1960s-70s). The college disappeared during the Revolution; the Institut, founded in 1795 in the Louvre, was eventually established here in 1805 under Napoleon. Mazarin had been an avid bibliophile, and his considerable collection formed the core of the celebrated Bibliotheque Mazarine, which not only survived but was augmented during the Revolution; it is housed in the east pavilion (the one to your left). This sumptuous room is open to the public and well worth seeing.

The Institut is in effect a kind of supreme authority in terms of literature and science; though often seen as monolithic and conservative, it is by no means an irrelevance. It incorporates five different *académies:*

- l'Académie Française, originally established 1635 by Cardinal Richelieu (1585–1642) and made up of writers (women are now accepted!), whose main responsibility is the updating of the *Dictionnaire* (before being officially admitted to any dictionary, new words must be approved by l'Académie)
- l'Académie des Inscriptions et Belles Lettres, originally established by Jean Baptiste Colbert (1619–1683) in 1664, specializing in history
- l'Académie des Sciences
- l'Académie des Beaux-Arts
- l'Académie des Sciences Morales et Politiques

Le Pont des Arts and the Louvre

The original Pont des Arts was the first cast-iron bridge in France (1802–4). It was designed to be a suspended garden, adorned with flowerpots, potted trees and benches. Its very light structure was supported by nine piles, into which the river barges had an unfortunate habit of crashing. In the early 1970s the bridge was declared unsafe, and demolished. It was replaced in 1983–4 by an entirely new bridge on the same site, spanning the river between the Institut and the Louvre.

The views offered from the bridge towards the Louvre, the Institut and the houses on the banks of the river are truly wonderful. Paris appears almost as a gentle city, the pressure of contemporary living a long way away. As you walk across, the perspectives change. Facing you is the Louvre's magnificent Galerie du Bord-de-l'Eau, initiated by Catherine de' Medici (1519–1589) to link the Louvre and the Tuileries palaces. On your right are Tour St-Jacques and Église St-Germain-l'Auxerrois, quite close by, and a lovely vista over Île de la Cité and Pont Neuf. To your left, as you walk on, are the Musée d'Orsay and Tour Eiffel. By this time you are almost to the other side; look back for a last view of the grandeur of the Institut.

Go down the steps at the end of the bridge, cross Quai du Louvre – there is a convenient pedestrian crossing – and enter the Palais du Louvre and the Cour Carrée. The *palais* is more fully discussed on p92; here we need mention only that this is the oldest section of it, started by the young Pierre Lescot (c1510–1578) for François I in the early part of the 16th century and decorated by Jean Goujon (c1510–1568), with subsequent alterations by Le Vau and Claude Perrault (1613–1688) during Louis XIV's reign, before its final completion in the 1800s.

Leave the Louvre through the Porte Marengo, directly ahead of you.

Designerland

Cross straight over Rue de Rivoli into Rue de Marengo and follow it to Rue St-Honoré, which you cross into Rue Jean-Jacques-Rousseau, slightly to the right. Continue down this pleasant street and then (at no 19) turn left into Galerie Véro-Dodat. This fine arcade has seen few changes in the past 150 years; note the painted ceiling, the mosaic floor, the marbled walls, and the brass and glass on the shop windows (see p169 for a fuller description). The Café de l'Époque at the end is a good place for lunch or a drink.

Turn right into Rue du Bouloi. As you cross Rue du Colonel-Driand, almost straight away you can see the Bourse du Commerce, the large rotunda on your right (see p77). The street dates from the 14th century and takes its name from the *jeu de boules* that used to be between nos 19 and 23. The courtyards of nos 21 and 22 are worth a glance.

Take a left into Rue Coquillière, which had already been entirely built up by the end of the 13th century. There is a nice old-fashioned brasserie, with original turn-of-the-century décor, on the corner of Rues Coquillière and Bouloi. At the end of Rue Coquillière is the HQ of the Banque de France.

Turn right almost immediately into Rue Hérold, where there are some old houses. Charlotte Corday (1768–1793) stayed at no 17 when she came from her village to assassinate the founder of the revolutionary newspaper, *L'Ami du Peuple*, Jean Paul Marat (1743–1793). Reach the busy Rue Étienne-Marcel, opened in 1880 and named for the long-ago Prévost of the Merchants, Étienne Marcel (*c*1316–1358). The street, especially this section of it, has changed considerably over the past few years; it and the nearby Place des Victoires provide a home to designers such as Kenzo and others.

Take a left to reach the oval Place des Victoires (1685), designed by Jules Hardouin-Mansart (1645–1708) but with the *hôtels* built, all to the same plan, by a different architect, called Prédot; they have since been brutally altered, so what you see now has little to do with the originals. Rue Étienne-Marcel tore through here in a singularly unplanned way. The *place* was conceived by an aristocrat, the Duc de la Feuillade, who wanted to toady to the king. The numerous Places Royales, of which this is one, were essentially designed to show off statues of the ruling king; the statue of Louis XIV now in the centre of the *place is* not the original but one installed under the Restoration in 1822 (the only original statue of Louis XIV is at Carnavalet – see p36).

Walk clockwise around the *place* – no 1 is the finest house – until you reach the short Rue Vide-Gousset which leads to Place des Petits-Pères, established in 1805 on the site of the *couvent* of the Augustins Déchaussés. Some 200 years earlier the fathers had been thrown out of their prosperous monastery – its extensive large library included a unique collection of maritime maps – by Queen Margot (Margaret de Valois; 1553–1615) under the pretext that they sang out of tune! All that remains is their chapel, now Église Notre-Dame-des-Victoires, facing you. Among the architects who worked on the church, which took over 100 years to complete (1629–1740), was Libéral Bruand (1635–1697). It is an interesting church, very symptomatic of the ultra-Catholic fervour that has always been such a feature of French life: the walls are covered with ex-votos (thanks to the Virgin Mary), and of the seven pictures in the choir by Carle Van Loo (1705–1765), painted in the 1750s, all but one (Louis XIII at the siege of La Rochelle) are scenes from the life of St Augustine (354–430). Among the people buried here is the musician Giovanni Battista Lully (1632–1687).

Leaving the church, go left into Rue du Mail, opened in the first half of the 17th century; the restaurant on the çorner, Chez Georges, gives reliable quality at mid-range prices. Many of the houses are 16th-century. Napoleon, while still a young general, lived somewhere in this street in 1790, the first year of the Revolution. Franz Liszt (1811–1886) stayed at no 13 many times between 1823 and 1878 (plaque). The street is now full of interior-design and upholstery shops.

La Bourse des Valeurs

At the top of the street, turn left into Rue Montmartre; this short section of it was opened in the 1630s, but the houses are mostly 19th-century. Carry on and cross Rue Réaumur. Facing you, slightly to the right, is an interesting example of early-20th-century iron architecture, built as an office block by George Cherdanne (1861–1940) in 1904–6. At no 136 is an amusing *hôtel,* built in 1760, with Classical-style statues inset in the façade. Pass Rue du Croissant, also opened in the 1630s, and turn left into the extremely short Rue Brongniart (exactly opposite Rue des Jeûneurs).

Cross Rue Notre-Dame-des-Victoires into Place de la Bourse, which occupies the site of Couvent des Filles-St-Thomas, demolished during the Revolution. The Palais de la Bourse-des-Valeurs was built in 1808–26 in typically imperial Neoclassical style. It was enlarged into the cruciform style seen today in 1902–3. Facing the Bourse is the good Brasserie Vaudeville, often full of brokers.

The Bibliothèque Nationale

Cross Rue du Quatre-Septembre/Rue Réaumur at the southwest corner of the *place*, by the newspaper kiosk, into Rue Vivienne, opened in 1652, which takes its name from a family that lived there in the 1750s. It has a few interesting old houses, especially that at nos 12–16, the second Hôtel Tubeuf (see below for the first), built in 1649 by Le Muet – walk in to have a look at its courtyard.

Turn right into Rue Colbert, opened in 1683 on the site of the stables of the Palais Mazarin, and then left into Rue de Richelieu. You are going round the Bibliothèque Nationale, the French equivalent of the British Library and the US Library of Congress. Square Louvois, on your right, with its lovely fountain by Lodovico Visconti (1791–1853) showing four rivers of France, was created in 1839.

The entrance to the Bibliothèque Nationale is opposite the *square*. The library is a complex collection of buildings dating back to the days of Cardinal Mazarin, with many additions by Robert de Cotte (1656–1735) in the 1720s and even more radical transformations (the reading-room, etc.) by Henri Labrouste (1801–1875) in 1857–73. You can go into the library itself only if you are already a reader at an institution like the British Library or are a researcher or by special appointment. However, you can visit the exhibition rooms, and it is worth doing so, even if the current exhibition is of no interest to you. Especially grand are the two galleries designed by Mansart for Mazarin in 1645 – Galerie Mansart downstairs and Galerie Mazarine upstairs – where the Cardinal intended to house his precious collections and his library.

The Bibliothèque Nationale's collection is one of the oldest and largest in the world, dating back to Charles V, whose collection was the first royal collection. It was greatly enhanced by successive French kings, and especially with the royal ordnance of 1537 obliging all printers in France to submit one copy of any volume they printed.

Carry on down Rue de Richelieu, passing a few old houses before you reach Rue des Petits-Champs, in which you turn left. Pass the fine gate and façade of the 17th-century Hôtel Tubeuf, now part of the Bibliothèque (and further discussed on p171), and go left again into Rue Vivienne; the splendid *hôtels* on your right date from the 17th century. Behind the railings on your left is what remains of the garden of Cardinal Mazarin's Hôtel. Also to the left is the back of the Hôtel Tubeuf, and facing you is the fine elevation of the two Mansart galleries. Opposite the gates, just by Jean Paul Gaultier's shop, is the entrance to Galerie Vivienne (see p171). A little before you reach there, turn right into Galerie Colbert (see p171), recently renovated for the Bibliothèque, which owns it. Both these *galeries* are early-19th-century.

The Palais-Royal

Leave Galerie Colbert and go back into Rue des Petits-Champs; turn right and left again down a few steps into Rue de Beaujolais. Here Colette (1873–1954), author of the *Claudine* series, lived in an apartment above Passage du Perron from 1938.

Enter the *passage* which leads into the Palais-Royal, another building that took a long time to raise, in this instance about 200 years. You are approaching it from the 19th-century end; the oldest part, built for Cardinal Richelieu (1585–1642) in 1629–35 by Jacques Lemercier (1585–1684) and then called the Palais Cardinal, is at the other end. The *palais* has a remarkably rich history (see below); but the person most responsible for converting it to its present state was Philippe Égalité (1747–1793). Terribly in debt, he reduced the garden considerably by bordering it on three sides with the monumental ensemble we see today. It was built in 1781–5 by the architect Victor Louis (1731–c1811), and numerous shops – all for rent – were housed under the arcades. On the fourth side of the rectangle were erected, temporarily, the notorious *galeries de bois* (wooden arcades), soon rife with prostitution, performing freaks and petty criminals.

The gardens were extremely lively, and many people came to shop, dine or drink. The infant Louis XIV almost drowned himself in the Grand Bassin in the centre, where children play today. Many royal balls and fêtes took place in the gardens from Louis's time onward. The three *galeries* – Galerie de Beaujolais to the north, Galerie de Montpensier to the west (i.e., to the right as you enter) and Galerie de Valois opposite it – are today rather quiet, containing mostly art galleries; it is difficult to imagine the throngs of 200 years ago.

The Restaurant du Grand Véfour, in Galerie de Beaujolais, was established from the *galerie's* inception, in 1784. Even if you do not plan to eat there, do walk in: with its columns, painted ceiling and mirrors, it has been little changed.

The gardens are an excellent place for a quiet stroll; for some extraordinary reason few people come here. On the far side of the fountain, in the middle of the lawn, is a curio: Le Petit Canon du Palais-Royal. This miniature cannon was installed in the early days of the arcades by a clockmaker from Galerie de Beaujolais; an appropriately placed lens ignited the device at noon each day. In 1914 the practice was stopped; it was reintroduced in 1990.

Walk through the colonnaded Galerie d'Orléans, erected on the site of the *galeries du bois* by Pierre Fontaine (1762–1853) in 1828–9, during the Restoration. You are now in the old Palais-Royale. The sculptures by Daniel Buren (b1938) – those grey and white columns – have filled the Cour d'Honneur since 1986; whatever one may feel about them (I quite like them), they are certainly better than the car park the sumptuous courtyard had become.

As noted, the history of the Palais-Royal is rather complex. Richelieu bequeathed it to Louis XIII; on his death Anne of Austria (1601–1666) moved in with her two young sons, the future Louis XIV and Philippe d'Orléans (1640–1701). The royal family lived here for a few years, through the vicissitudes of the Frondes (two rebellions, in 1648–9 and 1650–53), often having to flee to St-Germain-en-Laye, until, wearied by the insecurity, they finally moved to the Louvre, which then still looked like a fortified castle. The *palais* passed to Philippe and stayed with the Orléans until the revolution of 1848. During the Second Empire Napoleon III housed members of his family here, and the *palais* then became the property of the state. It now houses the Conseil Constitutionel (in Pavillon de l'Horloge), the Ministère de la Culture (in the Valois Wing) and the Conseil Economique (in the Montpensier Wing).

Thanks to the whims of princes, the spoliations of three revolutions, and various fires and lootings, hardly anything is left of the Palais Cardinal. As you stand under the colonnaded Galerie d'Orléans, the Valois Wing is on your left. There are traces of the original façade by Lemercier, with decorations showing anchors and prows (Richelieu was minister of the Navy), but all rather hidden by the 19th-century colonnade. The central Pavillon de l'Horloge, with its fine allegorical figures, was erected in the 18th century (with later alterations); the Montpensier Wing, started by Victor Louis, was completed in the 19th century.

On the right, on the corner with the Monpensier Wing, is the Théâtre de la Comédie-Française, originally built by Victor Louis in the 1780s. As you leave the Cour d'Honneur at its right-hand corner onto Place André-Malraux, you can see the theatre's entrance to your right. Take a left to look at the old *place d'armes*, which was in fact the entrance to the Palais-Royal, the Cour d'Honneur backing onto the gardens. This portion now houses the Conseil Constitutionel, the body regulating the French constitution, and dates mostly from the 18th century, with major alterations during the Restoration. The bas-reliefs on the central Pavillon de l'Horloge are by Augustin Pajou (1730–1809), as are those of the left wing. The other wing was burnt down during the Commune and rebuilt in 1875.

Your métro, Palais-Royal, is nearby, as are various bus-stops.

Assemblée Nationale, Concorde and Opéra

A walk through monumental Paris, with grand avenues, boulevards, *places* and perspectives. It is also a shopping walk, and culture is by no means absent, with the imposing Palais Bourbon – home to the Assemblée Nationale – and the stupendous Opéra, the most remarkable example of Second-Empire opulence.

Start: **Métro Assemblée-Nationale; buses 83 and 84.**
Finish: **Métro Tuileries; buses 72 and 81.**
Length: **3.5km (2¼ miles)**
Time: **1½hr.**
Refreshments: **No shortage, but little that is special. If money is no object, there are two great classic restaurants: Maxim's and Lucas Carton.**
Which day: **Saturday if you want to look at the Assemblée; weekdays are best if you want to shop (Saturdays are crowded); Sundays are dead.**
To visit:
- **Assemblée Nationale: Saturday only, guided tours at 10.00, 11.00 and 15.00; passport or identity card needed.**
- **Opera: daily 11.00–16.00.**

The Assemblée Nationale
Leave Assemblée-Nationale métro station (still sometimes referred to as Chambre-des-Députés) by the Rue de l'Université exit and find yourself in Boulevard St-Germain. A few steps along, go first right along Rue de l'Université to the charming leafy Place du Président-Édouard-Herriot. Continue into Place du Palais-Bourbon, created in 1776 by the Prince de Condé (1736–1818) to clear the entrance to his palace. The splendid *hôtels* around the trapezoidal *place* all date from those days. The fine street going south from the *place* is Rue de Bourgogne, opened in 1719.

The *palais* was built in 1722 by the architects Jacques-Ange Gabriel (1698–1782), Jean Aubert (d1741) and a third, called Ghirardini, for the Duchess de Bourbon, a daughter of Louis XIV and Mme de Montespan; it eventually passed into the Prince de Condé's hands before being bought by the state in the 1830s. It went through massive modifications in order to accommodate the desires of its various owners; only the Cour d'Honneur, which you can see through the gates (no entry), is original, and the building is now heavily Neoclassical.

Walk around the *palais* and down Rue Aristide-Briand until you reach the river. Turn left along Quai Anatole-France to face the front of the Assemblée. Its theatrical façade, destined to act as a symmetrical counterpoint to the Madeleine, was done in 1804–7, and Jean-Pierre Cortot (1787–1843) was responsible for the sculptures of the pediment. The Hémicycle where the deputies sit is open to the public when the Assemblée is in session.

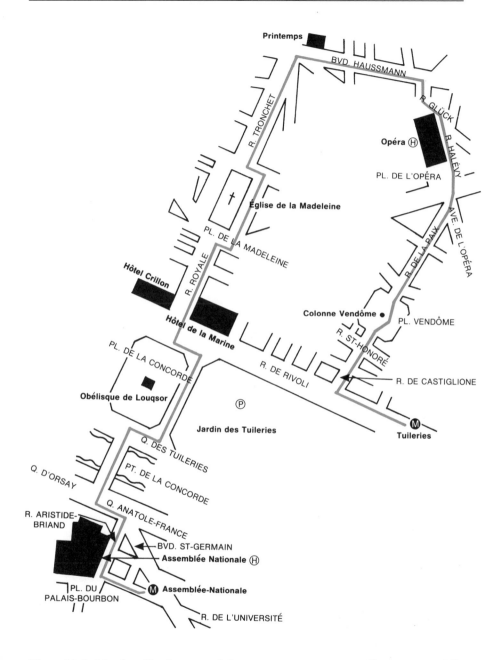

The guided visit takes 45 minutes, and there are numerous rooms of interest, especially the sumptuous Galerie des Fêtes (1848), the Salle des Quatre-Colonnes, the Salon Delacroix, the remarkable library – decorated by Eugène Delacroix (1798–1863), and with a large collection, including the original transcript of the trial of Joan of Arc (*c*1412–1431) and many manuscripts by Jean-Jacques Rousseau (1712–1778) – and finally the richly decorated Hémicycle.

On leaving the Assemblée, cross the river by Pont de la Concorde, built at the end of the 18th century with stones from the Bastille. To your right in the far distance is the Île de la Cité, while to the left of it and much nearer you can see the Louvre. On your left are the glass roofs of the Grand Palais and the gilded Pont Alexandre-III. As you keep walking, Tour Eiffel and the Trocadéro ensemble come into view.

Place de la Concorde
The Place de la Concorde, a triumph of urban design, is one of the city's Places Royales. It was designed by Jacques-Ange Gabriel in the 1770s to show off a statue of Louis XV that the merchants' provost had offered the king on his recovery from a bad illness; that statue was destroyed during the Revolution. Before the creation of the *place* there was little here except a large esplanade with the Jardin des Tuileries on one side and the *allée* up the Chaillot and Roule hills on the other. The celebrated Chevaux de Marly by Antoine Coysevox (1640–1720) flanked the rotating bridge that gave entrance to the gardens over a great moat, left from the Louis XIII fortified wall.

Gabriel decided to do his design on the grand scale, and was gloriously successful. The octagonal *place* was surrounded by a ditch, spanned here and there by stone bridges. At each of its eight angles was a small stone pavilion, with steps leading down into the ditch. On the north side Gabriel set two twin *hôtels* done in the style of the superb colonnade by Claude Perrault (1613–1688) at the Louvre, intending them as residences for foreign ambassadors. This aim went unrealized, and they were divided and sold in lots. There have been other transformations: a further set of horses, this time by Guillaume Coustou (1677–1746), was installed on the Champs-Élysées side (see p96); Pont de la Concorde was finished during the Revolution; and Rue de Rivoli was opened during the First Empire. But the more important improvements took place in Louis-Philippe's reign: the eight little pavilions were filled with statues, all by different sculptors, representing great cities of France – apparently Juliette Drouet (1806–1883), later for many years the mistress and muse of Victor Hugo (1802–1885), posed for the one representing Lille by her then lover James Pradier (1790–1852) – the lamp-posts appeared; the wonderful fountains – inspired by similar ones at St Peter's in Rome – were installed; the 13th-century-BC Obélisque, a present to the king from Mohammed 'Ali (*c*1769–1849), Viceroy of Egypt and the Sudan, was erected between the two fountains; and finally, during the Second Empire, the ditch, which had become a happy hunting-ground for prostitutes, was filled in.

The *place* changed its name from Place Royale to Place de la Révolution during the Revolution, and was one of the three *places* in Paris where the guillotine was in action: 1119 people were decapitated here (nearly half the total guillotined in Paris), including Louis XVI and Marie Antoinette (1755–1793), Georges Danton (1759–1794), Maximilien de Robespierre (1758–1794) and Louis de Saint-Just (1767–1794). It became Place de la Concorde in 1795.

Cross to Rue Royale, diametrically opposite from Pont de la Concorde. Go along the end of the Jardin des Tuileries, past the museums of the Orangerie and of the Jeu de Paume; on your right, as you go, you see the classic vista down to the Louvre, and, on your left, up to the Arc de Triomphe. Cross Rue de Rivoli, walk alongside the Ministry of the Navy and cross Rue Royale over to the Hôtel Crillon. Here a plaque tells you that on 6 February 1778 'Conrad Gérard, in the name of Louis XVI, and Benjamin Franklin, Silas Deane and Arthur Lee, in the name of the USA, signed a treaty of friendship, commerce and alliance between France and the USA, by which France, first of all nations, recognized the independence of the USA'.

The Madeleine

Walk up Rue Royale towards Église de la Madeleine, facing you. The street was opened in the early 18th century along the old Louis-XIII fortified wall. Gabriel imposed uniform façades on the houses that were built alongside the street. Rue Royale is now a street of luxury shops and is also home to the celebrated Café Maxim's, at no 3: walk in to look at the splendid 1899 Art-Nouveau décor, with later contributions from the great Louis Majorelle (1859–1926). But it was with the Lucas Carton restaurant at the top of Rue Royale, at no 11 Place de la Madeleine, that Majorelle excelled. This is Art-Nouveau interior decoration at its best: no frills and not much paint, just finely carved wood panels with arabesques and flowery motifs. It is an intimate décor, with images reflecting in the interplay of mirrors in the numerous niches.

From Lucas Carton, cross the wide Boulevard Malesherbes (Église St-Augustin appears in the distance) and walk over to Église de la Madeleine. There has been a church in this district – then known as Ville l'Evêque, as the Bishop of Paris owned the land – since the 6th century. Dedicated to Madeleine in the 13th century, the church proved too small to cope with the urban explosion of the 1700s, and was pulled down to make way for a larger and grander building, the present Madeleine, one of the most celebrated edifices in Paris. It was begun in the Ancien Régime by the architect Pierre Constant d'Ivry (1698–1777), the intention being to provide a proper finish to Rue Royale; work stopped at the Revolution; then it was transformed by Napoleon into a Greek temple (the *Temple de la Gloire* – 'I want a monument such as there are in Athens and none in Paris'), which was continued by Pierre Alexandre Vignon (1763–1828) and finished by Jean-Jacques Huvé in 1842. By now the building was a church again, but it kept its austere, massive and somewhat ungainly temple-like shape.

Inside there is a strong feeling of opulence: this was no poor parish. Marble predominates, but there are also painted ceilings, mosaics and sculptures by numerous artists of the time, including Pradier, Jules Claude Ziegler (1804–1856) – those on the large semi-dome at the back – and François Rude (1784–1855). The church has recently been restored, and so its sumptuous interior can be fully appreciated.

On leaving, admire the vista over the Obélisque and the Assemblée as you walk down the steps. Turn left at the bottom and left again along the eastern church wall. Just by the flower shops in the island is a public loo (underground), another Art-Nouveau monument, with stained glass, mosaics on the floor, fine white ceramics and mahogany doors – and all kept astonishingly clean.

In the corner of the *place* is Fauchon, one of the most celebrated delis in Paris (a little like London's Fortnum & Mason). There is a good restaurant on the first floor and an excellent Italian-style cafeteria downstairs.

Shopping

Turn right into Rue Tronchet, opened 1824 on the site of the Couvent des Bénédictines de la Ville-l'Évêque; it was built as a shopping street and has remained one. Carry on up towards Boulevard Haussmann. At no 102, on the left, Marcel Proust (1871–1922) lived in his cork-lined room – he suffered from asthma – and wrote a large part of *À la recherche du temps perdu*.

Cross over and go right on the boulevard. This is department-store land. Facing you is the splendid Magasin du Printemps, built at the turn of the century by Paul Sédille (1836–1900) and later converted by René Binet (1866–1911), another exponent of Art Nouveau; sadly, much of it was destroyed in a fire in the 1920s, but the store has kept some of its *fin de siècle* charm, and the large stained-glass roof is splendid. The next block is occupied by another of Paris's large department stores, the Galeries Lafayette; the building is of little interest but the store is good.

On reaching Rue de Mogador, cross the boulevard to reach the back of the French Opéra. Take Rue Glück and then Rue Halévy along the side of the building until you reach Place de l'Opéra.

The Opéra
Built at the behest of Napoleon III, this is one of the most remarkable architectural achievements of the 19th century. The quasi-Gothic use of material and the quality of voluptuousness, luxury and wealth epitomize the era. 172 architects competed to build it; the winner was Charles Garnier (1825–1898). Building began in 1861, was interrupted by the Franco-Prussian War (1870–71) and the Commune, and was finally completed in 1875.

The theatre, a monument to the glory of the triumphant bourgeois classes of the Industrial Revolution, is on the Italian model, with almost as much space outside the auditorium as inside. The Grand Foyer overlooking Place de l'Opéra is typical of that design. Walk along the entrance hall, past a copy of the famous *Groupe de la Danse* by Jean Baptiste Carpeaux (1827–1875) – the original is at the Louvre – and up the magnificent stairs, rich in onyx and marble, to the first floor, with its many halls. Garnier declared that what he had done was to provide 'sumptuousness', and he certainly created a perfect setting for those resplendent evenings when appearance was all that mattered.

Another interesting room is the Rotonde du Glacier, near the Buffet (first floor on the right), which has a painted ceiling by Georges Clairin (1843–1919) and Gobelins tapestries. The auditorium itself was hardly designed for visibility, and many seats leave a deal to be desired. In fact, most operas are nowadays shown at the Bastille Opéra (see p145), with the Palais Garnier being used for ballet. The ceiling was painted by Marc Chagall (1887–1985) in 1964.

Leaving the Opéra, cross to the central island and go right, towards Boulevard des Capucines, opened in the late 17th century. The Café de la Paix on the boulevard is a survival from the 19th century, when numerous such establishments bordered the boulevards from the Madeleine to the Faubourg Montmartre. With its attractive décor, this café is a good place to sit and watch the world go by. At no 14, a little way along, was the Grand Café where, on 28 December 1895 in the now celebrated *salon Indien*, the first ever cinematographic show took place.

Cross the boulevard, with Avenue de l'Opéra more or less facing you. Take a right into the handsome Rue de la Paix, opened in 1806 on the site of the Couvent des Capucines. The original convent was a little further south, but Louis XIV needed the space for what is now Place Vendôme (see below), and the nuns were moved to their bright new convent at the end of the 17th century. A century later, during the

Revolution, it was closed; its chapel became a theatre while the gardens were opened to the public. A few years afterwards it was decided to create Rue de la Paix, which cut right through the chapel.

Place Vendôme
Continue along Rue de la Paix, today lined with luxury shops. The first street you cross is Rue Daunou. To your left down it, at no 5, is Harry's Bar, made famous by one of its habitués, Ernest Hemingway (1899–1961). There is still a good atmosphere there, so you might think of stopping for a drink.

Carry on until you reach Place Vendôme, an elegant octagonal *place* surrounded by more luxury shops – Van Cleef and Arpels, Chaumet, Cartier and Boucheron – as well as the Ritz (no 15). The buildings have matching façades, with arcades, Corinthian pilasters and mansard roofs – one high, one low, alternately; an appropriate frame for the statue of the king. Another Place Royale, this was designed by Jules Hardouin-Mansart (1645–1708) and Germain Boffrand (1667–1754); it was called Place Louis-le-Grand and – for a few years during the Revolution – Place des Piques (pikes) before becoming Place Vendôme in 1799, after the Hôtel de Vendôme, demolished with the Couvent des Capucines to make way for the *place*. Only the façades were part of Hardouin-Mansart's design: the plots behind were sold to wealthy members of society, who could build on them as they wished. Many people of note lived here, including the financier John Law (1671–1729), Georges Danton (1759–1794), Frédéric Chopin (1810–1849), who died at no 12, and Giacomo Puccini (1858–1924). The Ministry of Justice is at no 13.

The king's statue, 7m (23ft) high in bronze, was melted down during the Revolution. The present 43m (140ft) column, aping Trajan's column in Rome, was erected in 1806 to celebrate the victory at Austerlitz; over 1200 Austrian cannon were melted for its manufacture. The spiral bas-reliefs depict scenes from the 1805 campaign and were designed by a pupil of Jacques Louis David (1748–1825) called Bergeret. Napoleon, in Roman costume, is at the top.

Leave the *place* by the fine arcaded Rue de Castiglione, opened in 1802 on the site of two *couvents*, the Couvent des Feuillants and the first Couvent des Capucines. At the bottom is Rue de Rivoli; a little way to the left is Tuileries métro station, where you can connect with the Faubourg St-Germain walk (p86). Alternatively, you could keep going along Rue de Rivoli to the Louvre station (5–10 minutes' stroll) and connect with the Louvre and Champs-Élysées walk (p91); on the way you pass the excellent Musée des Arts Décoratifs, which might be worth a detour.

Trocadéro, Tour Eiffel
and Invalides

This walk shows you grand, landscaped Paris at its best. Culturally rich – with six museums and three important monuments – it takes you twice across the Seine and along the gardens of the Champ-de-Mars.

Start: Métro Trocadéro; buses 22, 30, 32.
Finish: Métro Champs-Élysées-Clémenceau; buses 42, 73, 83, 93.
Length: 4.5km (2¾ miles).
Time: 2hr.
Refreshments: **Plenty of large cafés and brasseries, but few cheap-and-cheerful restaurants. The best are at the first stage of the walk on Place du Trocadéro, on Place Vauban just by the Invalides, halfway along the walk, and, at the end, on the Rond-Point des Champs-Élysées. The cafeterias in the Palais de Chaillot and at the Invalides offer an alternative to the cafés. The celebrated Restaurant de la Tour-Eiffel, on the first floor of the tower, though good, is expensive.**
Which day: **Most days; your choice of museums may disqualify Mondays and/ or Tuesdays (see below). A clear day is essential if you want to enjoy the view from Tour Eiffel.**
To visit:
● **Musée de l'Homme: daily (not Tuesday) 09.45–17.15.**
● **Musée de la Marine: daily (not Tuesday) 10.00–18.00.**
● **Cité de l'Architecture et du Patrimoine, opening in 2008 (check status on the web).**
● **Tour Eiffel: daily 10.00–23.00.**
● **Musée de l'Armée and Tombeau de Napoléon: daily 10.00–17.00, and to 18.00 from 1 April to 30 September.**
● **Palais de la Découverte: daily (not Monday) 10.00–18.00.**
● **Musée du Petit-Palais (Musée des Beaux-Arts de la Ville de Paris), now entirely renovated : daily (not Monday) 10.00–17.40.**

The Trocadéro
Leave the station by the Avenue Kléber exit to reach Place du Trocadéro (full name Place du Trocadéro-et-du-11-Novembre), created by Georges Haussmann (1809–1891) in 1869. The area gained its name from an 1827 re-enactment here of the French seizure of Fort Trocadéro, near Cadiz, in 1823.

In the central island you can see the statue of Marshal Foch (1851–1921) on horseback. Cross Avenues Kléber and du Président-Wilson to the Palais de Chaillot. Built in 1935–7, the current version was, like many other architectural ventures of the 1930s, a joint effort; its three architects were Léon Azéma (b1898), Louis Hippolyte Boileau (1893–1978) and Jacques Carlu (1890–1976)..

The *palais* has a long history. Catherine de' Medici (1519–1589) had the idea of building a country residence with landscaped gardens in the superb setting of the Chaillot hill. In the 17th century it passed into the hands of François de Bassompière (1579–1646), a great general and a great lover – he reputedly burnt over 6000 love letters before being sent to the Bastille for 12 years for conspiring against Cardinal Richelieu (1585–1642). On Bassompière's death the estate was bought by Henrietta Maria (1609–1669), queen to the British Charles I (reigned 1625–49); she turned it into a convent. It was closed during the Revolution and razed by Napoleon, who wanted to create 'a French Kremlin, a Napoleonic city'. His star waned before the project had got properly under way: the hilltop had been flattened and the slopes made gentler, but that was all. Little more was done until Gabriel Davioud (1823–1881) erected a *palais* – a 'neo-Byzantine pastry', according to one description – for the 1878 Exposition Universelle.

Davioud's Palais du Trocadéro – decaying genteelly, leaking and almost collapsing – remained until Azéma, Boileau and Carlu won the competition to revitalize the site for the 1937 Exposition Universelle; Le Corbusier (1887–1965) was one of the unlucky runners-up. The brief was reconstruction, not demolition. Carlu had the notion of opening the space out and getting rid of the central rotunda: there was no sense in trying to compete directly with Tour Eiffel, so the idea was to impress with empty space. The crescent-shaped wings were kept (they are now completely enveloped by the new building), two pavilions were added, and the rotunda was replaced by a *parvis*. Much effort went into the conception of the long rectangular space going down the hill towards the Seine and into the design of the gardens. The result is a great spot for museum-goers and skateboarders alike.

Access to the museums in the Palais de Chaillot is from the Place du Trocadéro side. The left-hand pavilion (Pavilion de Paris) takes you to the Cité de l'Architecture et du Patrimoine which will, among other things, house the collections of the defunct Musée National des Monuments Français – as well as a large gallery devoted to 19th- to 21st-century architecture, a public library on architecture and the French national heritage, and a research centre. It was due to open in 2005; will now open in 2008.

On the other side (Pavilion de Passy) are the Musée de l'Homme and the Musée de la Marine. The Musée de la Marine, quite small, contains superb models – some over 4m (13ft) long – of various celebrated French ships as well as many fine pictures, including prints by Jacques Callot (1593–1635) and a superb series of French harbours painted 1752–65 by Joseph Vernet (1714–1789).

The Musée de l'Homme, covering ethnography and anthropology, is enthralling. The earlier parts of the large collection are from the 19th century. Although many of the rooms have been redecorated, the museum still retains a sort of nostalgic charm. Guidebooks in English are available at the reception desk. You have a wide choice of exhibits, from Peruvian mummies to sculpted skulls and shrunken heads. There is a gallery devoted to human evolution, and a diversity of rooms arranged by provenance – Africa, Australasia, New Guinea, Afghanistan, etc. – all packed with artefacts, totems, masks, jewellery, pottery and ornaments. Also of interest is the music room, where ethnic instruments are on display; sometimes there are demonstrations.

Exit the museums onto the *parvis* and terrace. From the terrace you can see, on a clear day, the gilded dome of the Invalides (to the left of Tour Eiffel) and, in the distance, the dome of the Panthéon. The two pavilions have inscriptions by Paul Valéry (1871–1945). Walk down either through the gardens or along the pool – hemmed by statues – to

Place de Varsovie. Cross the river by Pont d'Iéna, built 1809–13, which has four large equestrian statues: an Arab and a Greek on this side and a Roman and a Gaul on the other. As you cross, the modern blocks of the Front de Seine and the steel structure of Pont de Bir-Hakeim appear on the right. Looking back from the other side you can see splendid views of the Palais de Chaillot and, framed by Avenue François-1er, of the Sacré-Coeur (see p140).

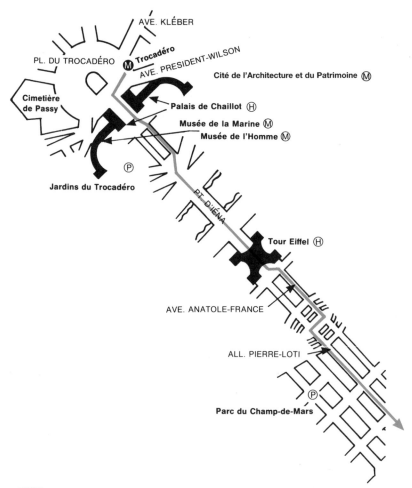

Tour Eiffel

Tour Eiffel, directly ahead of you, dominates Paris. The view from the tower on a clear day is exquisite – it is not worth going up on any other sort of day. Try to go to the third floor. The tower was built for the 1889 Exposition Universelle; 1889 was also the first centenary of the Revolution. The authorities launched a competition for a 300m (985ft) steel tower that would dominate the Champ-de-Mars. Out of 700 entries, Gustave Eiffel (1832–1923), an engineer from Dijon, emerged a close winner. It was erected in less

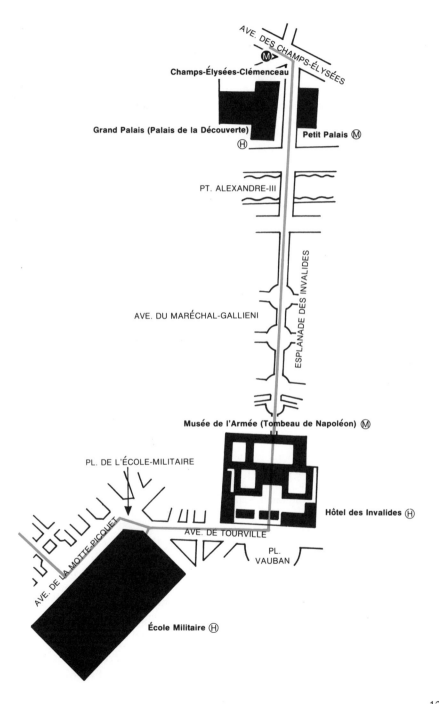

than two years, and was certainly ahead of its time: there were anti-Eiffel press campaigns, and the intelligentsia – including Alexandre Dumas fils (1824–1895), Guy de Maupassant (1850–1893), Léon Bloy (1846–1917) and Georges Clemenceau (1841–1929) – signed petitions against it; later Paul Verlaine (1844–1896) so loathed it that he habitually made detours to avoid it!

The lightness of the structure (a mere 7000 tonnes) becomes apparent at night when it is lit up. Lace-like and airy, made entirely of steel and cast-iron, if it were melted down into a square plaque the size of its base, between the four piles, that plaque would be a mere 6cm (2⅓in) thick! The four piles rest on a complex subterranean hydraulic system, which you can and should see: it is fascinatingly evocative of the weird contraptions dreamt up by Jules Verne (1828–1905). There are lifts in the north and west piles as well as, in the south pile, stairs and the special lift to the Restaurant de la Tour-Eiffel.

The Champ-de-Mars and the École Militaire

Leaving the tower, walk south across Parc du Champ-de-Mars. The Champ-de-Mars, established in the 18th century at the same time as the École Militaire (the imposing building in the near distance), was originally used for the students of the school to practise military manoeuvres. During the Revolution it was the scene of grand fêtes, including the Celebration of the Supreme Being, mounted in 1794 by Maximilien de Robespierre (1758–1794) to counter the spread of atheism (in fact it served to confirm in the minds of too many that he sought despotism, and thereby heralded his downfall); there were royal galas during the Restoration and horse races during the Second Empire. With the advent of the Republic it became the site for Expositions Universelles, of which there were six between 1867 and 1937. During the 19th century the Champ-de-Mars shrank as parts were developed; smart blocks today overlook the gardens, established in 1908–28 and containing statues, shrubberies and flowerbeds, children's playgrounds and *jeux de boules*.

Take Avenue Anatole-France (centre left), cross Place Jacques-Rueff and change over to Avenue Pierre-Loti (centre right); follow it to Place Joffre, which is in effect the *parvis* of the École Militaire. There is a gorgeous perspective from here back over Tour Eiffel and the Trocadéro.

The École Militaire is an impressive building. It was erected by Jacques-Ange Gabriel (1698–1782) during Louis XV's reign; Napoleon went to school there as a young officer. Today it houses the Institut des Hautes Études de Défence Nationale et d'Economie de Guerre and the École Supérieure de Guerre, among others, and can be visited only by appointment.

L'Hôtel des Invalides

Turn left down to the busy Place de l'École-Militaire, then right briefly around the school wall before crossing into the wide Avenue de Tourville, developed in the late 19th century. The semicircular Place Vauban, a couple of hundred metres along, sports a good brasserie. Leading off the south of the *place* is the elegant Avenue de Breteuil, opened 1680, the epitome of the *quartier chic*. That enormous building ahead of you is the Hôtel des Invalides, containing the Musée de l'Armée and Napoleon's tomb. The dome was, like many other monuments in Paris, regilded for the bicentenary of the Revolution.

The Hôtel Royal des Invalides was created in 1671 by Louis XIV to house disabled soldiers and officers, who until then had had to depend on the charity of religious institutions. Two of the best architects of the age were employed. The *hôtel*, designed by Libéral Bruand (1635–1697), is one of the finest 17th-century buildings in Paris, and Église du Dôme, by Jules Hardouin-Mansart (1645–1708), is almost certainly the best example of 17th-century religious architecture in the capital. When the *hôtel* was finished, in 1706, 6000 invalids moved in.

You are approaching it from the rear. The ticket office for the tomb and the museum is on this side, in the left-hand pavilion, as are loos and a cafeteria.

Two churches and a military museum

The façade of Église du Dôme is supremely Classical: Doric order for the lower half and Corinthian with triangular pediment for the upper. The large dome, set on 40 Corinthian columns, takes the church to a height of 107m (350ft).

Climb the steps and enter the church (ticket required). The plan is a Greek Cross; the marble marquetry of the floor is noteworthy. The dome rests on four large pillars separated by arcades. Hardouin-Mansart's original interior was greatly altered when it was decided to put Napoleon's tomb here. The new architect, Lodovico Visconti (1791–1853), dug an open circular crypt so as to enshrine the red porphyry sarcophagus, which is mounted on a block of green granite and contains six coffins inside each other, Russian-doll fashion: the innermost is of tin, the second mahogany, the next two lead, the fifth ebony and the outermost oak.

The side-chapels and the choir are as richly decorated as the rest of the interior, with pictures by Noël Coypel (1628–1707), among others.

On the far side of Église du Dôme is Église St-Louis-des-Invalides, the entrance to which is *via* the Cour d'Honneur. Originally the two churches shared the same choir and altar. The separation was made when the crypt was installed. Leave Église du Dôme, turn right and right again, and follow the short arcaded walkway past the ticket office to Galerie du Midi, which borders the sumptuous Cour d'Honneur. The entrance to Église St-Louis-des-Invalides is on the Cour du Midi, at the centre of the *galerie*. The church is often empty – tourists generally congregate in the *cour* or by the tomb.

Église St-Louis-des-Invalides, though less powerful than Église du Dôme, is another fine example of the religious architecture of the time; the architect is believed to have been Hardouin-Mansart, working on plans by Bruand. The church is in impeccable condition, having recently been cleaned up. The vast nave is supported by a series of Corinthian pillars, on which occasional plaques commemorate the many celebrated military leaders buried in the crypt – including Sébastien de Vauban (1633–1707), Théophile de La Tour D'Auvergne (1743–1800) and Jean Baptiste Kléber (1753–1800).

Leave the church and step into the Cour d'Honneur, where the Classical elegance of the *hôtel* and the genius of Libéral Bruand are much in evidence. The four sides of the *cour* are identical, with semicircular vaulted arcades and a mansard roof adorned with groups of horses. At each corner a stone stairway with cast-iron balustrades leads to the first-floor gallery. Take a walk around the quadrangle along the first-floor gallery.

The entrance to the Musée de l'Armée is in the western gallery (on the left when coming out of the church). Much larger than the Navy Museum, this is rather formally educational, providing a chronological military history from prehistoric times to the present. There are collections of swords, guns and armour (including Japanese and Ottoman), an assemblage of photographs of the Crimean and Franco-Prussian wars, pictures by artists drafted during the two world wars (including Jacques Villon [1875–

1963], Raoul Dufy [1877–1953], Pierre Bonnard [1867–1947] and Fernand Léger [1881–1955]), the famous Salle des Drapeaux and cannon from many campaigns.

A grand bridge

Leave the Cour d'Honneur *via* Galerie du Nord and cross the front *cour* to the main gates. Look back at the magnificent façade: the building is over 200m (220yd) long and is decorated with mascarons, helmets, armours and fireballs. Step into the esplanade, designed early in the 18th century, and walk down to Pont Alexandre-III.

This bridge was built in exactly two years for the 1900 Exposition Universelle. Tsar Alexander III (1845–1894) of Russia laid the first stone in 1898 as a symbol of the bonds between the two nations. The bridge is of metal, and the exuberant ornate decoration typifies a certain type of Third-Republic architecture: this was the heyday of Art Nouveau, which obviously had some effect on urban industrial engineering. Among the sculptors who took part in the decoration of the bridge were Georges Recipon (1860–1920) and the prolific Emmanuel Fremiet (1824–1910). As you cross, the Trocadéro becomes visible on the left while the Louvre and the Tuileries Gardens appear on the right. On the far side are the Grand Palais (left) and the Petit Palais (right), both built for the same exhibition.

The largest of the many halls in the Grand Palais is a brilliant innovative metallic structure by Henri Deglane (1855–1931), Gabriel Thomas (1854–1932) and an artist called Louvet, and is primarily devoted to trade fairs. Other galleries and halls are used for prestigious art exhibitions. As you cross the river you will note the stunning quadriga by Recipon on the roof. The garden on your right, as you reach the bank, is what is left of the Cours La Reine, created by Marie de' Medici (1573–1642) in 1616 and once an extremely fashionable promenade. The Palais de la Découverte is in the western part of the Grand Palais, with an entrance in Avenue Franklin-D.-Roosevelt – go left along the *quai* and right alongside the *palais*. All the sciences are represented in the displays, but the museum is probably best known for the planetarium.

The Petit Palais houses a strange, almost forgotten museum containing a most eclectic collection. Among its treasures are some stunning large canvases by Gustave Doré (1833–1883), fine works by Pieter Breughel (*c*1520–1569) and Jakob Jordaens 1593–1678), an excellent collection of ceramics and pottery, some early Alfred Sisley (1839–1899) and Johan Jongkind (1819–1891) pictures and, in the restored Galerie Zoubalof, works by many French 19th-century artists.

Walk along between the two *palais*, and then turn left into Avenue des Champs-Élysées. Your métro station, Champs-Élysées-Clémenceau, and an array of bus-stops are at the Rond-Point des Champs-Élysées.

You can easily connect this walk with the previous walk. On leaving the Petit Palais, instead of going to the Rond-Point, retrace your steps over Pont Alexandre-III, turn left along Quai d'Orsay to the Assemblée Nationale, and then right into the large Boulevard St-Germain to reach Assemblée-Nationale métro station, where the new walk starts.

Ternes and Parc Monceau

A fine walk across little known parts of Paris, from the Arc de Triomphe to Boulevard Haussmann. On the way are Art-Nouveau buildings, the charming Parc Monceau, and three superb small museums – each a gem in its own way. This is essentially 19th-century Paris, a Paris that few Parisians know, a Paris that is home to the bourgeoisie. Also on the way is Russian Paris, with the Russian Cathedral and the shops in Rue Daru.

Start: **Métro Charles-de-Gaulle-Étoile; bus 31.**
Finish: **Métro Miromesnil; buses 49, 80.**
Length: **6.5km (4 miles).**
Time: **2hr.**
Refreshments: **Quite a few cafés, especially in Place des Ternes at the beginning of the walk and Place Prosper-Goubaux later on.**
Which day: **Any day, but Wednesday–Sunday preferred.**
To visit:
- **Musée Cernuschi: daily (not Monday) 10.00–17.40.**
- **Musée Nissim-de-Camondo: daily (not Monday and Tuesday) 10.00–1200 and 14.00–17.00.**
- **Musée Jacquemart-André: daily 10.00–18.00.**

The Ceramic Hôtel
Leave the métro by the Avenue de Wagram exit to reach Place Charles-de-Gaulle (previously and still commonly called Place de l'Étoile). The avenue starts from the northern side of the Arc de Triomphe; if you are coming from the Champs-Élysées, the avenue is fourth on your right. Both the *place* and the Arc are described on p97.

Walk down the right-hand side of the avenue. This portion was opened in 1853, after the destruction of the Fermiers Généraux wall. There are many cafés at the beginning and some fast-food joints further down.

At no 34, decorated with the archetypal Art-Nouveau motifs of exuberant foliage, is the Ceramic Hôtel, the masterpiece of Jules Lavirotte (1864–1924), an eclectic architect who flirted for some time with Art Nouveau; he is regarded by many as second only to Hector Guimard (1867–1942). The two most celebrated of his many buildings, aside from this one, are in Avenue Rapp. The Ceramic Hôtel is like a gigantic piece of pottery. The ceramic decorations are by Alexandre Bigot (1862–1927), who also worked with Anatole de Baudot (1834–1915) on Église St-Jean-l'Évangéliste at Montmartre (see p139).

On the other side of the avenue is the celebrated Salle Wagram, a vast dancehall; it was here that the dance scenes of *Last Tango in Paris* (1972) by Bernardo Bertolucci (b1940) were shot. It is a great place, sometimes used for concerts or vast parties, and worth going to. Salle Wagram is on the site of the much older Bal Dourlan (1812).

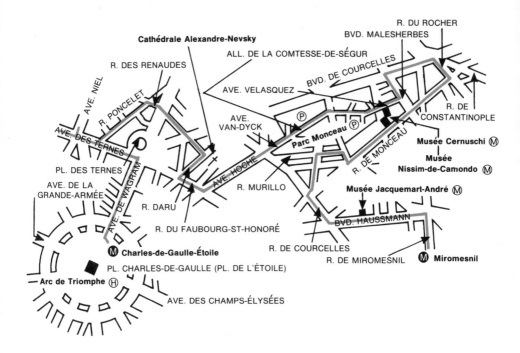

Flowers and culture

Reach the leafy Place des Ternes, created in 1864 over the Barrière du Roule, a tollgate of the Fermiers Généraux wall. In the central island is a flower market (daily except Monday). With its trees and cafés, the *place* has an agreeable atmosphere despite the maddening traffic.

Turn left into Avenue des Ternes, established on a track that led from Paris to the royal residence of St-Germain-en-Laye (see p188). Walk on the left-hand pavement to the first set of traffic lights and Avenue Mac-Mahon – the Comte de MacMahon (1808–1893) was the second President of the Third Republic. On your left is an interesting perspective over the Arc de Triomphe.

Cross Avenue des Ternes to the FNAC store on the corner with Avenue Niel. Built in 1912 as a department store for the local bourgeoisie, it now houses a wonderful book, record and hi-fi store. The building retains many of its original elements – especially the stained-glass roof at the top – but is decidedly modern inside and great fun to explore: it has an interactive video column, a room for photographic exhibitions, an English-language department on the fourth floor and a ticket hall where you can book for all the Parisian shows.

Russian Paris

Leave the store, turn left into Avenue des Ternes and, a little way along, left again into Rue Poncelet, traced over the old Chemin des Dames which led to the Abbaye des Dames-de-Montmartre. There is a good market in the morning (not Monday). The

Auberge des Dolomites restaurant (serious traditional food) is on the right at no 38. Turn right into Rue des Renaudes (just after a café) – at no 7 Captain Dreyfus (1859–1935) of the celebrated Dreyfus affair, and the famous *J'accuse* by Emile Zola (1840–1902), lived the last seven years of his life. Cross Avenue de Wagram and then Boulevard de Courcelles (on the site of the Fermiers Généraux wall) to reach Rue Pierre-le-Grand. Facing you is Cathédrale Alexandre-Nevsky (open to the public on Tuesday and Friday, 13.00–17.00), usually just called the Russian Cathedral. Built in 1862, it is Byzantine in inspiration; the interior decoration, richly ornamented with icons, mosaics and frescoes, is superb. The À la Ville de Petrograd restaurant (Russian food) is on the corner with Rue Daru, opposite the church.

With the cathedral behind you, go left along Rue Daru and turn left into Rue du Faubourg St-Honoré, one of Paris's longest streets. At no 252 is the Salle Pleyel, an exceptionally elegant concert hall. Turn left again into Avenue Hoche, which has typical, rather rich, Haussmanian buildings; nos 12, 15 and 6 are worth more than a passing look as representatives of the period's architecture.

Parc Monceau
At the end of the avenue are the gates of the delightful Parc Monceau. Just before, the avenue is crossed by Rue de Courcelles, established over an 18th-century track; at no 45, about 100m (110yd) away, was the Proust family apartment. This whole area is redolent of Marcel Proust (1871–1922) – Parc Monceau was a favourite haunt – and his contemporaries.

Cross the street to Avenue Van-Dyck, with its splendid cast-iron gates. Most of the *hôtels* built around the park date from the Second Empire. No 5 Avenue Van-Dyck is one of the most ostentatious *hôtels* in Paris; it was built for the then king of cocoa, Émile Menier (1826–1881). The whole decoration, by Jules Dalou (1838–1902), is a triumph of Baroque and pastiche.

The park itself covers about half of what used to be the estate of the Folie de Chartres, created by Carmontelle (1717–1806) for Louis-Philippe, Duc de Chartres and d'Orléans, later known as Philippe Égalité (1747–1793); as a member at the Convention during the Revolution, he voted for the beheading of Louis XVI before being guillotined himself in 1793. Carmontelle, a writer and an illustrator now chiefly remembered for his work as a landscaper, wanted to create here a 'land of illusion', and accordingly borrowed extensively from the classics – the references are numerous. The *folie* was eventually acquired by the state in 1852; one half was built on while the other was redesigned by Jean Charles Alphand (1817–1891) in the style of the English gardens so dear to Napoleon III, who had spent his years of exile (1846–8) at Ham House in Surrey.

It is a lovely park. There are beautiful shrubs, flowers and trees – some surviving from the original gardens – children's playgrounds and various weird and wonderful things. It is a good place for picnics, and there is a *buvette* near the rotunda. Wander as you will – the route described below is merely a suggestion – but make sure you rejoin the main walk by leaving the park on its eastern side, *via* Avenue Velasquez.

Walk along the central Allée de la Comtesse-de-Ségur; Sophie Rostopchine, Comtesse de Ségur (1799–1874) was a famous children's writer. Pass the statue of Alfred de Musset (1810–1857) by Antonin Mercié (1845–1916), showing the poet in a romantically depressed mood. At the junction with Avenue Ferdousi, you can see to your left the Fermiers Généraux Rotonde, one of three such monuments by Claude

Nicolas Ledoux (1736–1806) still surviving; the other two are at La Villette (see p143) and Place Denfert-Rochereau (see p153). This rotunda served as an apartment for the toll-keepers; the Duc de Chartres had an observation room in the cupola, over the keepers' flat. The Fermiers Généraux wall bordered the northern side of the *folie* (now Boulevard de Courcelles). Just after the junction, and almost opposite the monument to Ambroise Thomas (1811–1896), is a bridge in the middle of some artificial rockwork. From the bridge there is a view over the Naumachie, an artificial lake with mock colonnades, etc., one of the few surviving parts of Carmontelle's orginal park.

Walk around the lake and the Corinthian columns (17th-century or earlier) to return to Allée de la Comtesse-de-Ségur. Facing you is a rather weird pyramid, another of Carmontelle's constructions. Leave the gardens *via* Avenue Velasquez on the left.

At no 7 Avenue Velasquez is the Musée Cernuschi, devoted to Chinese Art. There is a fine collection of pottery, the most important part dating from the T'ang dynasty, as well as an important collection of ancient bronzes (14th-12th centuries BC). On the top floor is a room of contemporary Chinese paintings in traditional style.

Leave the museum and Avenue Velasquez and turn left into Boulevard Malesherbes. At no 9, down on the right, Proust spent his youth; when he was in his late twenties the family moved to Rue de Courcelles. It was in the house here that he had his second encounter with the ageing Oscar Wilde (1854–1900), who came to visit – and, to Proust's outrage, made a string of critical comments about the furniture.

At the traffic lights, turn right into Boulevard de Courcelles; the dome in the distance is that of the 19th-century Église St-Augustin. A splendid view over Montmartre and the Sacré-Coeur appears as you walk along the boulevard. The musician Ernest Chausson (1855–1899) lived at no 22 (on the other side), and at no 29 is a fascinating building, the only one left in Paris by the architect Xavier Schoellkopf (d1911). Very Art-Nouveau, it is so sculpted that the flat surfaces have almost disappeared and the junction-lines with the balconies are nearly invisible, as if the façade were of a whole, organic.

A communal grave
Continue to the busy Place Prosper-Goubaux, established on the site of the Barrière de Monceau, pulled down during the Second Empire.

Take the first turning to the right into Rue du Rocher, an old road that led from the city to the village of Argenteuil a few kilometres north, and very soon go right again into Rue de Monceau. Immediately to your right, at no 97, is a plaque commemorating the Cimetière des Errancis (cemetery of the cripples) there. This cemetery was established in 1794 as an overspill from the one at the Madeleine, nearby, which had become unable to cope with the results of an overactive guillotine, then set up on Place de la Révolution (today Place de la Concorde). All told, 1149 people were buried here, including Georges Danton (1759–1794), Antoine Lavoisier (1743–1794), Camille Desmoulins (1760–1794), Maximilien de Robespierre (1758–1794), Louis de Saint-Just (1767–1794) and Antoine Fouquier-Tinville (1747–1795). Understandably, the local population was not pleased, and the large communal grave was closed in 1797, the bones being later transported to the Catacombs (see p153).

An 18th-century reproduction and a Renaissance collection
Cross Boulevard Malesherbes at the traffic lights and continue along Rue de Monceau. At no 63 is the Musée Nissim-de-Camondo, an enchanting little museum dedicated to

the 18th century. The house, built in 1910–14 by René Sergent for Count Moïse de Camondo, was specifically designed to house some of the latter's collection, as with the remarkable room into which had to be exactly fitted seven painted panels by Jean-Baptiste Huet (1745–1811) depicting rural scenes. The *hôtel* and its collection were left to the state after the count's only son, Nissim, was killed in action in 1917.

Among other treasures are Sèvres china, an exceptional roll-top bureau in the style of André Charles Boulle (or Buhl; 1642–1732) – marquetry with chased bronze – by Jean François Oeben (c1720–1763), many fine pieces of furniture, Aubusson tapestries, paintings by Francesco Guardi (1712–1793) and a large assemblage of prints and engravings, etc.; in the Salon Bleu is a later collection of eight watercolours by Johan Jongkind (1819–1891). The authenticity of it all, and the perfection of the reconstruction – evoking a 19th-century wealthy aristocratic family living amidst an 18th-century décor – make this one of the most charming museums in Paris.

Turn right along Rue de Monceau as you leave the museum and reach Place Rio-de-Janeiro; turn right into Avenue Ruysdael and take the first left, Rue Murillo, which boasts many good-looking houses, then left again into Rue Rembrandt. The aspect of Imperial-bourgeois opulence eases somewhat as you cross Rue de Lisbonne and leave the environs of the park.

Continue along Rue Rembrandt to Place du Pérou, where you can see an odd-looking 19th-century red pagoda, now an Oriental art gallery. Turn left into Rue de Courcelles and reach Boulevard Haussmann. Stay on the left-hand pavement – there are a couple of interesting antiquarian and modern-first-edition bookshops – and continue until you reach no 158 Boulevard Haussmann, the Musée Jacquemart-André, now completely redecorated and reorganized. It was built by Henri Parent for the banker Édouard André (1833–1894) and his wife, the painter Nélie Jacquemart (1841–1912): they had the taste and the means to fill up their vast *hôtel* with a superb collection, including what may be the best selection of Italian paintings outside the Louvre, bequeathed to the Institut de France in 1914. There is a little of everything and almost every work is a masterpiece. Among the highlights of the Italian collection are *St George and the Dragon* by Paolo Uccello (1397–1475), *Christ* by Andrea Mantegna (c1431–1506), *Queen of the Amazons* by Vittore Carpaccio (c1455–1522), and an entire ceiling by Giovanni Tiepolo (1696–1770). The French collection has works by Jean Honoré Fragonard (1732–1806), Jean Baptiste Greuze (1725–1805), François Boucher (1703–1770) and Jacques Louis David (1748–1825); the Flemish collection has works by Rembrandt van Rijn (1606–1669) – including the celebrated *Pilgrims at Emmaus* – and Franz Hals (c1580–1666); and the British collection has works by Sir Joshua Reynolds (1723–1792) and Thomas Gainsborough (1727–1788). There are also fine pieces of furniture, carpets, tapestries and objets d'art.

Leave the museum and walk left along the boulevard until you reach Avenue de Messine. Cross the boulevard, continue in the same direction for a short while and turn right into Rue de Miromesnil; the Palais de l'Élysée is visible at the end.

This walk ends at Miromesnil métro station, a short way down the street. However, you can connect it with the Faubourg St-Honoré walk (p98), missing only a little bit at the start, by turning right at the métro station into Rue de La Boétie and walking along to Église St-Philippe-du-Roule.

Pigalle

A walk between two of the city's old fortified walls, mixing parts of Paris where few people go with others that are well trodden. A mixture also of times and of characters, from the boulevards to a Jewish quarter, some important Catholic churches, the Nouvelle Athènes, the sex shops of Pigalle and the important Cimetière du Nord, dit de Montmartre. The exquisite Musée Gustave-Moreau is on the way, as are the Folies-Bergère and the Casino de Paris. This is a part of Paris that was cherished by artists throughout the 19th century.

Start: **Métro Bonne-Nouvelle; buses 20 and 39.**
Finish: **Métro Place-de-Clichy; buses 68, 80, 81, 90.**
Length: **5.5km (3½ miles).**
Time: **2hr.**
Refreshments: **Many interesting places, especially if you like exotic food: there are Jewish, Greek, Turkish, North-African and Spanish restaurants - not to mention some good French ones. There are cafés all over the place on the boulevards at the walk's beginning and end.**
Which day: **Any day except, if you want to see the museum, Tuesday.**
To visit:
• **Musée Gustave-Moreau: Monday and Wednesday 11.00–17.15, other days (not Tuesday) 10.00–12.45 and 14.00–17.15.**

Boulevards and grocery stores
Leave the station *via* the Boulevard de Bonne-Nouvelle exit. Go left along the righthand side of the boulevard, created by Louis XIV as part of a ring of *cours* to enhance the city (see p15). For a long time tree-lined and a fashionable place for a *promenade,* they were gradually absorbed by the city's expansion, and were built up through the late 18th and 19th centuries. In the last century the boulevards from the République to the Madeleine were fashionable places for entertainment, with cafés and places of amusement everywhere, but today they are somewhat seedy.

Cross Rue du Faubourg-Poissonnière (previously Chemin de la Marée) – the road by which fish used to be delivered to the city's market – onto Boulevard Poissonière. At no 24 is the Max Linder Cinema, one of the best and most attractive in Paris. On the other side is another celebrated temple of the cinema, the Rex, built in 1932; there used to be many *hôtels* on that side of the street. In this part of the boulevard there are still lots of amusement stalls – shooting, fortune-telling, etc. – and people mill about until the small hours in search of fun.

When you reach the enormous Café Brébant, turn right into Rue du Faubourg-Montmartre, a section of the ancient track that led from Lutèce to Montmartre. There are many Neoclassical buildings. At no 4 is a late-18th-century *hôtel,* while on the other

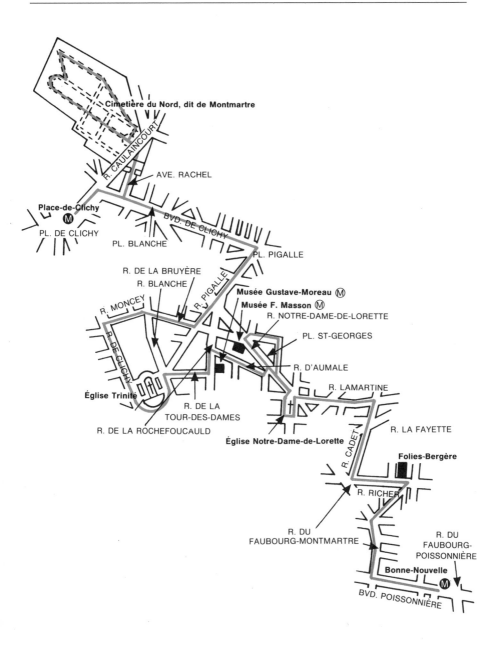

side there is the Restaurant Chartier – top-notch décor and ambience, not-so-top-notch cuisine – in the courtyard of no 7.

At no 6 you will find the entrance to Cité Bergère, which was created in 1825 at the same time as many of the other Parisian *passages* (see p169). This particular *cité* was primarily a residential development. Heinrich Heine (1797-1856) lived at no 3 and Frédéric Chopin (1810–1849) at no 4. At no 19 Rue du Faubourg-Montmartre is Rue de la Grange-Batelière, leading to the Hôtel Drouot, the French Sotheby's; there are many antiques shops nearby.

At no 20 Rue du Faubourg-Montmartre, turn right into Rue Geoffroy-Marie, opened 1835 on an estate given to the Hôtel Dieu hospital in the 13th century by a cobbler, Geoffroy, and his wife, Marie, on condition that the hospital feed and clothe them for the rest of their lives. In the 19th century the hospital sold the land for development and made quite a profit.

Get to Rue Richer at the end of the street: facing you is the famous Folies-Bergère, which dates from the 1860s, although the building received a comprehensive Art Deco conversion in the 1930s. Turn left along Rue Richer. Built on the site of the Grand Égout (large sewer), it dates from the late 18th century and is a lively shopping street; like Rue Geoffroy-Marie, it contains many Jewish restaurants and delicatessens.

When you reach Rue du Faubourg-Montmartre again you will find, facing you at the corner with Rue de Provence, a fine grocery store with original 19th-century décor: '*À la mère de famille, fondée en 1761*' ('The Housewife - Founded 1761') announces the sign outside.

At the junction of Rues Richer and du Faubourg-Montmartre, turn right into the busy Rue Cadet, where there is a good street market most mornings. Many of the houses on the right-hand side were demolished in 1857 to make way for the Grand Orient de France (French Masonic Great Lodge), also housing a museum of freemasonry. On the other side, at no 9, is a splendid 1750s *hôtel*.

Rue Cadet continues as Rue de Rochechouart; be careful as you cross the very busy Rue La Fayette, an important thoroughfare from the Opéra to the outskirts of Paris, created in the 19th century by Claude Rambuteau (1781–1869) and Georges Haussmann (1809-1891). Rue de Rochechouart is named for the abbess who ruled the Abbaye des Dames-de-Montmartre 1717–27.

Notre-Dame-de-Lorette

After crossing Rue La Fayette, turn left almost immediately into Rue Lamartine, a typical Parisian street of the 19th century.

Reach Rue Fléchier, on your left (opposite Rue des Martyrs), and walk down it to Église Notre-Dame-de-Lorette, built 1823–36 by Louis Hippolyte Le Bas (1782–1867) on the site of a 17th-century chapel. The building was inspired by Santa Maria Majora in Rome: it has an imposing portico supported by four large Corinthian columns and a pediment ornamented with symbolic statues. As with many other Parisian churches of the period, it has a richly decorated if somewhat severe interior. It takes its name from the *lorettes,* the young girls who thronged from the provinces in the 19th century to seek jobs in the capital, and who then often lurched into prostitution. A large contingent lived in this newly created *quartier.*

Take a turning to the right outside the church and walk along its western wall into Rue St-Lazare. Cross to Rue Notre-Dame-de-Lorette, going gently uphill. You are now in the Quartier St-Georges, home to many artists, including Jean Baptiste Pigalle (1714–1785), Théodore Géricault (1791–1824), Eugène Delacroix (1798–1863) and Paul Gauguin (1848–1903). Sometimes this part of the city is called Nouvelle Athènes, though strictly speaking that name should be applied only to the luxury development, done during the Restoration, a little further on (see below).

Rue Notre-Dame-de-Lorette, which was created in 1824–5, takes you to the circular Place St-Georges, developed at the same time. On the left is Hôtel Thiers (rebuilt in 1873), now housing a large library (visits only by appointment). On the other side is a fine neo-Renaissance *hôtel* (dating from 1840), heavily decorated with sculptures, pilasters, and so on. The street continues in the same vein after Place St-Georges. Delacroix had his studio at no 54 before moving to Place de Fürstenberg (see p67), and Gauguin was born at no 56.

A nearby street of interest is Rue Laferrière (first right in Rue Henri-Monnier after Place St-Georges, then first right again): the Symbolist poet Stéphane Mallarmé (1842–1898) lived at no 12. Follow Rue Laferrière round to return to Place St-Georges. If you need a rest, the half-hidden square recently created in the gardens of the Hôtel Thiers is very agreeable.

Now take a left down Rue St-Georges, developed haphazardly in the late 18th and 19th centuries. There is an interesting *trompe l'oeil* at the corner with Place St-Georges, and Auguste Renoir (1841–1919) had his studio at no 35. Take a right into Rue d'Aumale, developed in the first quarter of the 19th century – Richard Wagner (1813–1883) lived at no 3 – and go along to Rue de La Rochefoucauld, where you turn left.

Master of Symbolism

You are entering the real Nouvelle Athènes, completely developed with semi-luxury private houses in the 1820s, on the site of small market gardens and aristocratic *folies*. There are good *hôtels* at no 19 (1827) and no 11. At no 14 is the remarkable Musée Gustave-Moreau.

Gustave Moreau (1826–1898) was celebrated in his day by Joris Karl Huysmans (1848–1907) – the dandy writer of *À Rebours* (1884), used by Oscar Wilde (1854–1900) as a model for Dorian Gray – by Marcel Proust (1871–1922) – who used Moreau as a model for Elstir in *À la Recherche du Temps Perdu* – and by many other contemporaries. He remained perhaps too much of a painter's painter: he disliked *salons* and exhibited rarely. His work was largely forgotten until André Breton (1896–1966) and André Malraux (1901–1976) began to sing its praises, and slowly it regained the recognition it deserved. For a long time considered by history to have been more a pedagogue than an artist – he headed a workshop at the École des Beaux-Arts in the 1890s, his students including Henri Matisse (1869–1954), Georges Rouault (1871–1958) and Pierre Bonnard (1867–1947) – he is now recognized as one of the masters of the 19th century and a precursor of the Fauves.

The house in which he lived for 45 years – converted just a few years before his death, with the removal of his own studio and the addition of two new floors – was bequeathed by him to the École des Beaux-Arts. His apartment contains many fine objects, including a piece by Bernard Palissy (c1509–1589), aside from his own work: the museum has nearly 1200 oils and watercolours (many unfinished) as well as more than 12,000 drawings – he was a magnificent draughtsman – of which about 5000 are on show. It is fascinating work, perhaps a little perplexing at first since so many of the subjects are borrowed from the classics and the Bible. The large paintings are remarkable, but do take time to look at the watercolours and drawings in the innumerable drawers of the various cabinets.

Nouvelle Athènes

Leaving the museum, cross Rue de La Rochefoucauld over to Rue de la Tour-des-Dames, created in the 1820s over an ancient track, and the centre of the Nouvelle Athènes. The houses are typical of the 1820s, the more interesting ones being no 1, by Lodovico Visconti (1791–1853), no 3, no 5 and no 9, built for François Talma (1763–1826), Napoleon's favourite actor. The power station on the other side at nos 16–20 is an interesting example of early industrial design and architecture.

Turn left into Rue Blanche, which runs over the site of an old track that led to the quarries of Montmartre; the street's name probably refers to the white plaster dust from the carts. Reach Place d'Estienne-d'Orves, named for the Resistance hero Honoré d'Estienne d'Orves (1901–1941), killed by the Nazis; the *place* was created in 1860 (as Place de la Trinité) on the site of a then-celebrated café, the Grande Pinte, where important meetings took place preparing the revolution of the Trois Glorieuses in July 1830, which ended Bourbon rule.

The large church now facing you is Église de la Trinité, built by the official architect Théodore Ballu (1817–1885), a great unashamed mixer of style, a clever restorer (e.g, Tour St-Jacques – see p74) and the rebuilder of the Hôtel de Ville (see p74). The Trinité has recently been restored to its original splendour. Olivier Messiaen (1908–1992) was organist here for over 40 years until his death. The church, a light building with a large nave (ribbed vault) and small side-chapels, is as representative of the decoration and architecture of the Second Empire as is Garnier's Opéra (see p116). The rich ornamentation is by various artists of the time; a full description is supplied at the entrance.

On leaving the church, go around Place d'Estienne-d'Orves and then right into Rue de Clichy, another street opened on the site of a very old track, in this instance the one that led to the villages of Clichy and St-Ouen to the north. On the left are Rues de Londres and d'Athènes, both part of a large, mostly 1820s sector known as the Quartier de l'Europe. Carry on up the street until you reach the Casino de Paris, where Josephine Baker (1906–1975) made her name. The building dates from 1890; the great façade (recently restored), with mosaics and stained-glass windows was restored recently and is more Art Deco than Art Nouveau. Victor Hugo (1802–1885) lived for a while at no 21.

Pigalle

Turn right into Rue Moncey (at no 46 Rue de Clichy), opened and developed from 1843, and cross Rue Blanche into Rue de La Bruyère, opened from 1827; Hector Berlioz (1803–1869) and the poet and essayist Antonin Artaud (1896–1948) lived in this street. Turn left into Rue Pigalle, named after the sculptor, who lived here in 1757–70. The ancient track on which this street was laid led from one of the city gates of Paris to the Abbaye des Dames-de-Montmartre. The street is now full of cabarets and part of the red-light district, but in the 19th century it was, like other streets in the area, home to numerous artists and writers: Édouard Vuillard (1868–1940) and Pierre Bonnard (1867–1947) lived at no 28, George Sand (1804–1876) and Frédéric Chopin (1810–1849) at no 16, Victor Hugo (1802–1885) at no 55 and Charles Baudelaire (1821–1867) at no 60, while Vincent Van Gogh (1853–1890) lived in the Cité Pigalle until a few days before his suicide.

Walk up Rue Pigalle, passing the Cité Pigalle on your left at no 45, cross Rue Notre-Dame-de-Lorette and Rue Victor-Massé, where Bonnard had his studio (at no 12), and carry on until you reach Place Pigalle. Just here on your right, at an angle with Rue Pigalle, is the private Avenue Frochot: developed in 1830, it still contains many picturesque houses; Henri Toulouse-Lautrec (1864–1901) had his last studio at no 15. At no 9 Place Pigalle was the Nouvelle Athènes, the favourite café of the Impressionists. Place Pigalle was installed in 1827 on the site of the Barrière Montmartre of the Fermiers Généraux wall; the central pond (1862) occupies the site of the old gates.

You are now in coach-tripper land, but the boulevards still have an elusive decaying charm. Turn left into Boulevard de Clichy. Montmartre and the Sacré-Coeur are, as you can see, very close. Around the turn of the century many artists lived or had their studios on the boulevard's left-hand side, including Edgar Degas (1834–1917), Pablo Picasso (1881–1973), Van Gogh, Toulouse-Lautrec, Georges Seurat (1859–1891), Bonnard and Kees Van Dongen (1877–1968). This was the Paris so often painted by Toulouse-Lautrec, but the famous cabarets have all gone. On the right are various amusement stalls, cafés, restaurants and sex shops. At no 14 is the Café Wepler, now much changed but a landmark of Bohemian life well into the 1920s. Reach Place Blanche, home of the celebrated Moulin Rouge, now a cinema and cabaret, with nothing left of the original except the wings. Continue along the boulevard until you reach Avenue Rachel, on the right, leading to the Cimetière du Nord, more usually called Cimetière de Montmartre.

Cimetière du Nord, dit de Montmartre

Though less grand than Cimetière du Père-Lachaise (see p164), less architecturally curious and not as romantic, Cimetière de Montmartre is of much interest. Among those buried here are (in order of the walk suggested below) Émile Zola (1840–1902), Mme de Récamier (1777–1849), Stendhal (1783–1842), Jacques Offenbach (1819–1880), Léo Delibes (1836–1891), Henri Murger (1822–1861) – author of the novel *Scènes de la Vie de Bohème* (1845), which inspired Puccini's opera – Théophile Gautier (1811–1872), Jean Honoré Fragonard (1732–1806) and Berlioz.

Reach the main gates and continue until you reach the roundabout (Zola is on the west side). Go left along Avenue de la Croix (Mme de Récamier and Stendhal), cross Avenue Montmorency, continue into Avenue Travot, cross Avenue du Tunnel, carry on in the semicircular Avenue Samson and then go left along Avenue des Anglais (Offenbach and Delibes). Turn right at the end along Avenue des Carrières. Cross Avenue du Tunnel again into Avenue Cordier (Murger, Gautier, Fragonard), which you follow down to Avenue Berlioz (Berlioz at corner). Turn left along Avenue Berlioz and then right into Avenue Dubuisson which will lead you back towards the roundabout and the exit.

Back in Avenue Rachel, go down to the boulevard and turn right to get to the busy Place de Clichy, another *place* erected on an ancient Fermiers Généraux *barrière*.

You can connect this walk with the next one by either taking the métro to Château-Rouge or catching a bus (30 or 54) to Barbès and walking (five minutes) up Boulevard Barbès to Place du Château-Rouge.

Montmartre

'*Paris est une ville d'escaliers qui provoquent l'imagination*' ('Paris is a city of steps that spark the imagination'), wrote Julien Green in his book *Paris* (1983). Montmartre certainly is full of steps. Today, in spite of the tourists, there is still something quite magical about the *butte*. This walk takes you through circuitous alleyways, up steps and cobbled streets, and past ignored areas of the village as well as famous sights, such as the Sacré-Coeur and Place du Tertre.

Start: **Métro Château-Rouge; buses 31 and 56.**
Finish: **Métro Anvers; buses 30 and 54.**
Length: **5km (3 miles).**
Time: **3hr.**
Refreshments: **Countless cafés and restaurants.**
Which day: **Any day, although weekends can be too busy.**
To visit:
• **Musée de Montmartre: daily (not Monday) 11.00–18.00.**

Château Rouge
Exit the métro onto Place du Château-Rouge; behind you is the area known as the Goutte d'Or, which in spite of intense reconstruction, has kept some of its popular charm. It is home to diverse communities, mostly African and Maghreban.

Facing you, on the other side, is Montmartre. Cross Boulevard Barbès and go left along Rue Poulet. At the top, turn right into Rue de Clignancourt, a long street leading to the outskirts of the city and named after the Seigneurie de Clignancourt, less than 1 km (½ mile) away. The original Château Rouge – built mostly of red bricks, and later, in the 1840s–60s, an extremely popular dancehall – was at nos 42–54. Pass Rue Muller on your left, go left along Rue Ramey, and then turn left again into Rue du Chevalier-de-La-Barre. This very narrow 17th-century street is picturesque and charming, with steps, trees and an unusual view over the Sacré-Coeur.

Rue du Chevalier de-La-Barre carries straight on, now a normal-sized street; notice the narrow steps of Passage Cottin going downhill to your right. Cross Rue Lamarck and continue up the steps facing you, still Rue du Chevalier-de-La-Barre. At the top is Rue de la Bonne, which owes its name to the old fountain of the Bonne Eau.

Enter the new and attractive Parc de la Turlure, on your right. There are great views over northern Paris and its suburbs, and of course over the back of the Basilica. Leave this little park by the other side to return to Rue de la Bonne. Go left into Rue St-Vincent, an old street of the village, and the first street you come to is Rue du Mont-Cenis, another ancient path. The indifferent house on the corner sports a plaque indicating that Hector Berlioz (1803–1869) composed *Harold en Italie* (1834) and *Benvenuto Cellini* (1838) here; in fact, the lovely hermitage where he lived in 1834–7 with his young wife,

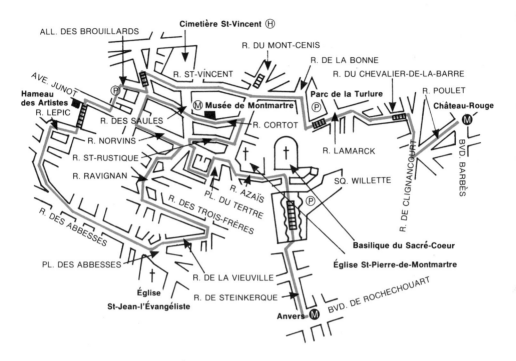

Harriet Smithson (1800–1854), was demolished in 1925 to make way for the existing building. There are also two restaurants at the bottom of Rue du Mont-Cenis and on the corner with Rue Lamarck: Le Relais and Beauvilliers.

Foggy street

Continue along Rue St-Vincent, a street rendered famous by the *chansonnier* Aristide Bruant (1851–1925) at the beginning of this century. On your left is first a small, rather wild-looking public garden, and then the last vineyard of Montmartre. When the abbey was still here (it was demolished during the Revolution, see p15), the *butte* was liberally covered with vines (the wine had a reputation for headiness). This one, much more recent, was planted in the 1930s to commemorate those that had disappeared.

Cross Rue des Saules. On your right are the famous Cabaret Lapin Agile, very much part of Montmartre's bohemian history, and the small Cimetière St-Vincent, where Arthur Honegger (1892–1956), Eugène Boudin (1824–1898) and Maurice Utrillo (1883–1985) are buried. The street goes downhill, turns sharply right, and leads into the small Square Dorgelès. Directly on your left, at the turn, are the steep steps of Rue Girardon, another ancient track of the *butte*. At the top of the steps, turn immediately right into the narrow Allée des Brouillards. On the left is the Château des Brouillards, a *folie* built at the end of the 18th century and recently renovated; the poet Gérard de Nerval (1808–1855) lived there a while. On the other side are charming mid-18th-century *cottages* established on the site of the outbuildings of the *château;* they are unique among the *cottages* of Paris in having front gardens.

Dada in Paris

The *allée* opens out onto Rue Simon-Dereure. Go into the public garden on the left, created in the 1930s, and walk through it until you find yourself on Avenue Junot, opened in 1909 and containing many fine contemporary houses; it is the northern way to the top of the hill. Turn right. At no 13 lived Francisque Poulbot (1879–1946), who became so famous for his paintings of urchins – every local souvenir shop sells reproductions of his rather gooey work – that for a long time the Paris street kids were called *poulbots*.

In the house at no 15 (not visitable) lived the Dada poet Tristan Tzara (1896–1963); this is also the only house built in France by the Viennese architect Adolf Loos (1870–1933), one of the pioneers of Modernism. It was created in the heyday of Art Deco and reflects Loos's preoccupations: there is no decoration on what is a rather arid façade, yet we have an intuitive feeling for what must be inside. The flatness is ameliorated by the triangular inset window – the converse of a bow window – and by the large rectangular opening on the two upper levels.

Further down the avenue, at no 25, is the rather delightful Villa Léandre, a series of small houses built in the 1920s.

Now retrace your steps to Poulbot's house at no 13, and go through the gate just to the left of the house into one of Montmartre's charming private *allées*. Climb the steps and carry on along the path – you have a good view of the back of Tzara's house – and then down some steps to Rue Lepic. (If this way is closed, there is another *passage* by Tzara's house leading to Rue Lepic.)

'Rue de l'Empereur'

Rue Lepic, one of the longer streets of Montmartre, was created at the instigation of Napoleon – hence its original name, 'de l'Empereur'. The story goes that he wanted to inspect the telegraph installed by Claude Chappe (1763–1805), inventor of the optical telegraph, on a tower built on Église St-Pierre. (Optical messages were relayed *via* 16 such constructions all the way to Lille.) At the time there was only one way up, Rue Ravignan (see below), but this was so bad and so steep that the Emperor had to dismount and walk. His disgruntlement was such that a new road was quickly started.

At no 77 is the Moulin de la Galette, a mill built on the site of an older medieval mill in 1621. Heavily restored but still the same shape, a dancehall from the 1820s until quite recently, it is one of the last two *moulins* – there used to be 30 – on the *butte*. The Impressionists made it famous not only by painting it but also by drinking there often. Walk down Rue Lepic, a busy shopping street with pleasant houses. Vincent Van Gogh (1853–1890) and his brother Théo (d1891) lived for two years on the 3rd floor of no 54. At no 42, just before you reach Rue des Abbesses, is La Pomponnette, an excellent old-fashioned restaurant.

Rue Lepic carries on steeply downhill to the busier part of Boulevard de Clichy, with food stores, butchers, grocers, etc.; instead, turn left into Rue des Abbesses. Rue Tholozé, first on your left, has a good perspective on the Moulin de la Galette. Also on Rue Tholozé, Studio 28, a few steps up on the right, was Paris's first 'repertory' cinema: here the seminal *L'Age d'Or* (1930) by Luis Buñuel (1900–1983) and Salvador Dali (1904–1989) received its première in 1930.

Continue along Rue des Abbesses to Place des Abbesses.

The Sanctum Martyrium

Place des Abbesses, with its pleasant cafés, is a great place to sit and watch the world go by. Just on the other side of the *place*, by Rue Yvonne-Le-Tac, used to be the entrance to the Abbaye des Dames-de-Montmartre (see p126). The Abbesses métro station is by Hector Guimard (1867–1942), with a roof and a Wallace fountain.

The red-brick church on the south side, Église St-Jean-l'Évangéliste, the first public building in France in which concrete was used as a construction material, was built in 1897–1904 by Anatole de Baudot (1834–1915), a pupil of Eugène Viollet-Le-Duc (1814–1879) and an exponent of the new architecture. Although the church was built when Art Nouveau was at its zenith, it is not truly speaking Art-Nouveau. The ceramic decoration both outside and inside was the work of Alexandre Bigot (1862–1927), also responsible for the Ceramic Hôtel (see p125). The interior is surprisingly light, airy and restful.

No 9 Rue Yvonne-Le-Tac was until very recently the Couvent des Auxiliaires-de-la-Rédemption, built on the site of the Sanctum Martyrium, a cemetery for persecuted Christians. It was on this site that St Denis is said to have been beheaded by the Romans (see p15); a chapel built in the 9th century quickly became a place of pilgrimage. In 1534 Ignatius de Loyola (1491–1556), St François Xavier (1506–1552) and five other friends met in the crypt of the chapel – it had been rebuilt in the 12th century and was by now part of the Abbaye des Dames-de-Montmartre – and decided to found a new order. This became the Society of Jesus, better known as the Jesuits.

The Bateau Lavoir

Cross the triangular *place*, go along Rue de La Vieuville (1840) and turn left into Rue des Trois-Frères. The second street on your right is Rue Ravignan (noted above), probably Montmartre's most ancient street; it was so busy with the ferrying of plaster that it was cobbled as early as the first half of the 17th century.

Rue Ravignan merges with Place Émile-Goudeau, a very shady little *place* with several cafés. At at no 13 is the famous Bateau Lavoir, the artists' colony where Max Jacob (1876–1944), André Salmon (1881–1969), Pablo Picasso (1881–1973), Juan Gris (1887–1927), Kees Van Dongen (1877–1968), Georges Braque (1882–1963), Guillaume Apollinaire (1880–1918) and others lived before WWI. It was in this house, in about 1906–7, that Picasso painted what is reckoned the first Cubist painting, the *Demoiselles d'Avignon*, now at the Museum of Modern Art in New York. The house, burnt down in 1970 but restored in 1978, was named by Max Jacob, probably because its unusual shape reminded him of the washing-boats of the Seine.

Facing you are the cobbled steps of Rue de la Mire, which leads into Place Jean-Baptiste-Clément, created at the turn of this century over the Bel-Air vineyard; Jean-Baptiste Clément (1836–1903) was a *chansonnier* and mayor of Montmartre during the Commune. The *place* is the top of Rue Lepic, and from it you can clearly see the other extant windmill, the Moulin Radet. Also on the left is an old water tower (1837). Staying on the left, take a left a little further on into the 11th-century Rue Norvins, the *butte*'s 'ridge' road and the high street of the original village.

The oldest house in Montmartre

At no 22 Rue Norvins, a fine 18th-century house known as the Folie Sandrin, the celebrated Dr Esprit Blanche (1796–1852) had his mental clinic from 1820 to 1847, when he moved it to Passy (see p160); one of his patients was the poet Gérard de Nerval, who had taken to going for walks with a live lobster on a lead.

Reach the new Place Marcel-Aymé, where there is a sculpture by the actor Jean Marais (1913–1998) of the *Passe Muraille*, after a story by Marcel Aymé (1902–1967), and turn right into Rue Girardon. Go down a few steps into Rue de l'Abreuvoir, along which cattle used to be driven to the public trough *(abreuvoir)* nearby. At no 2 is the Petite Maison Rose, painted by Maurice Utrillo (1883–1985); now done up, it is an average restaurant.

Cross Rue des Saules – again a good view of the vineyard – into Rue Cortot. Erik Satie (1866–1925) lived at no 6 for some years. No 12 is Montmartre's oldest house, built in the early 17th century and lived in by the actor Roze de Rosimond. From 1875 it was an artists' colony, and it is now the Musée de Montmartre, dedicated to the history of Montmartre; there are frequent exhibitions relating to people who have lived on the *butte*. The gardens are pretty and the house is almost intact.

Turn right into Rue du Mont-Cenis – the water-tower at the corner was built in 1927 – and immediately right again into Rue St-Rustique, one of Montmartre's best preserved streets. At the other end, on the corner with Rue des Saules, is what used to be the Billard en Bois, another pet place of the Impressionists. Van Gogh used the garden in his painting *La Ginguette* (plaque).

You are now, alas, deep in tourist-land, complete with souvenir shops and pseudy restaurants. Turn left and left again into Rue Norvins, then right into the narrow Rue Poulbot and along to the charming Place du Calvaire, where there is a superb perspective over Paris. Cross the *place*, turn left and reach Place du Tertre, the trendiest spot in Montmartre, now invaded by the *artistes Montmartrois* and by expensive cafés and restaurants.

Paris's first church

Cross diagonally over to Église St-Pierre-de-Montmartre, at the top of Rue du Mont-Cenis. This church, built at the same time as the abbey on the site of an older Roman temple and almost demolished in the last century, is one of Paris's two oldest churches (the other being St-Martin-des-Champs – see p41). Sadly, all that remains of the original 12th-century building is the choir, its ribbed vault, a bit of the transept and two of the apsidioles (subsidiary apses); the vault of the nave is 15th-century and the façade 18th-century. The bulk of the restoration was done at the turn of the century, after many years of neglect; it has been restored again recently. The Cimetière du Calvaire, to the left of the church, dates from Merovingian times (5th–8th centuries).

With the church behind you and Place du Tertre facing you, turn left along Rue Azaïs to the Basilique du Sacré-Coeur. What is perhaps most remarkable about this monument is that it can be seen from so many parts of Paris. On the steps of the church is an orientation table to help you make the best of the spectacular view from there over the city – even more spectacular is the view from the Galerie des Colonnes, in the church's dome. The basilica was begun in 1876 and eventually consecrated at the end of WWI. It is massive and rather ungainly, but certainly worth a visit.

Leave the Sacré-Coeur, walk down the steps and reach Place St-Pierre at the bottom of Square Willette. Those large warehouse-type buildings on the left house the Marché St-Pierre (fabrics only). Turn right at the bottom and first left into Rue de Steinkerque, which takes you down to the boulevard. Your metro station, Anvers, is there on the left.

République to La Villette

An unusual walk, from the 17th century to the 21st in a few hours. Really you are going through three *quartiers* of Paris, travelling through time and crossing borders. There are no museums *per se*, but the walk ends with the amazing Cité des Sciences et de l'Industrie at La Villette. The other landmark is Hôpital St-Louis, Paris's second oldest hospital and one of its finest early-17th-century edifices.

Start: **Métro République; buses 54, 56, 65, 75.**
Finish: **Métro Porte-de-Pantin** *or* **Porte-de-La-Villette; bus 75.**
Length: **6km (3³/₄ miles), but you may be able to go part of the way by boat (see text).**
Time: **2¹/₄hr.**
Refreshments: **Many cafés at the start of the walk on Place de la République and some pleasant cafeterias at the Cité des Sciences; no restaurants of note.**
Which day: **Tuesday-Sunday.**
To visit:
● **Cité des Sciences et de l'Industrie: daily (not Monday) 10.00–18.00, Sunday 10.00–19.00.**

The Canal
Leave the métro by the Place de la République exit. With the back of the Statue of the Republic to your back, walk towards the lively Rue du Faubourg-du-Temple, a very ancient track leading to Belleville. Pass Rue de Malte on your right and carry on until you reach the large Boulevard Jules-Ferry on your right and the Canal St-Martin on the left. Cross Quai de Valmy and turn left into Quai de Jemmapes. The canal, now halfcovered, links La Villette to the Seine. It was opened to traffic in 1825 and brought tremendous growth to the area; the Industrial Revolution transformed the sector completely, with many workshops and small industries being set up along its banks. Today half the canal is covered. With its locks, its fine arched footbridges and its treelined walkway, it gives the whole area a picturesque air.

Walk along the canal and take the second right into Avenue Richerand, leading to Hôpital St-Louis. (At weekends this entrance to the hospital is closed, so instead use the side entrance in Avenue Claude-Vellefaux – turn right on Place du Docteur-Alfred-Fournier and follow round along Rue Alibert into Avenue Claude-Vellefaux – and then, once inside the hospital, go to the modern block and turn left towards the older-looking part of the hospital.)

The *hôpital* was founded by Henri IV and built remarkably rapidly in 1607–11. During the nation-wide plague at the turn of the 17th century, Paris's sole hospital, the Hôtel Dieu in Île de la Cité, had been unable to cope – hence the need for a second. The original Hôtel Dieu was pulled down in the 19th century, but Hôpital St-Louis

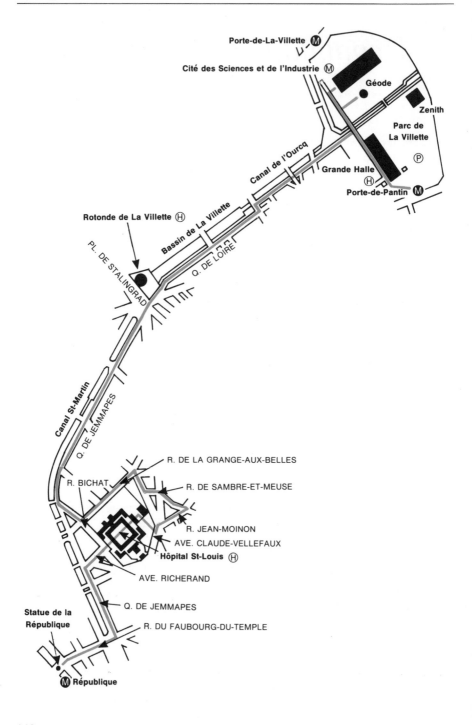

has remained intact, with the recent addition of a new block to house modern facilities. Go through the porch into a small courtyard and continue straight ahead *via* a narrow *passage* to the quadrangle. The building, completely restored, is extremely handsome, in the style of Place des Vosges, with stone and red brick and fine slate roofs. It is obvious why it is generally considered the finest ensemble of its age. Cross to the other side and you find the modern hospital facing you.

Turn right and leave the hospital by the exit into Avenue Claude-Vellefaux. Turn left, cross Rue St-Maur, and almost immediately to the right is Rue Jean-Moinon, down which you walk to Rue de Sambre-et-Meuse, which take to the left; both these streets evoke a 19th-century, working-class Paris. Cross Avenue Claude-Vellefaux and carry on to the right on Rue Juliette-Dodu, along the northeast side of the hospital.

At the end, turn left into the ancient Rue de la Grange-aux-Belles. Between this street and the canal stood the Monfaucon gibbet, which was in use from the 13th century to the 17th; as many as 50–60 prisoners were hanged simultaneously. The gibbet appears quite frequently in literature, both contemporary and in historical novels by such writers as Alexandre Dumas (1802–1870) and Théophile Gautier (1811–1872). The authorities stopped using it only when the newly created Hôpital St-Louis complained of the stench. The gallows were dismantled in 1760.

Walk down Rue de la Grange-aux-Belles until you reach the canal, and turn right. Just there at no 102 Quai de Jemmapes is the Hôtel du Nord, famous as the title and subject of *Hôtel du Nord* (1938) by Marcel Carné (1906–1996), a classic of French cinema and one of the most celebrated films of the inter-war period.

The Rotonde de La Villette
The canal now bends to the right and the sector changes from quietly residential to something more industrial. Pass Rue des Écluses-St-Martin, which marks the southern limit of the Gibet de Monfaucon, and continue until you reach Place de Stalingrad.

The 18th-century Rotonde is the finest example left of the tollgates Claude Nicolas Ledoux (1736–1806) did for the Fermiers Généraux wall. The best way to get there is to stay on the left, cross the canal and Rue La Fayette and then Boulevard de La Villette by the traffic light and the pedestrian crossing, going under the métro. Recently renovated, the Rotonde is now sometimes used for exhibitions. The space between the rotunda and the Bassin de La Villette, recently redesigned and landscaped, is a fine piece of contemporary design.

If you are doing this walk between 1 April and 30 October you can now take a boat along the canal to Parc de La Villette (check beforehand); departures are every half-hour. To reach the boatstop, cross the canal by means of the footbridge on the right. Otherwise, walk along the canal to the *parc* – about 20 minutes. The left-hand side is slightly the more interesting.

Parc de La Villette
This extraordinary place is vast (about 55 hectares [140 acres]) and packed with things to see and do. Until quite recently La Villette was a cattle-market and slaughterhouse, and in its heyday nearly 3000 people worked here. The structure of one of the markets, La Grande Halle, still stands, and is a fine example of 19th-century metal architecture; today it is used for concerts, theatrical productions, trade fairs and so on.

It would be impossible here to describe all the activities of the *parc*. You can get a free location map (in English) at the information centre, the pavilion on the right by the boatstop (next to the café), or you can buy a more comprehensive catalogue. Here, however, are some highlights:

- the Cité des Sciences et de l'Industrie, a huge complex with shops, library, temporary exhibition space and Explora, a permanent exhibition area with sections devoted to mathematics, acoustics, behavioural science, computer science, space photography, agriculture, automation, energy, aquaculture, a planetarium, oceanography, geophysics and much, much more;
- the Géode, an enormous ball housing a cinema with the biggest screen in the world (1000m^2 [9000 sq ft]) and 180° projection screen;
- the Parc, with lanes, follies, squares, restaurants, playgrounds and so on;
- the Cité de la Musique, designed by Christian de Portzampac (b1944), a great building which also houses the Conservatoire National de Musique.

Once you have seen all you want to see, you can leave the *parc* either on the left, on the other side of the Cité des Sciences, to reach Avenue Corentin-Cariou and the Porte-de-La-Villette métro station, or on the right, on the other side of the Grande Halle and Cité de la Musique, to reach Avenue Jean-Jaurès and the Porte-de-Pantin métro station.

Plate 17: Daniel Buren's modern sculpture in an elegant courtyard at the Palais-Royal (see the Odéon, Bourse, Palais-Royal walk, page 110).

Plate 18: The 19th-century Paris Opéra designed by Garnier (see the Assemblée Nationale, Concorde and Opéra walk, page 116).

Plate 19: Café life at the busy Trocadéro (see the Trocadéro, Tour Eiffel and Invalides walk, page 118).

Plate 20: The Eiffel Tower seen from the Palais de Chaillot (see the Trocadéro, Tour Eiffel and Invalides walk, page 120).

Plate 21: View from the Seine's Right Bank across Pont Alexandre-III to the Eiffel Tower (see the Trocadéro, Tour Eiffel and Invalides walk, page 120).

Plate 22: *The Naumachie in the Parc Monceau (see the Ternes and Parc Monceau walk, page 128).*

Plate 23: *Montmartre's lively Place du Tertre, with the Sacré-Coeur glimpsed beyond (see the Montmartre walk, page 140).*

Plate 24: *A hidden courtyard off Rue Norvins in Montmartre (see the Montmartre walk, page 139).*

Plate 25: The Géode at the vast Parc de La Villette (see the République to La Villette walk, page 144).

Plate 26: Le Lapin Agile, frequent haunt of Picasso and other artists (see the Montmartre walk, page 137).

Plate 27: The Rotonde de La Villette tollgate (see the République to La Villette walk, page 143).

Bastille and Faubourg St-Antoine

A fine circular walk in the Bastille and Faubourg St-Antoine *quartiers,* past modern architecture (the newly created Opéra de la Bastille), semi-industrial architecture (the many artisans' workshops) and domestic architecture (old houses). For a long time this was a rather seedy part of Paris, but its fortunes have completely changed with the advent and popularity of the Opéra. The Bastille is now one of the trendy spots of the capital and there are many fun places on the way, including the great Aligre market and Rue de Lappe, with its cafés and dancehalls.

Start and finish: **Métro Bastille; buses 20, 29, 69, 76, 86, 87, 91.**
Length: **5km (3 miles).**
Time: 2hr.
Refreshments: **In the first part of the walk there are many places offering excellent food at reasonable prices. The second half is not so well endowed, although the numerous cafés on Place de la Bastille are there to welcome you at the walk's end.**
Which day: **On Sundays the Aligre market is very active, but most of the workshops in Faubourg St-Antoine are closed, so that the *quartier* can seem a little dead.**

Place de la Bastille
Leave the métro by any of its numerous exits and look for the column in the middle of Place de la Bastille and then southeast for the Opéra de la Bastille, a large, modern, white building with a broad flight of steps.

This is not a formal place, like the Places des Vosges or Vendôme, which were planned and designed; rather, it evolved somewhat haphazardly over 60 years, from its origins in 1803 until the 1860s, when Georges Haussmann (1809–1891) opened Rue de Lyon and Boulevard Henri-IV, thereby giving the *place* the appearance it has today.

The column in the middle celebrates not the Revolution of 1789, as many believe, but the 1830 Revolution of the Trois Glorieuses (the last three days of July, 1830). The 504 dead of this short-lived uprising were placed in an ossuary underneath the column, as, later, were the dead of the 1848 revolution. The column was begun by Jean Antoine Alavoine (1776–1834) in 1831 and finished by Joseph Duc (1802–1879) 10 years later. It is bronze, 52m (171ft) high and 4m (13ft) wide, hollow and in three distinct parts, each symbolizing one of the three days. At the top is the recently regilded *Génie de la Liberté* (Spirit of Liberty). Scaling the column involves a steep climb up some 230 steps, but the view at the top is superb. It was, until fairly recently, possible to climb the column. Closed at present, it may re-open one day.

The Opéra de la Bastille, modern and yet not without Classical lines, was completed

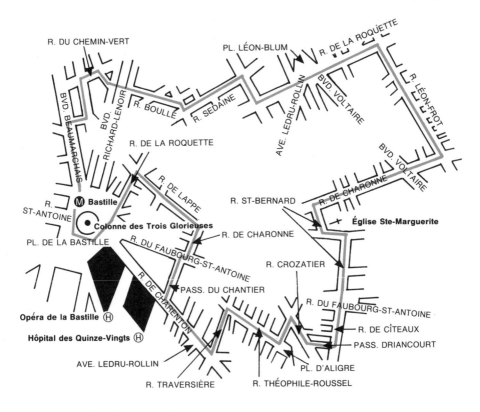

in 1989. It has taken over from the Palais Garnier (see p116), now dedicated almost exclusively to ballet. This is a fine place to enjoy opera, and the acoustics are excellent. The façade showing on Place de la Bastille does not reveal the true scale of the building, which goes back a long way, locked between Rues de Charenton and de Lyon. It is worth climbing the steps to have a look around the large foyer.

The Opéra was erected on the site of an old railway station, Gare de Vincennes (also called Gare de la Bastille). The track, which is an elevated viaduct built in the 19th century, still runs along Rue de Lyon and Avenue Daumesnil: it is now a lovely walk known as '*La coulée verte*'; underneath, craft shops occupy the arches.

A line of paving-stones in the *place* marks the site of the Bastille fortress, whose fall on 14 July 1789 is celebrated annually. Before being completely demolished during 1789–92, it had stood for more than 400 years as a symbol of royal despotism. It was erected in the 14th century to defend the Charles V wall, to the east, but its military role ended in the reign of Henri IV, and a few years later Cardinal Richelieu (1585–1642) converted it into a state prison.

The king alone had the prerogative of condemning people to the Bastille, which was effected using the notorious *lettres de cachet*. Among its many well known prisoners were Voltaire (1694–1778), the Sicilian alchemist and charlatan the Count di Cagliostro (1743–1795), the Man in the Iron Mask and the Marquis de Sade (1740–1814).

They were not badly treated, if they had the money: Cardinal Armand de Rohan (1674–1749), for instance, gave regular dinner parties from his incarceration! With your back to the Opéra, you can see the dome of Église St-Paul not far away. The ungainly skyscrapers in the distance to your left are those around Place d'Italie, in the 13th arrondissement.

Dancehalls and art galleries
Now leave the Opéra and go right, past the Restaurant La Grande Marche. Cross Rues de Charenton and Faubourg-St-Antoine to the 17th-century Rue de la Roquette, which has many old houses; it links the Bastille to Cimetière du Père-Lachaise (see pl64). This first section of the street is almost entirely devoted to commerce, cafés and restaurants. Paul Verlaine (1844–1896) lived with his mother for a while at no 17.

Reach the intersection and turn right into the narrow Rue de Lappe, again 17th century, and once the Parisian centre for *bals musettes* (dancehalls). One of these, the Balajo, has survived and is a must for all cognoscenti of Parisian nightlife. Celebrated by many writers, including Ernest Hemingway (1899–1961) and Leon-Paul Fargue (1876–1947), and named for the farmer who then owned the land, a certain Gérard de Lappe, the street can be expected soon to join the ranks of Parisian chic. Several bars and cafés of different styles line the street; most stay open until the early hours of the morning. Halfway down the street, in Passage Louis-Philippe, the Café de la Danse is also of interest.

Craft-land
Turn right into Rue de Charonne which, like most of the *quartier*, is 17th-century. Walk down to Rue du Faubourg-St-Antoine. This busy street has always been part of the city's life, one of the main ways eastward out of the centre and to the Abbaye St-Antoine-des-Champs, only 1km (½ mile) from the Bastille. Louis XI gave franchises to the artisans working under the patronage ot the abbey, and thus a large population of craftsmen and the like grew up in its vicinity. In the 17th century Jean Baptiste Colbert (1619–1683) renewed the edict, giving a further boost to the area, which quickly gained an even greater reputation for its craft tradition, which has continued to this day.

As you reach the Faubourg there is a fine fountain on the corner, the Fontaine Trogneux, one of four like it built in 1710 to provide fresh water for the local population. Cross to no 66, where you find the entrance to Passage du Chantier, which is, typically of many around here – such as the well known Passage de la Boule-Blanche – a home to crafts workshops; this is probably one of the pleasantest of them, and is still very active.

It leads to Rue de Charenton, also opened in the 17th century. At no 28, to your right, is a large hospital, Hôpital des Quinze-Vingts, established in the rather splendid Caserne des Mousquetaires Noirs (Barracks of the Black Musketeers) at the end of the 18th century after Louis XVI had put an end to that regiment.

Turn left out of the *passage* (or retrace your steps if you went to look at the hospital) and follow Rue de Charenton across the wide Avenue Ledru-Rollin; take the next left, Rue Traversière. Just there on the right, actually in Rue Emilio-Castelar, is a turn-of-the-century baker with original décor – and excellent bread. At the end of Rue Traversière, turn right into Rue Théophile-Roussel to reach Square Trousseau, established in 1905 on the site of the Hospice des Enfants Trouvés (hospice for abandoned children) established in the 17th century by Marie-Thérèse (1638–1683), Louis XIV's queen. All the buildings along the *square* were built by the Rothschild Foundation, and they are characteristic of the genre of social building ('for the improvement of workers' conditions') that philanthropic societies were building in the second half of the 19th century. Just before you reach the *square* you pass Square Trousseau, an old-fashioned restaurant which has great décor and serves good food at reasonable prices.

Le marché d'Aligre

Rue Théophile-Roussel leads to Place d'Aligre, one of the great Parisian markets, offering bric-à-brac, brocante, clothes, etc.; it is particularly good on Sunday mornings. The covered market was built in the 1840s. Étienne d'Aligre (1550–1635) was a chancellor whose wife was one of the principal benefactresses of the abandoned children's hospice.

Leave the *place* by Rue d'Aligre, on the left, which is also bordered with fruit and vegetable stalls and has a couple of good cafés. At the top, cross Rue Crozatier, turn right and then take second left into the narrow, busy Passage Driancourt, leading to Rue de Cïteaux. The ultramodern building at no 30, almost facing you as you exit the *passage*, houses the kitchens of Hôpital St-Antoine; built in 1985 by Henri Ciriani (b1936), it is a quite extraordinarily exciting bit of architecture.

A royal burial ground

Go left in Rue de Cïteaux and reach Rue du Faubourg-St-Antoine. Take a few steps to the right, into the triangular Place du Docteur-Antoine-Béclère, where you find the Fontaine de Montreuil, built at the same time as the Fontaine Trogneux. Behind the fountain is the entrance (at no 184) to Hôpital St-Antoine, established on the site of the celebrated Cistercian Abbaye de St-Antoine-des-Champs. Founded in the 12th century, the abbey was rebuilt many times; some of the 18th-century buildings by Alexandre Lenoir (1801–1891) still survive.

Retrace your steps to Rue de Cïteaux/Rue St-Bernard. Rue St-Bernard has many specialized furniture and cabinetmakers' shops and a few old-fashioned cafés. At the corner with Rue du Dahomey (first on the right) is an interesting-looking shop with an original 1900 façade (*Peintures décoratives* [decorative paints]).

Continue along Rue St-Bernard until you reach Église Ste-Marguerite, which you approach from the side. (If you want to skip the church, take the *passage* on the right, Impasse Charrière, to reach Rue de Charonne.) Although this 18th-century church does not look very inspiring, it has some interest – the harmonious decoration is almost entirely 18th-century – and certainly so has its cemetery (visitable by appointment), which contains what may be the tomb of Louis XVII (1785–1795), the unfortunate son of Louis XVI and Marie Antoinette (1755–1793). He died at the Temple Prison (see p42), but historians are not sure he was buried there – one theory suggests there was substitution at the prison. The tombstone is easy enough to find, being almost against the Chapelle des Âmes-du-Purgatoire.

Cyrano de Bergerac

Reach Rue de Charonne and turn right. On the other side of Rue Faidherbe is the Salvation Army Hostel for women, built in 1925, and a typical Le-Corbusier-influenced building of those days in steel and stone. At no 98, just after the hostel, is the site of the Couvent des Filles-de-La-Croix, demolished at the turn of the century; the poet, soldier and larger-than-life adventurer Cyrano de Bergerac (1619–1655) is said to have died in this convent.

Continue along Rue de Charonne. This is a very lively section of this long and busy street, with many bars and shops. Cross the enormous Boulevard Voltaire (opened by Haussmann), linking Place de la République (left) with Place de la Nation (right). Carry on to reach Rue Léon-Frot. A couple of houses further along, on the left at no 157–161, stood the *hôtel* which housed Dr Jacques Belhomme's celebrated clinic. Here wealthy patients sought refuge during the Terror, pleading illness and thereby escaping the guillotine – at least for a time: the daily rate was exorbitant and the good doctor had no compunction about throwing his patients out onto the street – and hence to the scaffold – once their money had run out.

Turn left into Rue Léon-Frot and almost immediately on your right, at no 42, is Jacques Melac's Bistrot à Vins – excellent wines, food (simple), décor and atmosphere. Carry on until you reach Passage Courtois, on the right. At the top of the *passage* is an old gate overlooking some disused land which was once the entrance to a royal hunting-lodge. Continue on Rue Léon-Frot to reach Rue de la Roquette.

Maigret and a market

You turn left here to follow the rest of this walk, which will take you slowly back to your starting point at Place de la Bastille. Alternatively, you might opt to turn right and head for the start of the Père Lachaise to Buttes Chaumont walk (p164). If you do so, on the way you will see the five paving stones where the guillotine was installed in the 19th century (on the corner with Rue de la Croix-Faubin) and, opposite, the site of the Roquette Prison, demolished not so long ago to make way for a modern housing estate.

To continue with the present walk, go left along Rue de la Roquette, crossing to Boulevard Voltaire and Place Léon-Blum, with the town hall of the 11th arrondissement on the right. Take the first right into the 17th-century Rue Popincourt, which led to the Abbaye St-Antoine-des-Champs; it is now mostly devoted to the rag trade. Take first left into the busy Rue Sedaine and walk along to reach Rue Froment, on the right. Cross to Rue Boulle, at an angle to the right, which takes you to Boulevard Richard-Lenoir, the home of Inspector Maigret, created by Georges Simenon (1903–1989). A good market is held in the mornings on the boulevard's central island, actually a cover over the Canal St-Martin (see p141).

There is a fine view over the Bastille column as you cross the boulevard to Rue St-Sabin. Turn immediately left into Rue du Chemin-Vert and left again into Rue Amelot, a long street sited in the ditch that ran along the Louis XIII wall. To reach Place de la Bastille, where the walk ends, turn right into Rue du Pasteur-Wagner and then left into Boulevard Beaumarchais. Most of the buildings on the boulevard date from the first part of the 19th century.

You can connect this walk with the République and Temple walk (p 39) by taking a no 20 or 29 bus from Boulevard Beaumarchais (travelling away from the Bastille) to Place de la République (otherwise a 20–minute walk), or with the Îles St Louis and de la Cité walk (p19) by taking a no 86 or 87 bus down Boulevard Henri-IV – second on the right from Boulevard Beaumarchais going anticlockwise – to Île St-Louis (otherwise a 10-minute walk).

Montparnasse, Montsouris and Butte aux Cailles

Paris has always been a city of pleasure, and Montparnasse is testimony to this. Today, La Grande Chaumière and La Closerie des Lilas may have given way to more sedate places of entertainment, but brasseries, cinemas, clubs, cafés of all sorts and restaurants are still very much in evidence. This is a walk through 19th-century villages and past artists' studios, a walk full of literary and artistic reminiscences, from the *cours* of Louis XIV to the Fermiers Généraux wall and beyond to the Thiers fortifications. On the way are the Catacombs, the Villa Seurat and the delightful Square Montsouris, where Le Corbusier (1887–1965) built his first house in Paris. After a walk across Parc Montsouris you reach the Butte aux Cailles, a charming village of yesteryear.

Start: **Métro Montparnasse-Bienvenue, buses 82, 91, 92, 94, 95, 96.**
Finish: **Métro Place-d'Italie.**
Length: **7km (4¼ miles).**
Time: **3hr.**
Refreshments: **Plenty of places along this walk, especially the famous brasseries on Boulevard Montparnasse, the cheap but cheerful crêperies of Rue Delambre, the restaurants of Rue Raymond-Losserand, the winebars of Rue Boulard and Rue Daguerre, and finally the fun cafés of Rue de la Butte aux Cailles.**
Which day: **Not Monday.**
To visit:
● **Les Catacombes: Saturday and Sunday 09.00–11.00 and 14.00–16.00, other days (not Monday) 14.00–16.00.**
● **Fondation Cartier pour l'art contemporain: daily (not Monday) 12.00–20.00, Thursday 12.00–22.00.**

The new Bohemia
Exit the station onto Boulevard du Montparnasse, part of the Boulevards du Midi, the southern section of the circular *cours* that Louis XIV wanted to build around the city. Long ago, at nearby Carrefour Vavin (see below) there was a small manmade hill – really a glorified rubbish tip – which the students of the Latin Quarter derisively nicknamed Parnassus; the nickname stuck, and the area became called Montparnasse.

Walk east along the boulevard, past various cinemas and Église Notre-Dame-des-Champs (1896) to La Coupole, at no 102, one of the great Parisian brasseries, famous for its *thés dansants* and a high spot of the capital (especially in the evenings). Opened in 1927 with superb décor – over 30 artists contributed – it was instantly successful. On the other side, around Carrefour Vavin, are Le Sélect, Le Dôme and La Rotonde. Pablo Picasso (1881–1973) was the one who signalled the exodus from Montmartre to Montparnasse. La Rotonde became the place of predilection of the New Bohemia – Vladimir Ilyich

Lenin (1870–1924) and Leon Trotsky (1879–1940) were often seen there (not together!) – until La Coupole took over in the late 1920s.

Carrefour Vavin is the important crossroads of Boulevards Raspail and Montparnasse and an array of smaller streets. On the northern edge of the *carrefour* is the famous statue of Honoré de Balzac (1799–1850) by Auguste Rodin (1840–1917).

The tradition of the large brasserie was not entirely novel to the New Bohemia: one previous establishment, La Grande Chaumière, also on the *carrefour*, reigned supreme in the life of gay Parisians from 1783 to 1853, when the Closerie des Lilas took over: it was really an enormous dancehall with gardens, big dipper, swings and other amusements, bars and restaurants. Here the Cancan was invented in the 1840s, and here also came the intelligentsia and artists: Armand Barbès (1809–1870), Louis Thiers (1797–1877), Horace Vernet (1789–1863), etc. Just on the other side is Rue de la Grande-Chaumière, a small street well known for the art academy of that name.

Hemingway and Fitzgerald
Take a sharp right at the *carrefour* into Rue Delambre, opened in 1839 through a field of cornflowers and poppies, and now known for its cafés and cheerful crêperies. *Crêpes* are a speciality of Britanny: traditionally Montparnasse was a refuge for Bretons, who would arrive at the railway station and settle nearby. It was in this street, at the now defunct Dingo Bar, that Ernest Hemingway (1899–1961) and F. Scott Fitzgerald (1896–1940) met, talked about *The Great Gatsby* (1925) and baseball and got drunk. At no 9 are Art Deco artists' studios, and at no 31 is the Hôtel Delambre, where André Breton (1896–1966) lived in 1921. Note the rare 'modern Della Robbia' ceramic medallions on the second floor.

At the end of the street, cross Boulevard Edgar-Quinet (good market in the morning and good cafés on junction) to the 19th-century Rue de la Gaîté. Like the boulevard nearby, the street used to be one huge funhouse (hence the name), with restaurants, *ginguettes* and dancehalls galore. It has changed, particularly over the past 20 years, and in so doing has lost much of its charm. Many of the theatres have closed, but Montparnasse Théâtre (1886) at no 31, the favourite of Jean Anouilh (1910–1987), survives as a reminder of a more glorious past.

Rue de la Gaîté joins up with Avenue du Maine, created by the Duc de Maine (1670–1736), the illegitimate son of Louis XIV and Mme de Montespan (1641–1707), at the same time as the Boulevards du Midi: he needed a quicker way from his Parisian home (today's Musée Rodin in Rue de Varenne) to his rural retreat in the village of Sceaux (now a smart southern suburb of Paris). On the southern side of the avenue is an enormous new development, Maine Montparnasse. Turn left, pass the brasserie Les Mousquetaires at no 79 – it has been done up, but you can still have a game of French billiards in the back room – and left again into Rue Froidevaux. The wall on the left is that of Cimetière de Montparnasse, created 1824, the third largest cemetery in Paris, containing the graves of Charles Baudelaire (1821–1867), Robert Desnos (1900–1945), Chaïm Soutine (1893–1943), Simone de Beauvoir (1908–1986), Jean-Paul Sartre (1905–1980), Guy de Maupassant (1850–1893), the great chess master Alexandre Alekhine (1892–1946) – with a chessboard decorating his tombstone – César Franck (1822–1890), Camille Saint-Saëns (1835–1921), Constantin Brancusi (1876–1957) and many other distinguished individuals. There are important monuments by sculptors such as David d'Angers (1789–1856), Rodin and Brancusi – whose celebrated Cubist *Baiser* is on the far side from the Rue Froidevaux entrance.

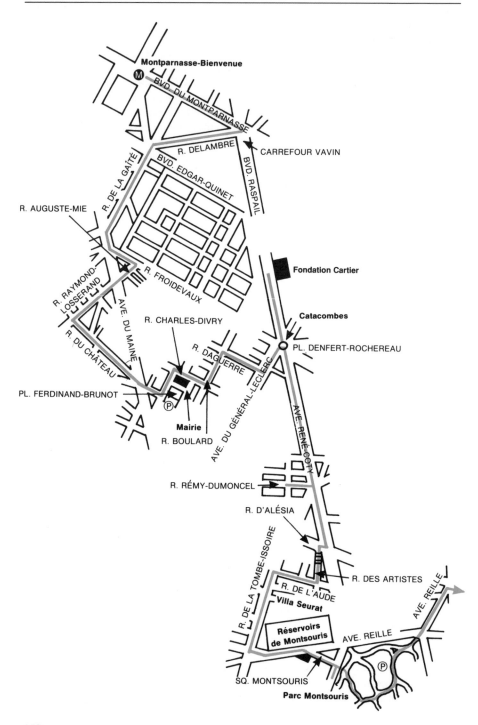

Take the short Rue Auguste-Mie on the right and cross Avenue du Maine to Rue Raymond-Losserand, an old medieval track and the limit of the 19th-century Petit Montrouge. Reach Rue du Château and turn left. Here the Château du Maine, really a large hunting-lodge, was built by the Duc de Maine. It was pulled down in the 1850s and the sector, known as Plaisance, was developed. It is a lively part of Paris with a rich *quartier* life. Halfway down Rue du Château is a bakery with an original painted-glass décor.

The street leads to Avenue du Maine; cross the avenue by the pedestrian crossing and go right. Now look back to the side of Avenue du Maine you have just left: at nos 29–31 is a late-Art-Nouveau block (1913), almost a pastiche with its balconies, canopies, foliage, gold mosaic, etc. Turn left into Place Ferdinand-Brunot and left again towards the *mairie* (town hall). Walk around the right-hand side of the *mairie,* turn right into Rue Charles-Divry and left again into Rue Boulard, where you will find, at no 21, the Vin des Rues, an excellent winebar. All these streets, part of the old village of Montrouge, were created in the 1840s. Turn right into Rue Daguerre, now a pedestrian precinct with a morning market, foodstores and cafés, including the good La Chope Daguerre, still the best, and another winebar, the Rallye. Cross Avenue du Général-Leclerc at the traffic lights and go left to Place Denfert-Rochereau.

The Catacombs
Place Denfert-Rochereau was established over what was the Barrière d'Enfer (Hell's tollgate) of the 18th-century Fermiers Généraux wall. Like most of the monuments along the wall, the two stone pavilions were built by Claude Nicolas Ledoux (1736–1806). The *barrière* served as the setting for the second act of *La Bohème* by Giacomo Puccini (1858–1924).

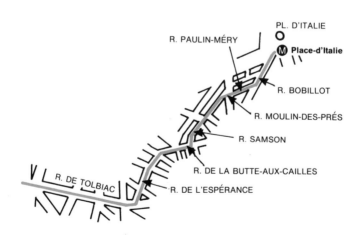

Before going to the Catacombs, modern art afficionados may want to visit the newly built (1994) Fondation Cartier pour l'art contemporain, designed by architect Jean Nouvel. It is quite a stupendous building, with an inner garden. The *fondation* houses various modern art exhibitions and an interesting, ever-growing permanent collection. From your point of arrival on the *place*, walk clockwise past Rue Froidevaux and then take a left into Boulevard Raspail. The *fondation* is three minutes walk away at no 261. After your visit return to the pavilions on the Place Denfert-Rochereau.

The entrance to the Catacombs is *via* the west pavilion. (If you want to skip the Catacombs, walk towards the railway station – the old Gare du Chemin-de-Fer-de-Sceaux, established 1846, in the very early days of train locomotion – and turn right into Avenue René-Coty, a continuation of Boulevard Raspail; at no 10 in the avenue is the Maison de Retraite de La Rochefoucauld, an old people's home founded in 1781. Then walk along the leafy central island until you reach the first busy intersection - Rues Remy-Dumoncel and de la Tombe-Issoire.)

The Catacombs were established at the end of the 18th century in the Montrouge quarries. Vast tracts of land around here were occupied by underground stone quarries, and a large portion of medieval Paris was built from stone extracted from the Plaine Montsouris. As the city expanded, little supervision was exercised over the quarries, with the result that in the 18th and 19th centuries it was not rare for entire buildings, sometimes entire streets, suddenly to vanish underground. Exploitation of underground quarries was completely forbidden from 1823 (1860 for the communes attached in that year to the capital). Paris has often been compared to a piece of Gruyère cheese: today there are some 325 hectares (800 acres) of underground quarries and 300km (185 miles) of galleries.

The installation of the Catacombs was completed in 1811. After walking down some 90 steps you find yourself in a narrow gallery, nearly 20m (65ft) underground. The entrance to the ossuary itself, 1km (½ mile) further along the narrow winding passage (mind your head!), is impressive, with its inscription: '*Arrête c'est ici l'empire de la Mort*' ('Stop: This is the Empire of Death').

The first cemetery whose contents were transferred here was the Cimetière des Innocents (see p80), whose stench had become too much for the local residents. Many others followed, until, all told, the bones of over 6 million people were placed here, piled sometimes to a depth of 30m (100ft). The charming decorative bone arrangements – circles of skulls, rows of tibias and femurs, the occasional cross and other clever inventions – were the idea of Louis, Vicomte Héricart de Thury (1776–1854), an Inspector General of the Quarry in 1810, who obviously had a Gothic sense of humour.

Another bohemia

The exit from the Catacombs brings you out on Rue Rémy-Dumoncel. Turn left and walk down to Avenue René-Coty, opened in the late 19th century. Cross the Tombe-Issoire intersection, going away from Place Denfert-Rochereau. There are a couple of interesting turn-of-the-century blocks at nos 34 and 36. The next crossing is Rue d'Alésia; go left and up a set of steps that seems to be almost part of the wall to Rue des Artistes, a village street of small houses – another and quieter world. Turn right. We are going to take the first right, into Rue de l'Aude, but it is worth first walking a little further along to have a look at Rue Gauguet, where there are three interesting artists' studios (1930) and where Nicolas de Staël (1914-1955) lived at no 7.

Rue de l'Aude takes you to Rue de la Tombe-Issoire, a 17th-century street leading out of Paris and then known as the Route d'Orléans; it has been greatly spoiled. Between the wars this whole area was another seat of literary Bohemia.

Turn left and left again into Villa Seurat, a charming cobbled alley bordered with small houses, almost all artists' studios. Seven of these (nos 1, 3, 3bis, 4, 5, 9 and 11) were done in 1924–5 by the architect André Lurçat (1894–1970), and share a pleasingly uncanny quality; no 3, built for the artist Marcel Gromaire (1892–1971), has a round bow window reminiscent of Villa Laroche by Le Corbusier (see p162). No 7bis, an astonishing little house with an unusual brick decoration on the first floor, is by Auguste Perret (1874–1954), another champion of modern architecture and of concrete.

Henry Miller (1891–1980) wrote the two *Tropic* novels and a few other works at no 18. Among those who came to visit him were Lawrence Durrell (1912–1990), fresh out of Greece and in the middle of writing his *Black Book* (1938), Anaïs Nin (1903–1977), Raymond Queneau (1903–1976) and Blaise Cendrars (1887–1961) – the first to praise Miller in France. Others who lived at Villa Seurat included Salvador Dali (1904–1989) and Chaïm Soutine.

Back on Rue de la Tombe-Issoire you see, almost facing Villa Seurat, a small street (Rue Marie-Rose) where the exiled Lenin lived in 1909–12 (plaque at no 4). Continue left along Rue de la Tombe-Issoire until you reach Place Jules-Hénaffe. Before you reach the *place* you see a large reservoir, built 1871–4, with pavilions typical of the period's industrial architecture.

Walk left along the reservoir wall into Avenue Reille. Cross the street to the small cobbled Square Montsouris. The white house on the corner at no 53 is Le Corbusier's first Parisian construction, built in 1922 for his friend the artist Amédée Ozenfant (1886–1966). The bottom two levels are for services while the top floor, with the corner bay window, has living quarters and the studio. As later at Villa Laroche (see p162), this is an organization of volumes and spaces around simple lines and with great attention to light. Like all Le Corbusier's buildings, this is without historical links or references, a truly modern piece of architecture.

Square Montsouris itself is remarkable, locked in a timewarp; small villas or *cottages* in various provincial styles border the cobbled *allée* on either side. At the far end, on the corner with Rue Nansouty, is the Maison Gaut, again by Perret: this house, unfortunately hidden by dense foliage half the year, was built a year after Ozenfant's *atelier*. The skewed symmetry – both studios are at an end of the alley, with one each on left and right – seems to symbolize two divergent and opposed conceptions of architecture: one rooted in tradition, the other believing in the plasticity of pure shapes.

Parc Montsouris faces you. Before you go in, take a detour to look at three other houses. Go right and right again into Rue Georges-Braque, another delightful cobbled tree-lined alley; at no 6 is a studio built by Perret in 1927 for Georges Braque (1882–1963), who worked there for 35 years. At 14 Rue Nansouty is another splendid studio by Lurçat, who here had more freedom than in the contrived space of Villa Seurat.

Parc de Montsouris

This park, the second largest in Paris, was designed by Jean Charles Alphand (1817–1891) and completed in record time in 1875–8. Though less inventive than Buttes Chaumont, also by Alphand, it is a lovely place, with fine trees and shrubs, green lawns, rocks and a lake. Go in through the small gate opposite Square Montsouris. Turn right, bear to the left at the fork and follow the crescent-shaped path until you reach the railway. Cross by the bridge and walk down the steps to the lake. Go left around the lake all the way down to the gates leading out of the park.

You are back in Avenue Reille. Walk rightish to the busy intersection with Rue d'Alésia and Rue de la Glacière. Turn right into Rue de Tolbiac, in effect a continuation of Rue d'Alésia. You are now in the 13th arrondissement, a part of Paris that has been extensively re-urbanized. Some way further along, turn left into Rue de l'Espérance, which leads to the top of the Butte aux Cailles, a charming forgotten spot with narrow picturesque streets and nice cafés. Pass the *cottage*-lined Rues Michal and Buot and enter Rue de la Butte-aux-Cailles. The *butte* first entered history when François Pilâtre de Rozier (1754–1785) landed a hot-air balloon here on 21 October 1783, thus ending the first controlled aerial journey in history; the flight's start had been 8km (5 miles) away on the Muette lawn (see p161). The *butte* was developed in the mid-19th century; before then it had been, like most of the Montsouris Quartier, dotted with windmills. When the Industrial Revolution came, many small tanneries and other factories settled along the Bièvre River (now underground), which ran on either side of the *butte,* and the whole area enjoyed tremendous growth. The wonderful view has been somewhat disfigured by nearby skyscrapers.

Take the second left, just after Rue des Cinq-Diamants, into the narrow Rue Samson, which changes name to become Rue Gérard. Reach Rue du Moulin-des-Prés, built over one arm of the Bièvre, and cross directly over to another narrow street, Rue Paulin-Méry. At its end, turn left into Rue Bobillot and walk along to the massive Place d'Italie, established on the site of the Barrière de Fontainebleau but in fact an important crossroads since Roman times, when the road to Italy started here. The cinema in the modern block behind you, by Tange Kenzo (b1913), completed 1990, has one of the largest screens of any commercial cinema in Europe.

The walk ends at the nearby Place-d'Italie métro station.

Passy and Auteuil

A longish walk through a rarely explored part of Paris, the rather elegant 16th arrondissement. Along the way are a few jewels of modern architecture, from Art-Nouveau masterpieces to Le Corbusier villas, as well as Honoré de Balzac's house, the exquisite Musée Marmottan and reminders of the two villages of Passy and Auteuil.

Start: **Métro Passy; buses 22 and 62.**
Finish: **Métro Jasmin (for a curtailed walk) or Michel-Ange-Auteuil.**
Length: **5.5km (3½ miles).**
Time: **2½hr.**
Refreshments: **Many cafés – especially the bar Antoine in Rue La Fontaine (designed by Guimard), but also in Rue de Passy, Place de la Muette and Place Jean Lorrain at the end of the walk – and some not uninteresting restaurants.**
Which day: **Tuesday-Friday is best; Sundays are a little dead.**
To visit:
• **Maison de la Radio: guided tours daily (not Sunday) 10.30, 11.30, 15.30, 16.30.**
• **Maison de Balzac: daily (not Monday) 10.00–17.40.**
• **Mushe Marmottan: daily (not Monday) 10.00–17.30.**
• **Fondation Le Corbusier: Monday to Friday 10.00–18.00, but closed for lunch.**

Last Tango in Paris

The two small villages of Passy and Auteuil date back to Gaulish and Roman times. Large estates, châteaux and abbeys flourished around here in the Middle Ages and after. The two villages became officially a part of Paris in 1860 Many famous people lived or had their country houses in the area, among them Molière (1622–1673), Jean Racine (1639–1699), Chateaubriand (1768–1848), Victor Hugo (1802–1885) and Marcel Proust (1871–1922).

Leave the métro and walk down the steps of Rue de l'Alboni towards the river. This is classic turn-of-the-century Paris, vaguely boring but not inelegant. The street merits a footnote in cinematographic history: in a flat on the first floor of no 1 Marlon Brando and Maria Schneider performed the steamy scenes of Bernardo Bertolucci's *Last Tango in Paris* (1972). The café on the corner (unfortunately done up since) was the setting for their illicit meetings. A dentist used to have his surgery in no 1, and his brass plaque was vaguely discernible in one sequence; he sued the film-makers over what he regarded as adverse publicity!

Under the railway, walk up the steps and across the bridge over the large Avenue du Président-Kennedy to Pont de Bir-Hakeim; its old name, Viaduc de Passy, is engraved in stone in the middle of the bridge. This quite remarkable example of post-Eiffel

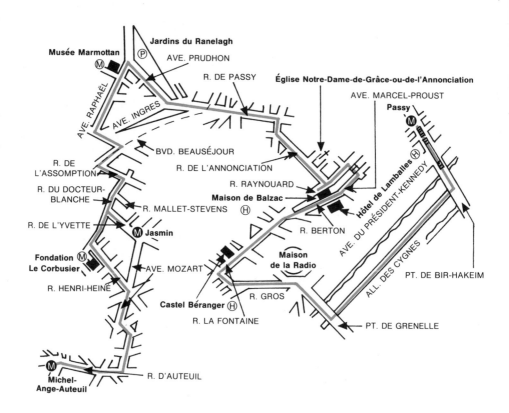

engineering is the only Parisian bridge to serve cars, pedestrians and the métro. It takes its name from the battle where the Free French opposed Rommel's troops in the Libyan desert in 1942; there is a commemorative inscription at the centre of the bridge. The four massive bas-reliefs on the bridge's stonework represent (upstream) the Seine and Labour and (downstream) Electricity and Commerce.

Stay in the middle section of the bridge, with cars on either side of you and the railway over your head. You have quite a view on your left, with Tour Eiffel and, on a clear day, the unmistakable white domes of the Sacré-Coeur in the distance, at the top of Montmartre. The spire nearer to you is that of St-Pierre-de-Chaillot. The bridge in the foreground is Pont d'Iéna (see p120).

Carry on to the centre of the bridge. On your right are the steps leading down to Allée des Cygnes.

Allée des Cygnes

Especially lovely in springtime, with its borders of trees, this artificial island was created in 1825 as a dyke to the Grenelle Harbour on the Right Bank, a reminder of the important industrial role that the Seine has played for centuries – as indeed it still does, albeit to a lesser extent. It takes its name from a natural one a little upstream, Île des Cygnes (Swan Island), which is now part of the 'mainland', just by Tour Eiffel; Louis XIV had a colony of swans from Sweden and Denmark installed on it. Before then the island had a reputation as a meeting place for duellists and was called Île Maquerelle (Mackerel Island), a corruption of *mâle querelle* (male quarrel).

Follow the *allée* to the other bridge, Pont de Grenelle. On your left is the Front de Seine, a rather dull 1970s residential and commercial development. Glance back now and again to appreciate Pont Bir-Hakeim, which really does look rather wonderful. As you approach Pont de Grenelle you can see on your right the round Maison de la Radio. At the end of the island is a small-scale Statue of Liberty, the original model by Auguste Bartholdi (1834–1904) for the one given by the French Republic to the USA to mark its first centenary.

Leave the island by going to your right across Pont de Grenelle, entirely rebuilt in 1968. On your left in the distance are the trees of Parc de St-Cloud. The Maison de la Radio, now facing you, houses what is to all intents and purposes the French broadcasting corporation (its statutes have recently changed in a rather complex way). Designed by Henry Bernard (b1912) and completed in 1963, the building owes its existence to the vision of General de Gaulle (1890–1970) and was intended as a 'symbol of the organization, concentration and cohesion' of French radio and tv. The façade is covered in aluminium plating, and the temperature inside is maintained by a warm spring (27°C [81°F]) coming up from a depth of some 550m (1800ft). The guided tours around this impressive building are recommended.

Afterwards, with the Maison de la Radio on your right, cross Rue de Boulainvilliers into Rue Gros, where you will find the more than average Restaurant Chaumette; this has been around since the mid-1930s and, though it has no great reputation, offers classic, unpretentious cooking and a deal of character. The writer Théophile Gautier (1811–1872) lived in this street, although his house has long gone.

Follow Rue Gros to its end, and enter Rue La Fontaine. (Watch out for the sharp bend in Rue Gros, or you may find yourself in Avenue Théophile-Gautier.) You have a treat in store – probably the finest building by Hector Guimard (1867–1942), the celebrated Castel Béranger – but before you go and look at it do have a coffee or a drink in the exquisite bar Antoine on the corner of Rues Gros and La Fontaine. It has not changed since Guimard designed it, and – rare for 1990s Paris – the interior décor is still intact, with its glass painted ceilings and flowery wall ceramics. The building as a whole was also designed by Guimard.

Hector Guimard

Castel Béranger is on the other side of the road, at no 14 Rue La Fontaine. Hector Guimard was one of the high priests of French Art Nouveau. A brilliant designer (he designed the métro entrances) and architect, he drew his inspiration from many sources, not least from the UK, both from people such as Norman Shaw (1831–1912), of Chiswick's Bedford Park fame, and from more conventional Victorian houses, especially at Farnham. Castel Béranger is a poem. Here are passion, ingenuity and brilliance – and yet this is after all only a block of flats. It is the detail that does it: note the masks in the iron arabesque on the balconies, a restatement of the mascaron tradition of a more Classical Paris; and then there are, along the wall, those small cast-iron decorations that look like birds of prey . . . or are they sea-horses?

Walk down the *allée* (Hameau Béranger) bordering Castel Béranger to appreciate the intensity of the building and its wall decorations. The fountain in the courtyard is worth more than a passing glance. Although the building is a private block, you can go in through the front door as far as the foyer to see its dense and intricate wall, ceiling and floor decorations.

Practically opposite Castel Béranger is the not uninteresting contemporary Conservatoire de Musique du 16ème-Francis Poulenc by Tailleb Tyber.

Nerval, Maupassant and Balzac
Continue up Rue La Fontaine and cross Place du Dr-Hayem into Rue Raynouard, with the back of the Maison de la Radio on your right. This street, one of the oldest and busiest of the old village of Passy, was known in the 18th century as the Rue qui Conduit du Monastère des Pères Minimes à la Maison de la Seigneurie de Passy (the street leading from the monastery of the Pères Minimes to the Seigniorial House of Passy) – quite a mouthful.

Keeping to the left-hand pavement, climb a short but steep hill to an intersection. Cross Rue des Vignes, pass École St-Jean-de-Passy, one of Paris's most prestigious private RC schools, and use the pedestrian crossing to get over to the right-hand side of the street. Walk down the five steps and turn immediately left into the narrow, cobbled Rue Berton; as you enter there is a wonderful vista over Tour Eiffel, perfectly framed by two buildings at the end. In the distance, gleaming over the rooftops, is the gilded dome of the Invalides. Rue Berton is rare in Passy in that it has hardly changed since the 18th century, retaining a sort of Ancien-Régime flavour. The first half was called Rue du Roc until 1865. Some 170 years ago, while the area was being redeveloped, some stone and plaster coffins dating back to the 14th century were found at the corner of Rues Berton and Raynouard.

Walk down the narrow street until you reach the green gate on your left. Behind it is the house where Honoré de Balzac (1799–1850) lived 1841–7; in a few minutes we shall go round to the main entrance in Rue Raynouard. Next to the gate is a boundary stone indicating the division between the seigniories of Auteuil and Passy (*Borne posée en 1731 pour indiquer la limite des seigneuries d'Auteuil et de Passy*).

On the other side of the wall are the Hôtel de Lamballes and what is left of its once huge park. At the end of the street take a few steps to your right to look through the gates. The *hôtel* has an extremely complex past. A certain Jean de Paci lived there in 1400. In the 17th century it belonged to Claude Chahu, Seigneur de Passy, before becoming the property of the Duc de Lauzun (1633–1723), whose famous brother-in-law, the Duc de Saint-Simon (1675–1755) – the French Pepys – stayed there in 1711. It then became the home of the notorious Princesse de Lamballe (1749–1792), confidante to Marie Antoinette (1755–1793), who like her queen went to the guillotine. In the mid-19th century Dr Esprit Blanche (1796–1852) transferred his mental institution here from Montmartre (see p139). Among his inmates were Gérard de Nerval (1808–1855), in 1853 and 1854, Charles Gounod (1818–1893), in 1857, and Guy de Maupassant (1850–1893), for the last year of his life. Today the *hôtel* houses the Turkish Embassy.

Go on to Avenue Marcel-Proust, the continuation of Rue Berton, and then up the 100 or so steps of Avenue du Parc-de-Passy; both streets were opened in 1930 in what used to be the thermal Parc de Passy. At the top of the steps, turn left in Rue Raynouard. Pass two 18th-century houses, at nos 38 and 39, and at no 47 you find the entrance to

Balzac's house. This is an enchanting and enchanted place, an oasis of times past. Here Balzac wrote some of the most famous novels of his *Comédie Humaine*, such as *Splendeurs et Misères des Courtisanes* (1843–7) and *Le Cousin Pons* (1847). There are manuscripts, photographs by Eugène Atget (1856–1927) and prints by Gustave Doré (1833–1883), among others. Among the letters on view are some truly wonderful ones to the Comtesse Hanska (1801–1882), Balzac's great passion, who finally married him when he had only six months to live.

Coming out of the house, cross the road and enter another old Passy street, Rue de l'Annonciation, today containing mainly 19th-century buildings. Along to your right is the 19th-century Église Notre-Dame-de-Grâce-ou-de-l'Annonciation. After you cross Rue Lekain, on the left, the street becomes a pedestrian precinct, with shops, some rather fine delicatessens, cafés and restaurants. At the top is the busy Place de Passy; turn left into Rue de Passy, which is now full of designer shops but was once the main artery of the village of Passy.

La Muette
Rue de Passy takes you into Chaussée de la Muette, one of the roads which led out of Paris to the Porte de la Muette. Château de la Muette used to stand at no 20. The name probably came from *meute* (hunting pack): Charles IX had a lodge here from which he hunted deer in the nearby Bois de Boulogne. At the hands of Philibert Delorme (*c*1510–1570) the lodge became a small *château*, belonging to Queen Margot (Margaret de Valois; 1553–1615), wife of Henri IV, before becoming crown property.

The grounds of the *château* were enormous and from one of the lawns François Pilâtre de Rozier (1754–1785) and François, Marquis d'Arlandes (1742–1809) set off in 1783 to make the world's first controlled aerial journey, in a hot-air balloon, the *Montgolfière*, so-named because it was designed – with wallpaper as an envelope and straw as fuel – by the brothers Joseph (1740–1810) and Jacques (1745–1799) Montgolfier. The entire court was there to watch the occasion, including Louis XVI and Marie Antoinette. Nine years later came the Revolution, and the estate was divided up and sold in lots, eventually to be developed.

However, there is a bit of the park left, now called the Jardins du Ranelagh. Lord Ranelagh had installed in the park of his Chelsea mansion in 1750 a rotunda where music was played daily for public enjoyment, and a little later two French officers of the king asked to be allowed to set up a similar 'Pleasure Dome' on the Pelouse de la Muette. The Petit Ranelagh soon became a favourite place of the court. It had a second lease of life during the Directoire, when people like Mme de Récamier (1777–1849), Joséphine de Beauharnais (1763–1814; later Empress Joséphine) and Talleyrand (1754–1838) disported themselves here. The dancehall was demolished in the mid-1850s.

Three large avenues now cut through the gardens. Take Avenue Prudhon and, at the end, use the pedestrian crossing to the other side of Avenue Raphaël, where you turn left and then right into the small Rue Louis-Boilly.

At no 2 is the Musée Marmottan, a little jewel of a museum – not too well known and somewhat dated, but full of treasures. It is rather poorly organized and there are four distinct *donations*, giving the place a rather jumbled feel. The house itself is an early 19th-century *hôtel*, given to the state by Paul Marmottan (1856–1932), a collector and historian, and in its oldest, unrenovated part is very evocative of its opulent times, with panelled rooms and fine parquet floors. Though set up to house Marmottan's Empire collection, the museum is now primarily known for its remarkable Impressionist collection. Over 50 paintings by Claude Monet (1840–1926) – including the celebrated *Soleil Levant* (1873) – are housed in the brilliantly refurbished basement. The top floor has a fine series of drawings and washes by Eugène Boudin (1824–1898), Édouard Manet (1832–1883), Auguste Renoir (1841–1919), Henri Toulouse-Lautrec (1864–1901) – including a stunning colour wash of a girl on a beach – Johan Jongkind (1819–1891), Paul Signac (1863–1935), Eugène Delacroix (1798–1863) and Jean François Millet (1814–1875). But you should also look at the magnificent 16th-century tapestries on the ground floor and the impressive Empire furniture, as well as the good collection of illuminated manuscripts, the Wildenstein Donation.

The Village d'Auteuil, Mallet-Stevens and Le Corbusier
Outside the museum, go back into the Jardins du Ranelagh and follow Avenue Raphaël to your right in order to reach Avenue Ingres. Cross the avenue over to the walkway under the disused railway line. You then turn into Boulevard Beauséjour on your right for 100m (110yd) until you reach Rue de l'Assomption, on your left. Known in the 18th century as Rue des Tombereaux (tip-carts), this is one of Auteuil's oldest streets. Its current name is from a convent situated there in the second half of the 19th century, Couvent des Dames-de-l'Assomption, whose church, Notre-Dame-de-l'Assomption-de-Passy, still stands.

Facing the church is Rue du Docteur-Blanche, the same Dr Blanche whose mental institution we noted earlier. Backing onto the street used to be the large garden of the Proust family's country house, where Marcel was born. Also of interest are two *allées* leading off the street. The first is immediately on your left, Rue Mallet-Stevens, a stunning example of inter-war architecture. Not as well known as Le Corbusier (1887–1965), Robert Mallet-Stevens (1886–1945) built little during his brief career (1923–34), and then almost exclusively for the rich or for the film industry. Of the houses in this *allée*, six are his – nos 1, 5, 7, 8, 10 and 12. His approach was essentially one of simplicity (we are far from Guimard) and that of a sculptor: overhangs, terraces, towers and porches all seem to combine to make a vast sculpture based on a single driving principle, the cube. Some of his houses here have been spoiled – especially no 12, which now looks almost like any old block of flats – but do walk down the *allée*: there is a wonderful, almost tangible feeling of space. At the end of the *allée* is a small bend, and as you go round it you find a cottage in the middle of a large garden, as if you were somewhere in the country. The contrast is startling.

The *allée* is a dead end. Go back to Rue du Docteur-Blanche and about 100m (110yd) along it and in through the gates of Square du Docteur-Blanche. At the end are Villas Laroche and Jeanneret, designed by Le Corbusier in the 1920s and remarkably well preserved, thanks to the Fondation Le Corbusier, now housed there. Villa Jeanneret holds the administration offices and the library (open to the public), devoted to works on architecture and Le Corbusier's own writings. In fact, he would have designed the entire street had his plans not been rejected except for these two houses, one for his brother and the other for a banker friend called La Roche.

From the outside Villa Laroche (also open to the public, although the public rarely goes there) looks a little like a ship sailing to worlds unknown. Part of it is built on piles, the first-floor window is full-length, and there is a roof terrace – all elements that were fairly innovative at the time but became part of Le Corbusier's architectural canon. La Roche was a keen collector of pictures, and the interior reflects his need to show them off. There are original pieces of furniture, and lithographs and oils on the walls, but perhaps it is the feeling of being in a perfect space that makes Villa La Roche so special. Everything seems to *work*.

Retrace your steps to Rue du Docteur-Blanche; go right and right again along the rather charmingly quaint Rue Henri-Heine to Rue Jasmin, which used to be called Rue de la Cure because of the curing waters of the nearby Auteuil spring, which were exploited from the 17th century until 1894 for the digestive qualities of their sulphur and iron salts.

If you want you can now call a halt to your walk: take Rue Jasmin to your left until you reach Avenue Mozart, with métro Jasmin and the no 22 bus line.

Otherwise, follow Rue Henri-Heine – there is a strange-looking 1920s Guimard block at no 18 – to the bottom, where it meets with Avenue Mozart. Go right and stay on the right-hand pavement. At no 122 is another, but earlier (1905–12), specimen of Guimard's brilliance, the fine Hôtel Guimard, still very much embedded in Art-Nouveau principles. Triangular in shape to optimize the very limited ground space, and less decorated than Castel Béranger, it is nevertheless quite remarkable: look at the bow windows, the studio window on the top floor and the various corbels.

Follow Avenue Mozart to another busy intersection, then go left past the Crédit Lyonnais Bank, briefly into Rue La Fontaine, and right into the tiny Rue du Général Largeau, which takes you into the 14th-century Rue des Perchamps, another of the oldest streets in Auteuil. Just there, on the corner with Rue Leconte-de-Lisle, is an amazing block of artists' studios, which was built by Henri Sauvage (1839–1928) in 1926, in the final stage of his career. The quality of the façade is remarkable: time seems to have left no mark.

Go up Rue des Perchamps to Rue d'Auteuil, a good shopping street that has retained a village atmosphere, many of its ancient houses having been preserved. On your left, a little distance away, is the rather uninspiring Église d'Auteuil, built in 1870 to replace the original 11th-century church. Molière lived at no 2 Rue d'Auteuil. On the other side of Rue des Perchamps is the Lycée Jean Baptiste-Say, established in the remains of an 18th-century mansion; only the front courtyard and the central pavilion remain.

Walk on up the street. On your right is the renewed Auberge du Mouton-Blanc, where people like Racine, Molière, Nicolas Boileau (1636–1711), Jean de La Fontaine (1621–1695) and Ninon de Lenclos (1616–1706) used to meet. Further along is Place Jean-Lorrain, previously called Place de la Fontaine, where the water was so good that Louis XV paused to drink whenever he came to Auteuil. At no 43 is the fine 18th-century Hôtel Antier-ou-des-Demoiselles-de-Verrière, where John Adams (1735–1826) and John Quincy Adams (1767–1848) stayed during their Parisian sojourns. The *place* has good cafés and an excellent fruit and vegetable market on Wednesday and Saturday mornings. Métro Michel-Ange-Auteuil is beside the Monoprix supermarket.

Alternatively, you can continue straight on down Rue d'Auteuil to visit the Serres d'Auteuil, an exquisite garden with a series of greenhouses dating from the late 19th century, containing exotic plants and palm trees. Walk down the street until you reach Porte d'Auteuil. You have, in effect, reached the limit of the city, and this is an important cross-section of thoroughfares. Stay on the left-hand side of the street; cross Boulevard Exelmans, and then Boulevard Murat and Rue du Général-Sarrail. On your right on the other side of the road is the Auteuil flat race course, one of the two Hippodromes of the city. A five-minute walk straight on is the Roland Garros stadium, where the French tennis open takes place. However, you should now turn left into Avenue du Général-Sarrail. 50m (55yd) along, turn right into a small garden, the *jardin des poètes*, leading to the Serres d'Auteuil.

Père-Lachaise to
Buttes Chaumont

A walk through three *quartiers populaires*, three old villages to the east of the city – Charonne, Ménilmontant and Belleville – and across Cimetière du Père-Lachaise (also called Cimetière de l'Est) and the great Parc des Buttes-Chaumont.

Start: Métro Père-Lachaise; buses 60 and 69.
Finish: Métro Danube; bus 75.
Length: 5.5km (3½ miles).
Time: 2½–3hr.
Refreshments: Pleasant cafés at the beginning of the walk in Avenue du Père-Lachaise and at the end of the walk in Place Rhin-et-Danube; excellent Thai and Chinese restaurants halfway along, in Rue de Belleville.
Which day: Any day.

Cimetière du Père-Lachaise
Leave the métro *via* the Boulevard de Ménilmontant exit. The boulevard was opened in the 19th century, on the site of the Fermiers Généraux wall, and developed as part of Haussmann's strategic network of circular boulevards. Walk along the central island until you see, on your left, the massive entrance gates of the Cimetière Père-Lachaise.

This is the largest – about 45 hectares (110 acres) – and most visited Parisian cemetery. Indeed, it is more than a cemetery: it is more of a park, full of romantic *allées*, fine trees, mausoleums and funeral sculptures by many artists of note including David d'Angers (1789–1856), François Rude (1784–1855) and Charles Garnier (1825–1898).

In the 12th century the Bishop of Paris had his wine-press here. 200 years later the estate was bought by a rich burgher, who built a country house on it; it became known as the Folie Regnault (*folie* then meant *feuillu* – leafy). It was sold to the Jesuits early in the 17th century and became Mont Louis, a country residence for Jesuit clergy. Père François Lachaise (1624–1709), Louis XIV's confessor, bought more land for the estate. The whole property was sold when the Jesuits were expelled in 1763. In the early 1800s, when burying of the dead had become a serious problem, it was decided that Paris should have three large cemeteries. The state bought Mont Louis to be the one on the city's east. It was reorganized and landscaped by Alexandre Brongniart (1739–1813).

Needless to say, hardly anything is left from the gardens of the Jesuit days, although the main *allée* going up from the gates is original and the chapel on the far side of the monument to those who died during WWII in concentration camps or fighting for the Resistance (the Monument du Souvenir) is on the site of Lachaise's chapel.

We are going for a 45–minute walk in the cemetery (a full tour would take 2–3 hours), but feel free to wander as you please. It is a confusing place so it is a good idea to buy a map at the bookshop by the entrance.

164

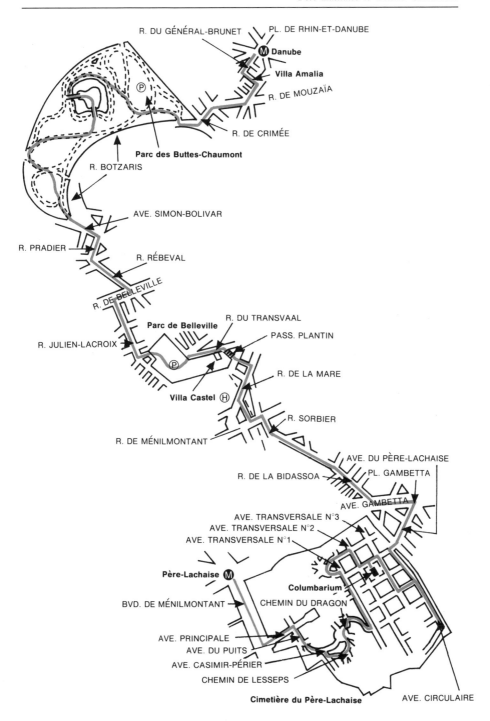

Walk through the gates and up Avenue Principale to a T-junction with Avenue du Puits. To your left, a few metres along on the right, is the grave of Colette (1873–1954), while straight ahead, towards the Monument du Souvenir, are the tombs of Giacchino Rossini (1792–1868) – a largish monument with red doors – and Alfred de Musset (1810–1857), both on the left-hand side.

Turn right into Avenue du Puits, which becomes Avenue Casimir-Périer and veers left. Go first right and then first left up a small *allée*. At a T-junction with Chemin Lauriston is the grave of Jim Morrison (1943–1971), the lead singer of the Doors, who died in Paris from an overdose of everything. His tomb is a makeshift affair: until a few years ago there was no stone, just a wooden cross in the bare earth. Most of the graves nearby are covered with graffiti done by people who have come from all over the world to pay tribute to him.

Back in Chemin Lauriston, keep going and then turn left into Chemin de Lesseps, up to Carrefour du Grand Rond and over into Avenue de la Chapelle. Two tombstones further on, go right into a small path, Chemin de la Vierge. Pass a few derelict graves and then climb a few steps to another narrow *allée,* Chemin du Dragon, which takes you to the sandy, crescent-shaped Chemin Molière (marked *24ème division),* which you follow to the right. Soon you come to a rather large mausoleum on the right and, opposite it, the sarcophagi of Molière (1622–1673) and Jean de La Fontaine (1621–1695) – although it is doubtful if they are really buried there.

Continue along the path to Avenue Transversale No 1. Go left along the avenue to the second turning on the right, Avenue des Anciens-Combattants. A little way up it, on the corner with Chemin du Quinconce, you can see the tomb of the remarkable Allan Kardek (1804–1869), the pseudonymous founder of Spiritualism in France and something of a cult figure.

Continue along Avenue Transversale No 1 and take the first turning to the left, downhill along the crescent-shaped Allée Eugène-Delacroix; the imposing black tombstone of Delacroix (1798–1863) is along on the right, almost opposite Chemin de la Gare. Turn almost immediately right into Chemin du Mont-Louis, beside the monument to Casimir Delavigne (1793–1843). Here you find Honoré de Balzac (1799–1850) and Gérard de Nerval (1808–1855) facing each other. Carry on in what is now called Avenue des Thuyas and turn right into Avenue Transversale No 2. Along on the left is the black marble gravestone of Marcel Proust (1871–1922).

Cross Avenue des Anciens-Combattants and take the first left to the Columbarium, which is organized around a square with a central island – the crematorium is in the middle. Walk in and you will see to your left a few steps, almost a ladder. At no 6796, by the floor, is a rather moving plaque for Isadora Duncan (1878–1927). Now climb down some large steps and find, underground as it were, the modest, curiously touching white plaque of Maria Callas (1923–1977) at the other end, in the left-hand corner at no 16258.

Go up the steps near the Callas plaque and leave the Columbarium *via* Avenue des Anciens-Combattants. Turn right into Avenue Transversale No 3 and follow it to Avenue Carette, second on your left. A little way down on your left you will find the monument by Jacob Epstein (1880–1950) to Oscar Wilde (1854–1900), who died in a small *hôtel* in the Latin Quarter. Continue down to Avenue Circulaire. Gertrude Stein (1874–1946), Edith Piaf (1915–1963) and Paul Éluard (1895–1952) are to be found down the avenue to the right, as is the Mur des Fédérés.

Take Avenue Circulaire left all the way round to the eastern gates and exit into Avenue du Père-Lachaise, where there are a couple of decent cafés.

The villages

The villages to the east of Paris never suffered the same degree of development and urbanization as those to the west. Besides the *châteaux* of Charonne and Ménilmontant, the Folie Regnault and the quarries of Belleville, the population was essentially a fragmented one of market gardeners, millers – there were windmills at the top of the hills – craftsmen-shopkeepers, and so on. When the Fermiers Généraux wall was built in the late 18th century, the villages grew rapidly, since the cost of living was so much lower outside the wall. The Industrial Revolution was beginning to bite, and the population of the villages of Charonne, Belleville and Ménilmontant, all eventually incorporated into Paris in 1860, became a mixture of peasantry and working class. There was only scattered development thereafter, except for a few major access roads and the great Parc des Buttes-Chaumont. Today the villages are subject to not always wise development. The remainder of this walk tries to capture something of what they used to be.

On leaving the cemetery, go down Avenue du Père-Lachaise to Place Gambetta, created in Haussmann's days. Turn left into the bustling Avenue Gambetta, created in the last quarter of the 19th century. Just before you reach Place Martin-Nadaud, take a right into the narrow Rue de la Bidassoa, which takes you past two much altered old streets, Rue Villiers-de-l'Isle-Adam and Rue d'Annam. Rue de la Bidassoa takes you downhill past a small public garden and into Rue Sorbier.

Reach Rue de Ménilmontant. In the Middle Ages this was a track leading to a small hamlet at the top, and was surrounded by vineyards and woods, many belonging to rich abbeys down in the city. Château Ménilmontant, built in the 17th century, was further up. Jean-Jacques Rousseau (1712–1778), a keen botanist – he collected an impressive herbarium – sometimes gathered plants on the hill.

Cross Rue de Ménilmontant by the pedestrian crossing, and turn left and then right into Rue de la Mare, just before the large Église Notre-Dame-de-la-Croix, built in 1869–80. Rue de la Mare, in use as long ago as 1672, owes its name to a nearby pond that collected the waters from the hill. The street continues on the other side of the pedestrian bridge over the disused railway line, and here you can sadly view what the 1970s did to old Belleville, regarded not so many decades ago as possibly Paris's most picturesque village. Cross Rue Henri-Chevreau and turn left into Cité Antoine-Loubeyre, a small craft and workshop centre. Cross Rue des Couronnes, another old street of the village, and walk up the steps of the narrow Passage Plantin, with small cottages on one side and, on the other, the long back wall of the houses of Villa Castel.

Turn left into Rue du Transvaal and immediately on your left, at no 16, is Villa Castel itself, a narrow cul-de-sac bordered by quaint cottages. Both it and Passage Plantin are typical of the way Belleville used to be.

Walk up Rue du Transvaal until you reach Rue Piat, a path that until the beginning of this century led to two windmills. Things have changed beyond recognition: this side of the hill was recently razed to make way for Parc de Belleville: 4 hectares (10 acres), more than 1200 trees and a few fountains.

This is the highest eastern point of the city. Working clockwise, you can view the Panthéon, Notre-Dame, Tour Montparnasse, the blue-and-red pipes of the Centre Georges-Pompidou, the Dôme of the Invalides, and Tour Eiffel.

Walk down the park steps and take the third *allée* to the right to reach the bottom of the garden, where you come out into Rue Julien-Lacroix, opened during the Restoration. Follow this street to the right until you reach Rue de Belleville, the main street of the old village of Belleville. The bottom end has given way to 1970s buildings, but the middle and top sections have retained some character. Down the street on the left are some excellent restaurants.

Walk up Rue de Belleville, passing the entrance to Rue Julien-Lacroix again, and immediately turn left into Rue Rébeval. Turn right into Rue Pradier and so to Avenue Simon-Bolivar, a typical Haussmann product. The nature of the area changes here, becoming quasi-bourgeois. Just north of the avenue, used to be a couple of paths – one called Chemin des Moulins (now Rue Clavel) – bordered by at least nine windmills that were visible from a great distance.

Les Buttes Chaumont

Almost immediately comes the entrance to the marvellous Parc des Buttes-Chaumont. It is hard to realize that such an attractive place was until 150 years ago one of the most unsavoury areas of Paris – matters not being helped by the presence of the Gibet de Montfaucon down the hill.

The park covers 22 hectares (55 acres) and has lakes, bridges, grottoes, restaurants and cafés. It was created in 1863–5 at the behest of Napolean III, who wanted another park for the forthcoming Exposition Universelle (1870), not to mention a bit more greenery for the local working people – most of Paris's parks were then concentrated to the west.

Enter the gardens by Porte Bolivar. To continue the walk you should exit *via* Porte de La Villette, on the Rue Botzaris side; otherwise, wander as you will, although the route described here will take you round the main sights. Go along Avenue Jacques-Liniers and take the steps up the hill almost immediately on your left; there is a nice view from the top. Come downhill to a children's playground and cross Avenue du Général-Puebla to a small path on the next hillside, facing you. Go up and over this hill; on the other side, turn right into Avenue des Marnes, then left across a bridge to the island. Take the steps to the right up to the Belvédère and the small temple (a copy of the Sybil temple at Tivoli). There is a stunning view over Paris and especially the Sacré-Coeur.

Go down some steep steps in a grotto-like *passage* (mind your head), cross another bridge and turn left by the Pavillion du Lac. About 100m (110yd) along on the left, take a narrow path that runs beside along a stream until you reach the lake again. Take Route Circulaire du Lac to the right and pass the large grotto to reach the music kiosk. Take the avenue to the right of the kiosk; a little along, some steps to the right lead to Avenue J.C.-Cavé, which you take to the right to reach a T-junction. Turn left into Avenue de la Cascade and leave the park by Porte de La Villette.

You find yourself in Rue Botzaris. Go left to Rue de Crimée and cross to Rue du Général-Brunet. This entire sector has escaped the bulldozer, and has retained a quiet charm. You are now going gently downhill on the northern side of the Butte de Beauregard. Go second right into Rue de Mouzaïa, which is, like Rue du Général-Brunet, bordered with *villas* – i.e., picturesque little alleyways lined with cottages. For an especially pretty one, pass Église St-François-d'Assise, take the first left, Rue de la Liberté, and go into the third *villa* on your left, Villa Amalia.

This takes you back to Rue du Général-Brunet. Go right to the rather sleepy Place de Rhin-et-Danube, where you find a couple of cafés, métro Danube and the bus-stop.

Plate 28: *The Opéra de la Bastille, completed in 1989 (see the Bastille and Faubourg St-Antoine walk, page 145).*

Plate 29: *A popular bakery in Rue Emilio-Castelar (see the Bastille and Faubourg St-Antoine walk, page 147).*

Plate 30: *Hector Guimard's Art Nouveau doorway at Castel Béranger in the Rue La Fontaine (see the Passy and Auteuil walk, page 159).*

Plate 31: *The Père-Lachaise cemetery (see the Père-Lachaise to Buttes Chaumont walk, page 164).*

Plate 32: The Parc des Buttes-Chaumont (see the *Père-Lachaise to Buttes Chaumont walk,* page 168).

Plate 33: The elegant Galerie Vivienne arcade (see *The* Passages *walk,* page 171).

Plate 34: The Grande Arche de la Fraternité at La Défense (see *Other Outings,* page 192).

Plate 35: *The château at Fontainebleau (see the Fontainebleau walk, page 179).*

Plate 36: *A richly ornamented courtyard at the château of Versailles (see the Versailles walk, page 183).*

Plates 37 and 38: No tour of Paris is complete without a visit to an exclusive shopping area such as the Place Vendôme. Afterwards you can turn your steps to one of the city's many pavement cafés. Here you can relax over a coffee or an aperitif and simply watch the world go by.

The Passages

A long, meandering walk through *Paris inconnu* – some of its numerous *passages* (arcades). Some, like Passage Brady, have been largely forgotten; others, like Galerie Vivienne, are being revitalized and are enjoying a new lease of life: all are worth seeing.

Start: **Métro Louvre; buses 69, 72, 76.**
Finish: **Métro Réaumur-Sébastopol; buses 20, 38, 39, 47.**
Length: **5.5km (3½ miles).**
Time: **2½-3hr.**
Refreshments: **Numerous cafés on the way. There are excellent tearooms in the Galerie de Montpensier, in Galerie Vivienne and in Passage des Panoramas.**
Which day: **Any day except Sunday, when most shops are shut.**
To visit:
● **Musée Grevin: daily 13.00–19.00, school holidays daily 10.00–19.00.**

Véro-Dodat
Exit the métro into the arcaded Rue de Rivoli, a fine example of imperial architecture, created 1811–35 on the estate of the Couvent des Feuillants, which had been razed in 1804. Go over the street and left under the arcades; cross Rue de l'Oratoire, with the back of Église de l'Oratoire (see p77) on your right. The impressive monument you see was erected in 1889 to the memory of Gaspard de Coligny (1519–1572), the austere head of the Huguenots, murdered along with thousands of his flock in the St Bartholomew's Day Massacre. Turn right into Rue de Marengo, cross Rue St-Honoré and carry on into the 13th-century Rue Jean-Jacques-Rousseau, formerly Rue Grenelle-St-Honoré, where a few old houses can still be seen. Stay on the left-hand pavement. At no 19, beside a Chinese restaurant, is the entrance to Galerie Véro-Dodat.

This *passage* is perfectly untouched and as a result perhaps a little moribund, but it is full of charm, with its marble columns and large glass panels. It is 80m (88yd) long and 4m (13ft) wide. The Restaurant Véro-Dodat, halfway down, is good. At the other end is the excellent Café de l'Époque, where the poet Gerard de Nerval (1808–1855) is said to have had his last drink before hanging himself. Otherwise the *galerie* contains art and craft shops, bookshops, etc. Created in 1822 by two *charcutiers* called Véro and Dodat, it was, unusually, a 'total concept' from the start: the external decoration is identical for all 38 shops. One of the first *galeries* to get gas lighting, in the 1830s, its success was immediate, and it remained busy for the next 60 or so years before falling into decline.

At the end, go straight across Rue du Bouloi into short Rue Montesquieu. Cross Rue des Bons-Enfants – where Anthelme Brillat-Savarin (1755–1826) and later Gérard de Nerval lived – and go through the arch facing you into Passage Vérité. This leads to the small but pleasing Place de Valois, opened in honour of the Duc de Valois, the father of Philippe Égalité (1747–1793), on the site of the kitchen courtyard of the Palais-Royal.

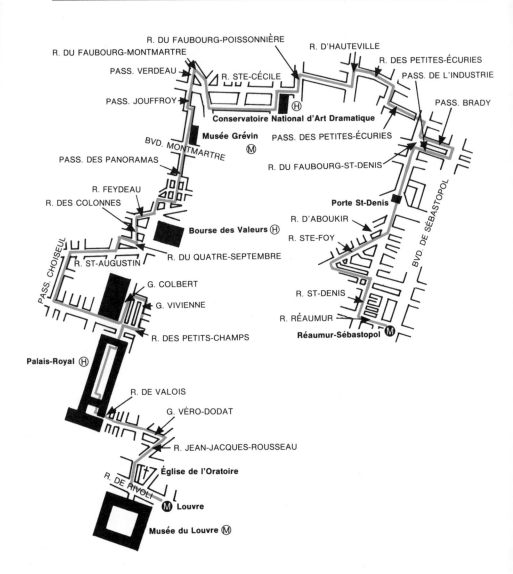

The Palais-Royal

Enter the Palais-Royal through Passage Valois. For a fuller discussion of the Palais-Royal, built for Cardinal Richelieu (1585–1642) in 1629–35 by Jacques Lemercier (1585–1684) and then called the Palais-Cardinal, see p110. The monumental ensemble that we see today was built by the architect Victor Louis (1731–*c*1811) in 1781–3, with numerous shops housed under its arcade. There were in fact some 60 almost identical pavilions all for rent. On the fourth side of the rectangle were the infamous *galeries de bois* (wooden arcades), rife with prostitutes and other lowlife.

Cross the colonnaded Galerie d'Orléans – the black-and-white columns in the Cour d'Honneur on your left were done by Daniel Buren (b1938) in 1986 – and reach the quiet Galerie de Montpensier, which contains art galleries plus the occasional coin and medal shop. Nothing remains of the café here where such revolutionaries as Camille Desmoulins (1760–1794) used to harangue the crowds. There are some nice mosaics on the floor, especially at no 13.

The *galerie* turns at a right angle, the second 'leg' being Galerie de Beaujolais, where you find the wonderful Restaurant du Grand Véfour (see p110). The *galerie* leads round to Galerie de Valois, a reprise of Galerie de Montpensier, with art galleries and antiques shops.

Vivienne, Colbert and Choiseul
At the corner of Galeries de Beaujolais and de Valois is your exit from the *palais*. Cross the narrow Rue de Beaujolais, walk up the steps of Passage des Deux Pavillons (1820), and cross Rue des Petits-Champs. On your right you can see, as if framed by the street, the statue in Place des Victoires of Louis XIV on his horse (see p108).

Facing you is Galerie Vivienne, another exquisite Parisian *passage*. Twice the size of Galerie Véro-Dodat – it is 176m (193yd) long – the *galerie* was opened in 1826, and its proximity to the Palais-Royal ensured its success throughout the 19th century. A few years ago it had become a little down-at-heel, but, faced by the threat of demolition, it pulled itself together and is now a gay, busy, bustling and beautiful *passage* housing many fine shops – including the fun Jean-Paul Gaultier shop at the far end – an excellent tearoom, À Priori Thé, and a good second-hand bookshop. The recent renovation has preserved almost all the original features. The mosaic floor is especially fine, as are the stairs at no 13, where Eugène Vidocq (1775–1857) lived in 1840: a criminal who turned informer and eventually became prefect of police, he was the model for Vautrin, the arch-villain in *La Comédie Humaine* by Honoré de Balzac (1799–1850).

Meander down. Just by Jean-Paul Gaultier's shop, take a left into Galerie Colbert, which has been completely restored and now houses the art gallery and bookshop of the Bibliothèque Nationale (the BN – the equivalent to the British Library). The art gallery often has excellent exhibitions of little-known prints; the bulk of the collection is exhibited from time to time at the library itself in nearby Rue de Richelieu (see p109). This *galerie* lies parallel to Galerie Vivienne and was likewise opened in 1826, both being built on the grounds of an *hôtel* which had belonged to the Marquis de Seigneulay, son of Jean-Baptiste Colbert (1619–1683). Galerie Colbert, too, was successful from the outset, though it suffered in the competition with Galerie Vivienne and effectively died around the turn of the century. Eventually the Bibliothèque Nationale bought the entire plot in 1986 and recreated the *galerie* according to original plans and drawings.

Come out of the *galerie* into Rue des Petits-Champs. Facing you is a good winebar, Aux Bons Crus. Turn right. At no 8, with the imposing gates, is the Classical first Hôtel Tubeuf built by Pierre Le Muet (1591–1669) in 1634 for the Président de la Cour des Comptes (the Revenue Court), and today part of the Bibliothèque Nationale; the front elevation, steps and trophies are original. Cardinal Mazarin (1602–1661), wanting to be near Anne of Austria (1601–1666) – rumoured to be his mistress – and the young Louis XIV, residing in the nearby Palais-Cardinal, bought it in 1649. It was then called the Hôtel Mazarin, and as such was often described in the works of Alexandre Dumas (1802–1870). It eventually became the property of the state. Mme de Récamier (1777–1849) died here of cholera.

There are a few other old houses, including nos 20 and 26, two early-18th-century *hôtels*. Follow the street, cross Rue Ste-Anne and carry on to Passage de Choiseul, on your right, at 44 Rue des Petits-Champs; the entrance is that of a 17th-century *hôtel*. Almost facing you on the other side of the street (no 57) stood the house where Jean-Jacques Rousseau (1712–1778) lived with his mistress Marie-Thérèse Levasseur (1721–1801). Passage de Choiseul, full of small businesses and shops and consequently very lively, is slightly more urban, less chic than the three we have just seen. It is probably less interesting architecturally and décor-wise than the others, but has an old-fashioned charm. Almost 200m (220yd) long, it was opened in 1827 and was another link between the Palais-Royal and the 'Grands Boulevards', where so much was going on. The Théâtre des Enfants-de-Monsieur-Comte had an entrance here and still does, though rechristened the Théâtre des Bouffes Parisiens by Jacques Offenbach (1819–1880), who bought it in 1855 to stage his ever more successful operettas, including *Orphée aux Enfers* (1858). A few years later Alphonse Lemerre (1838–1912) set up shop in the *galerie* and published from here almost all of the 'Parnassians', such as Villiers-de-l'Isle-Adam (1838–1889), François Coppée (1842–1908) and José Maria de Heredia (1842–1905), poets who were extremely influential then but are not much read today – although Villiers-de-l'Isle-Adam's novel *L'Ève future* (1886) and some of his *contes cruels* (a term that originated with him) are still known. Lemerre also spotted the talent of Paul Verlaine (1844–1896), whose poems he published as early as 1864. Thereafter the *passage* met harder times, if we are to believe Louis Ferdinand Céline (1884–1961), whose *Mort à Crédit* (1936) describes a dark smelly, airless childhood spent here.

Panoramas, Jouffroy and Verdeau
Come out into Rue St-Augustin and turn right. The Neoclassical building in the near distance is the Bourse. Rue St-Augustin, opened in 1633, takes its name from the monastery whose wall it followed. Some way along, turn left into Rue Richelieu and immediately right into the wide Rue du Quatre-Septembre, which you cross before going left into the charming Rue des Colonnes. This street is what remains of Passage des Colonnes, opened in 1791 and widened into a street in 1797, from which year date the houses at nos 1, 2, 6 and 7. At the end of the street, turn right into Rue Feydeau, opened in 1650, and follow it across Rue Vivienne (with a view of the Bourse again, to your right). Almost immediately afterwards you see on your left the short Rue des Panoramas, which takes you into Rue St-Marc.

More or less facing you, at no 10, is Passage des Panoramas, one of the oldest *passages* in Paris, opened on the site of an early-18th-century *hôtel* in 1800 by the US inventor Robert Fulton (1765–1815). He had come over to France to offer the Directoire two of his inventions, the torpedo and a submarine, the *Nautilus*. While waiting for a decision, he had the *passage* specially designed to house two large rotundas, 20m (66ft) high and 17m (56ft) wide, for the mounting of another project, the 'Panoramas', whereby epic-size topographical views could be displayed. His success was immediate: all Paris flocked to see the spectacular effects. Spectators stood on a platform inside one or other of the rotundas to view an enormous circular painting which filled the entire rotunda. Perspectives and lighting were cleverly worked out, so that the illusion was of being aboard a hot-air balloon. The quality of reproduction was excellent, as attested to by Chateaubriand (1768–1848), who, on returning from a journey in Greece, exclaimed that he recognized all the monuments down to their most intricate detail.

The *passage* was extended in 1834 with branching *galeries* being opened at the same time – Galeries Feydeau, des Variétés, Montmartre and St-Marc, as well as Galerie de la Bourse, since disappeared. Although it is a long *passage* – over 130m (142yd) – its glass roof gives it quite a lot of light. It is full of small businesses and there is a good tearoom, L'Arbre à Canelle, at no 57 on the left. The decoration of the print-shop at no 47 is original and well worth a look.

Come out and cross Boulevard Montmartre into Passage Jouffroy, built in 1847 on the site of the estate of the Russian Prince Tuffakine and about 140m (153yd) in length. To the right of the entrance is the Musée Grévin, founded 1882 and the French equivalent of London's Madame Tussaud's; in addition to the waxworks there are distorting mirrors and various fun events. Passage Jouffroy is less busy than Passage des Panoramas but perhaps more charming and quaint. There are lots of shops selling curios, second-hand books, toys, antiques and so on.

Coming out of the far end of the *passage*, cross Rue de la Grange-Batelière into Passage Verdeau, a continuation of Passage des Panoramas. Rue de la Grange-Batelière ('battling barn') is so-named because built across an estate (dating back to 800) where a fortified barn once stood. Passage Verdeau, 75m (82yd) long and opened in 1846, is a paradise for collectors of all kinds: books, antiques, photographs, prints, postcards . . . It has enjoyed an upsurge of interest since the establishment nearby of Hôtel Drouot (the French Auction House), at 9 Rue Drouot.

Les Petites Écuries

We now temporarily leave the *passages* to enter a part of Paris that was developed in the 18th and early 19th centuries. Come out of Passage Verdeau and turn right into Rue du Faubourg-Montmartre, a section of the ancient track that led from Lutèce to Montmartre. Take the third left into Rue Bergère, which dates back to the mid-1700s. At no 23 is the Cité Bergère, built in 1825, where Heinrich Heine (1797–1856) lived. At no 12 is the Conservatoire National d'Art Dramatique, the old Conservatoire National de Musique et de Déclamation, founded in 1784 by the Baron de Breteuil (1730–1807) in what was delightfully named the Hôtel des Menus-Plaisirs-du-Roi (Hôtel of the King's Little Pleasures); the main entrance is in Rue du Conservatoire (see below). At no 1 Rue Bergère is the fine 18th-century Hôtel de Sénac de Meilhan.

Retrace your steps slightly and go up Rue du Conservatoire, created along with Rue Ste-Cécile in 1853 on the site of the outbuildings of the Hôtel des Menus-Plaisirs-du-Roi. This opened up the Conservatoire National de Musique et de Déclamation, and the building was given a new façade. Much later, just before WWI, the school moved to larger premises in the nearby Rue de Madrid (and to the Cité at La Villette in 1992), but you can still see the old *salle de concert* (the Salle Pompéenne), done in 1811, as well as traces of Imperial decoration, as in the foyer and on the staircase.

Turn right into Rue Ste-Cécile and have a quick look in Église St-Eugène-et-St-Cécile on the corner. Architecturally, this church, done by Louis Auguste Boileau (1812–1896), was a Parisian first, as its structure is entirely cast-iron.

You now enter Rue du Faubourg-Poissonnière, a section of the ancient road by which fish from the northern seaports was delivered to the Halles; it is still a busy street, being one of the main routes from the north to the city centre. Go under the arch at no 36 into the narrow Rue Gabriel-Laumain (formerly Passage Violet), a quiet street with, at no 6bis, a fine 1840 pavilion.

At the bottom, turn left briefly into Rue d'Hauteville, opened in 1772 – straight ahead in the distance is Église St-Vincent-de-Paul, built 1824–44 – and then right into Rue des Petites-Écuries, which owes its name to the royal stables (*écuries*), some 400m (¼ mile) further down. Built in 1780 on the site of the 'New Sewer' (*Grand Égout*), which had been covered up in 1769, the street is now slightly shabby but has character. There is a fine 18th-century *hôtel* in the courtyard at no 44.

Turn right into Passage/Cour des Petites-Écuries at no 15, almost opposite Rue Martel. The *cour* is exactly where the royal stables stood. A few metres down, where it widens, turn left. This cobbled *passage* has been greatly spoiled by the modern blocks on the left, but on the right is the highly recommended Brasserie Flo: even if you do not plan to eat there, ask for a quick look at the splendid décor.

Rue du Faubourg-St-Denis and further passages

Cour des Petites-Écuries leads into Rue du Faubourg-St-Denis. This is an appealing street – not so much for its questionable beauty but because it is full of life and somehow still rings true. It contains a few interesting old houses, especially at nos 50, 48, 43 and 25. Before their demolition during the Revolution, two *couvents* stood at the north end of the street. This is part of one of the city's oldest routes, leading from the centre out to the rich Abbaye St-Denis and to one of the most important medieval fairs, the Foire du Lendit, held annually from the time of Dagobert I (reigned 628–39) until the Revolution. It lasted some four weeks and attracted merchants from all over Europe.

Turn right, cross the street and, at no 46, enter Passage Brady. The *passage* has changed completely over the last few years, today being devoted almost exclusively to oriental shops. It was opened in 1828, linking Faubourg St-Denis and Faubourg St-Martin, and is 216m (236yd) long. A rotunda at its centre disappeared in the 1850s when Boulevard de Sébastopol was built, bisecting the *passage*. Passage Brady has not enjoyed the new found *éclat* of the other *passages* and certainly could do with a spring-clean!

Coming out of it, turn right into Boulevard de Strasbourg – the continuation of Boulevard de Sébastopol and one of the city's main arteries – and then quickly right into Passage de l'Industrie, which takes you back into Rue du Faubourg-St-Denis. The wonderful Restaurant Julien is on your left at no 16; once again the décor is very impressive, especially the painted ceilings. Walk left to the monumental Porte St-Denis, built in 1672 by François Blondel (1618–1686); it and the neighbouring Porte St-Martin replaced a fortified medieval gate. The new Porte St-Denis still served as the kings' official entrance to the city, and was hence relatively splendid.

Cross the boulevard into Rue St-Denis and turn right into Rue Ste-Foy, built on the fortified Charles V wall. The two *rues* parallel to it, d'Aboukir and de Cléry, are also on the site of the wall (see p13). It becomes Rue du Caire, and at no 44 is the entrance to the city's longest *passage*, the multi-galleried Passage du Caire, created in 1799. Much appreciated by the public from the start as a protection from rain, mud and horses, this was built on the site of the Couvent des Filles-Dieu, abolished at the Revolution and demolished during the Directoire. Dating from 1276, the convent was for street girls who had 'abused their bodies' – prostitution was rife (and still is in nearby Rue St-Denis). The *passage* is now almost entirely devoted to the wholesale clothes trade.

Walk down it to the end, where you come out on Rue St-Denis. Turn right to reach Rue Réaumur some little way along. Buses and métro Réaumur-Sébastopol are nearby, on the corner with Boulevard de Sébastopol.

Étoile to Trocadéro

This walk takes you for a gentle stroll from Place Charles-de-Gaulle (Place de l'Étoile) down the Champs-Élysées and Avenue George-V to the river and back up to the Trocadéro, taking in three great museums and three important 1930s monuments. It links two of the city's hills: Colline du Roule – now with Place Charles-de-Gaulle at its top – and Colline de Chaillot, overlooking the Seine – now with Place du Trocadéro at its top. The whole area has a scent of opulence and wealth.

Start: **Métro Charles-de-Gaulle- Étoile; buses 22, 31, 52, 72, 92.**
Finish: **Métro Trocadéro; buses 22, 30, 32, 63.**
Length: **3km (1¼, miles).**
Time: **lhr.**
Refreshments: **Cafés on the Champs-Élysées and on Place de l'Alma, plus the three museum cafeterias, especially that at the Trocadéro.**
Which day: **Wednesday–Sunday is best.**
To visit:
• **Musee d'Art Moderne de la Ville de Paris: daily (not Monday) 10.00-17.40.**
• **Musee Galliera de la Mode et du Costume: when exhibitions are on, daily (not Monday) 10.00-17.40.**
• **Musée Guimet: daily (not Tuesday) 10.00–18.00**

Haute Couture
Leave the métro by the Champs-Élysées exit and at the traffic lights cross the avenue to the odd-number side. Behind you is the Arc de Triomphe, erected 1806–36 to celebrate the Napoleonic armies' victories, and the wide Place Charles-de-Gaulle (formerly and still commonly called Place de l'Étoile), with its 12 symmetrical avenues, designed during the Second Empire.

Facing you is one of the great urban perspectives, all the way down to the Louvre. For a full description of the Champs, the *place* and the Arc, see p94.

Walk down the avenue to Avenue George-V, on your right. On the corner is Fouquet's famous café – expensive, but probably the best on the avenue. Turn right into Avenue George-V, a typical wide avenue of the area, bordered by a few smart couturier shops and well known for the Hôtel George-V (good bar). At no 23 is the American-Protestant Church of the Holy Trinity. Nos 13 and 11 are opulent 19th-century houses dressed in Louis-Quinze style, now housing the Spanish and Chinese embassies respectively. On the other side, at no 12, is the celebrated Crazy Horse cabaret.

Carry on down to Place de l'Alma, where there are a couple of good cafés and where painters such as Gustave Courbet (1819–1877) and a little later Édouard Manet (1832–1883) exhibited their works outside the official circuit. The elegant leafy Avenue

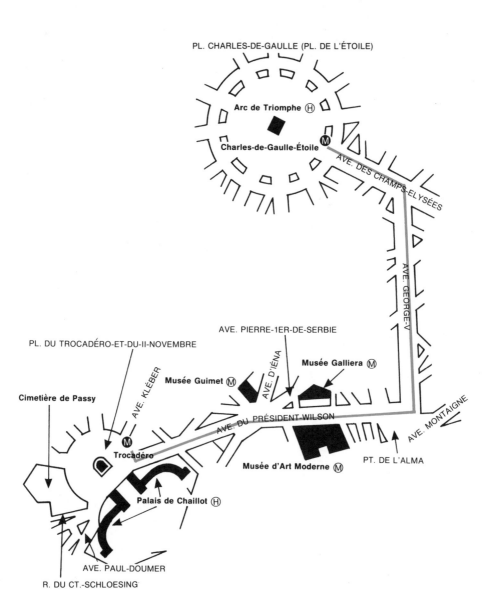

Montaigne leads off from the left of the *place* towards the Rond-Point des Champs-Élysées. The gilded torch near the Guimard métro entrance is an exact replica of that held by the Statue of Liberty in New York, and was given to the French nation as a symbol of Franco-American friendship. Pont de l'Alma (1974), nearby, is a rather ugly-looking affair which replaced a stone bridge (1854) commemorating the Franco-British victory over the Russian army at the Alma during the Crimean War (1854-6). In more recent years the Alma tunnel was the scene of the tragic car accident in which Diana, Princess of Wales, died on 30 August 1997.

Le Palais de New York et Tokyo

Turn right from the *place* into Avenue du Président-Wilson. The avenue bears left where Avenue Marceau goes uphill to the right. At no 5 lived Alphonse Bertillon (1853–1914), the police officer who invented bertillonage, a widely used precursor of fingerprinting in which criminals were identified by means of a set of bodily measurements.

At no 13 is one of the three 1930s buildings on the Chaillot hill, the Palais de New York et de Tokyo, now housing the Musée d'Art Moderne de la Ville de Paris (as opposed to the Musée National d'Art Moderne at Beaubourg – see p72). Built in two years for the 1937 Exposition Universelle and now completely restored to its original glory, the *palais* was designed by four little-remembered architects – A. Aubert, D. Dastugue, J.C. Dondel, and P. Viard – who won a competition against 120 other contenders, including Robert Mallet-Stevens (1886–1945) and Le Corbusier (1887–1965), both deemed too modern. Like the Palais de Chaillot (see below), it overlooks the river and is composed of two wings articulated around a vast open space, with an imposing colonnade as a link. Walk onto the terrace and around the rectangular *bassin*. A massive bronze by Émile Antoine Bourdelle (1861–1929) - one of the great French sculptors - dominates this splendid space, now little used except by skateboarders. Under the peristyle are two other allegorical statues (Force and Victory), also by Bourdelle.

The west wing, i.e. the Palais de Tokyo, now houses a museum dedicated to ultra contemporary art. Good library and great restaurant.

The Musée d'Art Moderne is in the east wing. Although the architects were Classicist in their overall design, they were Modernist in their use of space, and certainly had studied Le Corbusier: the spaces are superb and a joy to walk through. The first floor is devoted to temporary exhibitions. Downstairs is the small but fascinating permanent collection, representative of contemporary European art, with a strong bias towards French artists. Highlights include large canvases by Raoul Dufy (1877–1953) – the *Fée Electricité*- and by Sonia (1884–1979) and Robert (1885–1941) Delaunay - *Rythmes* and *Tour Eiffel* – as well as a good Cubist collection. There is also a room of works by the unjustly neglected Jean Fautrier (1898–1964) – *Les Otapes* - and other modern paintings by the likes of Pierre Soulages (b1919) and Yves Klein (1928–1962).

Le Palais Galliera

When you leave the museum you see, facing you on the other side of Avenue du Président-Wilson, the Italian Renaissance-like Palais Galliera, built in the last quarter of the 19th century by Léon Ginain (1825–1898) for the Duchess Galliera, who wanted it as a home for her collection of 17th-century Italian Art, which she intended to bequeath to the French nation. In the end she gave the collection to Genoa and the empty *palais* to France. Since 1977 the *palais*, which has a lovely little garden, has housed the Musée de la Mode et du Costume (Fashion and Costume), whose core collection comes from Carnavalet. Due to problems of conservation, it holds only temporary exhibitions.

Chinoiseries

Carry on up the avenue, staying on the same side as the Musée Galliera, until you reach Place d'Iéna. At the centre of the *place* is an equestrian statue of George Washington (1732–1799) done in 1900 by two US sculptors called French and Potter, and given to the city by the Society of the Daughters of the Revolution. Go right around the *place,* crossing Avenue Pierre-ler-de-Serbie and Avenue d'Iena.

At the angle of Avenue d'Iéna and Rue Boissière is the Musée National des Arts Asiatiques, or Musée Guimet, founded by Emile Guimet (1836–1918), a 19th-century businessman with a passion for the Orient. Though the building has no architectural value, the museum is an unalloyed pleasure. Completely restored and reorganized – chronologically and by nations – in 1983, it now contains one of the largest collections of its kind in the world. Especially remarkable is the Khmer collection on the ground floor – the largest ensemble outside. Kampuchea, and including the stunning 10th-century pediment from the Bantey Srey temple - and there are also works from central Vietnam, Thailand, Laos, Burma and Bali. In addition, there are rooms devoted to the esoteric arts of Nepal and Tibet (among the world's finest such collections, with some 70 paintings and 30 illuminated manuscripts), India, China and Japan.

Leaving the museum, cross Rue de Longchamp and Avenue du Président-Wilson. At the corner of Avenues d'Iéna and du Président-Wilson is the Conseil Economique et Social (Social Economic Council) building, designed by Auguste Perret (1874–1954) in 1936 and an architectural landmark for its unequivocal and unashamed use of concrete – no decoration, just the raw material.

Carry on up Avenue du Président-Wilson until you reach Place du Trocadéro-et-du-11-Novembre, established at the top of the Chaillot hill in 1869. On your left, with a superb view over the river, is the Palais de Chaillot (see p119), the third of our great 1930s buildings on the hill and another for which Le Corbusier failed to get the commission.

The wall straight ahead is that of the Cimetière de Passy, whose entrance is in the small Rue du Commandant-Schloesing, off Avenue Paul-Doumer. Along those buried there are the artists Édouard Manet (1832–1883) and Berthe Morisot (1841–1895), the writer Octave Mirbeau (1850–1917) and the composers Gabriel Fauré (1845–1924) and Claude Debussy (1862–1918). The place sees the intersection of four other avenues, also opened during the 1800s, and there are a couple of agreeable cafés.

Your walk ends here, at métro Trocadéro, although instead you could connect from here to the Trocadéro, Tour Eiffel and Invalides walk (p118).

As a footnote to this walk, when at the Palais de Tokyo, you could also decide to make an incursion to the remarkable Museum des Arts Primitifs (open 2006) just there on the other side of the river. To do so walk across the terrace, down the steps, and then make a right. Cross the rather busy 'quai' and cross the Seine via the passerelle Debilly erected in 1906.

Fontainebleau

After Versailles (see p183), Fontainebleau is probably the most remarkable *château* near Paris. Furthermore the setting is impressive, the town itself rather charming, and the vast forest unique.

Start and finish: **Trains go every half-hour at peak time, and every hour otherwise from Gare de Lyon (on métro line 1) to Fontainebleau station, and then a bus takes you to the *château*, 2.5km (1½ miles) away.**
Length: **4km (2½ miles).**
Time: **1½hr.**
Refreshments: **Many cafés and brasseries in town, especially near the *château*, on Rue Denecourt and on Place Napoléon-Bonaparte.**
Which day: **Any day, though weekends get very busy.**
To visit:
• **Château de Fontainebleau: daily (not Tuesday) 09.30–12.30 and 14.00– 17.00.**

Two kings, François I and Henri IV, and one emperor, Napoléon I, dominate the history of the *château*. There are historical parallels with St-Germain-en-Laye (see p188). Louis VI, a great hunter, built the first mansion here in order to enjoy the rich hunting grounds. A century later, Louis IX (St Louis) established a religious community and enlarged the building. Though the kings used Fontainebleau during the autumn hunting season, it was not until the 16th century that Fontainebleau really grew in size and munificence.

François I had the master builder Gilles Le Breton (*c*1500–1553) create a new *château* on the foundations of the old, around the Cour Ovale (oval court), and added the wings that border the Cour du Cheval-Blanc (Court of the White Horse) – named after a huge plaster horse that Catherine de' Medici (1519–1589) installed in the centre of the *cour*. François engaged Giovanni Battista Rosso (1494–1540) and Francesco Primaticcio (1504–1570) for the interior decoration. Work carried on desultorily after his death, although Henri II added a few bits and pieces, including the superb ballroom, painted by Primaticcio. But then came Henri IV, who sank an enormous amount of money into the palace: he added galleries, created a vast array of buildings for pantries, kitchens and other services, opened the Cour Ovale, created Cour Henri-IV, installed the Jeu de Paume, etc.; outside, the gardens were enlarged and the canal dug. Prominent French artists of the time were hired for the interior decoration. With Louis XIII, born at Fontainebleau, came further transformations, including the rebuilding by Jean Androuet de Cerceau (1585–1649) of the impressive horseshoe staircase which now dominates Cour du Cheval-Blanc (today the palace's main entrance). Louis XIV modified the gardens before Versailles took over all his available energy, and Louis XV made some additions,

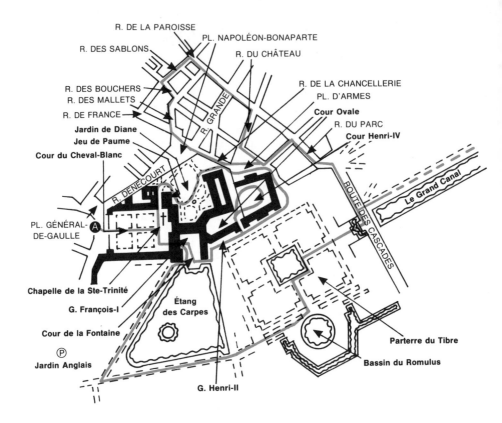

including a wing of the Cour du Cheval-Blanc by Jacques-Ange Gabriel (1698–1782), one of the most eminent architects of the time.

The palace enjoyed a new lease of life when Napoleon refurbished parts of it. He also signed his abdication here before going to Elba in 1814. He bade his old guard farewell at the bottom of the steps in the Cour du Cheval-Blanc, which is consequently sometimes called Cour des Adieux. In his *St Helena Memorial* he described the *château* as 'a residence fit for kings, a residence of time'.

The château

Since Fontainebleau is really a collection of *châteaux* without any unifying building plan, the ensemble can be puzzling. Before going on the walk as outlined on the map, you may want to have a brisk look around the entire palace, as outlined below, to get a feel for the place.

Go through the gates into Cour du Cheval-Blanc. The gates were installed by Napoleon, who had to demolish one wing of the closed Renaissance courtyard; the main entrance to the *palais* had previously been on the other side. You are confronted by classic French Renaissance architecture. Both the pavilion facing you and the wing to your left date from François I; the one on the right was built by Gabriel in Louis XV's days, the original Renaissance wing having burnt down. Jean Androuet de Cerceau's horseshoe steps date from 1634. Cross the courtyard and go through the *passage* at the right-hand corner into Cour de la Fontaine (courtyard of the fountain), where most of the façades date from the time of François I. Then walk around to the left along the Henri-II (1552) gallery. On the other side is the famous Cour Ovale, which you will see when you visit the palace.

Turn left at the end of the gallery to reach the remarkable Cour Henri-IV, known also as Cour des Offices (courtyard of pantries). This ensemble is very reminiscent of the architecture found at Place des Vosges (see p34) and Hôpital St-Louis (see p141).

Retrace your steps, turn left, and walk around the outside of Cour Henri-IV until you reach the rather fine Jardin de Diane, bordering the other side of the Cour Ovale and Cour de la Fontaine. These wings were added by Louis XV and by Louis XVI. Walk along and re-enter Cour du Cheval-Blanc *via* the *allée* between the Jeu de Paume (on your left), partly rebuilt during the 18th century, and the François I north wing.

Internal visit

Now visit the *château*. There are some splendid rooms, perfect examples of three centuries of architecture and royal decoration. The Galerie François-I, decorated by Rosso and Primaticcio, is stunning, and the Imperial apartments are fascinating. It is outside the remit of this book to provide a full description of the interior: the visit is extremely well signposted and there are multilingual explanation sheets in most rooms.

The grounds

Return to the Cour de la Fontaine and walk over to the pond, the Étang des Carpes, which also marks the start of the Jardin Anglais, covering some 12 hectares (30 acres), designed by André Le Nôtre (1613–1700) in the 17th century and modified during Napoleon I's reign. Walk along the right-hand side of the pond. There are many *allées*, down which feel free to wander. On the other side of the pond is the Carrousel, built by Louis XV for the royal stables.

Back at the pond, walk over to the royal garden, the square Parterre du Tibre, 2.4 hectares (6 acres) in area, designed in Henri IV's reign and later altered by Louis Le Vau (1612–1670), who created the terrace. Its central pond, the Bassin du Tibre, is named for the bronze statue, designed by Primaticcio. As you approach the Parterre you see an attractive horseshoe-shaped ornamental pond and fountain encircling another round pond, the Bassin du Romulus. The Parterre leads to a grand view over the canal, dug in Henri IV's days.

Walk down the steps of the terrace towards the canal and reach Route des Cascades. Feel free to walk into the park, which is rather wild; the grounds are really limited to the Jardin Anglais, the Parterre and the Jardin de Diane. The park's main interest is as a provider of perspectives, and there are also many places for picnics.

The town

Fontainebleau is pretty, but not much else. This route gives you a flavour of the place.

Turn left along Route des Cascades and go uphill to Rue du Parc. Take the first left into Rue d'Avon, reach Place d'Armes (another entrance to the *palais*), cross into Rue de la Chancellerie, which flanks the *château*, and reach the busy Place Napoléon-Bonaparte where most of the action in Fontainebleau takes place: there are cafés and brasseries.

Carry on straight over into the busy Rue de France and the pedestrian shopping precinct; turn immediately right into the narrow Rue des Mallets, then first left into Rue des Bouchers. At the crossroads, turn right into Rue des Sablons, another pleasant shopping street; continue for a while before turning right along Rue de la Paroisse to Rue Grande, which you cross to Rue du Parc. A little way along, turn right into Rue du Château, which leads you back to Place d'Armes.

If you feel you have walked enough, re-enter the *château*, turn right, cross the Jardin de Diane diagonally, reach the Jeu de Paume and Cour du Cheval-Blanc, and go through the gate to catch your bus. Alternatively, you could stroll back to the station. Retrace your steps to the canal and walk down it across the park. Turn left at the bottom and come out *via* Porte de Changis onto Rue Remy-Dumoncel, which cross to Rue du Montceau. Cross Rue des Déportés and reach Rue du Viaduc, which runs by the railway line. Turn left to reach the railway station, less than 1km (½ mile) along.

The enormous forest of Fontainebleau – about 16,000 hectares (40,000 acres) – lies to the west of the town, at the bottom of Rue de France. It is a unique place, full of remarkable trees – notably many ancient oaks – but is especially well known for its rocks. The only way to visit it is by car or bicycle, and you need a good map.

Versailles

A long circular walk taking you to the *château* and then on to the superb landscaped grounds, along the Grand Canal, past the two Trianons and Marie Antoinette's hamlet. The walk ends with a short tour through the fine Classical town, past one of the birthplaces of the French Revolution (the Jeu de Paume), the fine 18th-century Cathédrale St-Louis, and many charming old streets.

Start and finish: **RER Versailles-Rive-Gauche.**
Length: **8.5km (5 ¼ miles).**
Time: **There is so much to see and do in Versailles that you should spend at least a day there. This walk takes 2½–3hr.**
Refreshments: **Numerous cafés and restaurants in town and on either side of Place d'Armes, by the *château*, plus *buvettes* in the grounds.**
Which day: **Not Monday, unless you are interested only in the gardens.**
To visit:

- **Château de Versailles: daily (not Monday) 9.00–17.30 from 1 October to 30 April, 9.00–18.30 from 2 May to 30 September.**
- **Trianons: daily (not Monday) 10.00–12.30 and 14.00–17.30 from 1 October to 30 April, 11.00–18.30 from 2 May to 30 September.**

Versailles, a testimony to the most opulent phase of French history, is the epitome of Classical architecture and of landscaped gardening. For nearly a century it occupied a supreme position in the political, artistic and spiritual life of France.

In 1624 Louis XIII wanted to build a hunting lodge to enjoy the rich hunting grounds of Versailles, and one Philibert le Roy was appointed to build a small mansion. Nearly 40 years later, Louis XIV decided to embellish and enlarge it. He employed the team that had been so successful in another *château*, the exquisite Vaux-le-Vicomte, which belonged to Nicolas Fouquet (1615–1680), Superintendent of Finance. Louis Le Vau (1612–1670) was responsible for the design, Charles Le Brun (1619–1690) for the interior decoration and André Le Nôtre (1613–1700) for landscaping the gardens.

In 1678 Jules Hardouin-Mansart (1645–1708) took over and greatly enlarged the palace, building the famed Galerie des Glaces (hall of mirrors) and the north and south wings. Nearly 200,000 craftsmen, builders, sculptors, painters, decorators and gardeners worked on the site. At the end of the 17th century Hardouin-Mansart started work on the Royal Chapel (completed in 1710 by Robert de Cotte [1656–1735]).

On the king's death the Regent, Philippe d'Orléans (1674–1723), moved the court back to the Palais-Royal in Paris, but Louis XV returned to the *château*, appointing Jacques-Ange Gabriel (1698–1782) to transform the royal apartments. Gabriel also built the new Opéra and the Little Trianon. Little changed during Louis XVI's reign, except for the creation of a rural hamlet for Marie Antoinette (1755–1793). On 5 October 1789

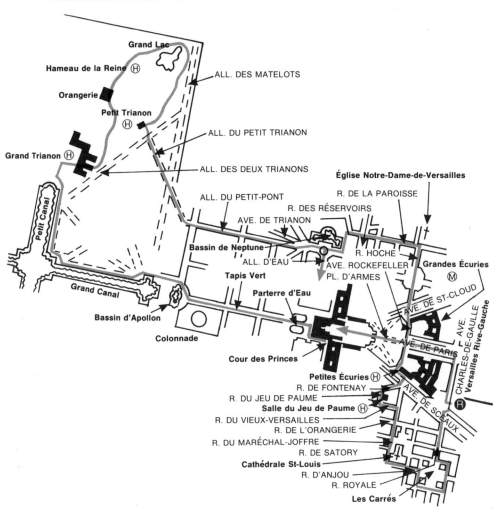

the people of Paris marched on Versailles to demand bread. The queen's celebrated retort – 'They have no bread? Give them brioches, then' – is a much misquoted and misunderstood part of French history.

After the guillotining of the king and queen, the contents of the *château* were auctioned off. Napoleon had little to do with Versailles, probably because its identification with monarchy was too strong, and thereafter no head of government lived in Versailles again – indeed, the *château* came close to being pulled down in the early 19th century. Eventually Louis-Philippe ordered that a museum be installed, but it was not until 1952 that the palace underwent a full restoration programme.

The Grandes and Petites Écuries

Exit the station into Avenue Charles-de-Gaulle. Turn right and reach the magnificent Avenue de Paris, the main artery of the town. The *château* is there at the bottom.

Take the left-hand side of the avenue until you reach the Petites Écuries (small stables), built 1679–82 by Hardouin-Mansart on the site of the Hôtel de Lauzun; it is worth entering the courtyard of this fine building. Cross the avenue to the Grandes Écuries, a mirror image of the Petites Écuries and likewise by Hardouin-Mansart. The Petites Écuries housed workhorses and the Grandes Écuries riding horses; while today the former building is used hardly at all, the latter contains the archives of the *département* of Yvelines, a few exhibition rooms and the Musée des Carosses (coaches and carriages), open 14.00–16.30. Go into the stables, turn left and reach the large cobbled courtyard opening out on Place d'Armes, which fronts the palace.

The château

Cross Place d'Armes to the main gates. This *place* is in effect the focus of Versailles. Three avenues spread out from it – Avenue de Paris (centre), Avenue de Sceaux (left) and Avenue de St-Cloud (right) – and if you look back you can enjoy the fine perspective over them. Enter the Cour d'Honneur; the entrance to the *château* is to the right.

Visiting the interior takes a long time – a couple of hours, perhaps, if you merely scamper round. There are stupendous rooms: the Galerie des Glaces is the most celebrated, but the Royal Apartments, the Opéra and the Royal Chapel are also a joy. Guidebooks and free location maps are available at the entrance.

Leave the *château* and enter the gardens *via* the Cour des Princes, a large *passage* between the Aile du Midi (south wing) and the Aile Vieille (old wing), situated opposite the entrance to the palace. Feel free to wander. The route suggested here takes you past some of the most beautiful spots, but there are countless other things to see and do.

The small formal garden on the other side of Cour des Princes is the Parterre du Midi (southern garden). Versailles is acknowledged as Le Nôtre's masterpiece and the acme of the *jardin à la française*. His style was one of strict formalism, but is not without beauty. The gardens, organized around a central axis, are rich in statues, fountains, etc., many celebrating the cult and myth of Apollo, an obvious symbol for the Sun King.

Turn right, walk along the palace and reach the terrace, where you have a superb view over the grounds and canal, and another over the garden façades of the palace (by Hardouin-Mansart). Walk across the Parterre d'Eau (water gardens). Most of the animal statues in the ornamental ponds – known as the Cabinet des Animaux – are by Le Brun.

Go down some steps to another water garden (the Parterre de Latone; i.e., Apollo's mother), where there are three ponds, and walk down the left-hand side of the wide central *allée* at the bottom, the Tapis Vert (green carpet). On your left are the Bosquets du Midi and on your right the Bosquets du Nord. Both cover a sizeable area and have various centres of interest. Three-quarters of the way down, follow a sign leftwards to Hardouin-Mansart's superb circular Colonnade, where Louis XIV held picnics and garden parties: there are 32 arcades, marble Ionic columns of different colours and, at the top, bas-reliefs showing various *jeux d'enfants*, sculpted by 13 different artists including Antoine Coysevox (1640–1720), Étienne Le Hongre (1628–1690) and Félix Le Comte (1737–1817).

Retrace your steps to the Tapis Vert and carry on down it to the gardens' masterpiece, the Bassin d'Apollon, done in gilded lead by an artist called Tuby; the astonishing vitality of the figures never ceases to charm. The Bassin d'Apollon is a pivotal point in the orchestral arrangement of the gardens, which are from here onwards dominated by water: by the Grand Canal and by the Petit Canal, crossing it. Venice had given the Sun

King a flotilla of gondolas, and he and the court would go for boating parties. More mundane rowing boats are now available for hire (as are bicycles).

Go through the gates and walk along the canal on the right-hand side (if you go the other way you face an extra 3km [2-mile] walk) to reach the Petit Canal, which you follow to the right.

The Trianons and the Hameau

The Grand Trianon's gardens appear at the end; walk up the steps. This ravishing building was created by Hardouin-Mansart in the 1680s and provided a less formal setting where Louis XIV could entertain his courtiers. One is immediately awestruck by the building's pinkness, due to the special Languedoc marble. Of special interest within are the Salon des Glaces and the Salon de Musique. The *jardins à la française*, by Le Nôtre and Hardouin-Mansart, contain many fine flowerbeds and a fine topiary. The original contents were dispersed during the Revolution, and the present arrangement dates from Napoleon – his only significant contribution to Versailles.

Leave the Grand Trianon *via* the main central gates onto the Trianon esplanade. Facing you is Allée des Deux Trianons, giving another lovely perspective. Take the diagonal *allée* on the left to the Jardin du Roi (small door in wall). Follow the *allée* slightly to the left through a second gate and then the path leading to the Orangerie (signposted).

Leave the Orangerie by the small gates and take the *allée* to the right. You are now in a much wilder garden, part of the grounds of Marie Antoinette's Petit Trianon and Hameau. The *allée* goes slowly downhill and the Hameau de la Reine, to give it its full name, becomes visible. Reach the lake and enjoy the rural setting, where the queen played shepherdesses with her courtiers.

The Hameau, an ersatz hamlet, was designed by the architect Richard Mique (1728–1794) in 1783–5; the concept had been borrowed from Jean-Jacques Rousseau (1712–1778) and his ideas of a return to Nature, but this was a real working farm, with sheep, cows, a mill and so on. It is an idyllic setting, but also rather unnatural.

Walk around the lake to the left, pass the quaint cottages, go over a small bridge, pass the water mill, cross the second bridge and take an *allée* which veers to the left. Turn right at the fork and go uphill across the grounds to the Petit Trianon. These grounds contain a large variety of splendid ancient trees, many planted by the leading botanist of the time, Bernard de Jussieu (*c*1699–1777).

The Petit Trianon, whose entrance is on the other side through a handsome courtyard, lacks the charm of the Grand Trianon. It is a cubic edifice, a perfection of Neoclassicism completed by Gabriel in 1768 for Mme de Pompadour (1721–1764), Louis XV's favourite, though she did not live to see it. Louis XVI gave it to Marie Antoinette, and it has been associated with her ever since. Napoleon gave it to his sister, Pauline Borghese (1780–1825); the original contents had by then been dispersed.

Also of interest is the *jardin à la française* on the other side of the building, bordered by the Ménagerie on one side and Marie Antoinette's Théâtre de la Reine on the other. In the centre of the garden is the Pavillon Français, built by Gabriel for Louis XV and Mme de Pompadour.

Leave the Petit Trianon *via* Allée du Petit Trianon and follow this across sweeping tracts of open farmland, where cattle and sheep often graze: it is easy to forget that Paris is only 15km (10 miles) away. Reach the large crossroads, cross Avenue de Trianon and Allée St-Antoine, both fairly busy (some roads in the park are open to traffic), and keep along Allée du Petit Trianon. Turn left at the bottom and re-enter the *château* grounds by the small lodge-gates. Walk up Allée du Petit-Pont, with a wall on your left and, on your right, the Bosquets du Nord and fine views over the *château*. At the top is another wonderful water display: the small circular Bassin du Dragon straight in front of you and, to your left, the magnificent half-moon Bassin de Neptune, started by Le Nôtre in 1679 and transformed later under Louis XV. To your right is Allée d'Eau, which leads to the Parterre du Nord and the terrace from which you set off to explore the gardens.

Into town

Leave the *château* grounds *via* the Grille de Neptune, on the other side of the pond. Cross Rue des Réservoirs into Rue de la Paroisse, a busy shopping street. Old Versailles has two distinct *quartiers*, separated by Place d'Armes and Avenue de Paris: the Quartier Notre-Dame, where you are now, and the Quartier St-Louis.

Walk on to Église Notre-Dame-de-Versailles, the royal parish church of Versailles, built by Hardouin-Mansart in the 1680s. Most of its decoration is 18th-century – there is an interesting *San Sebastian* by Carle Van Loo (1705–1765); most of its original contents were lost during the Revolution.

Leaving the church, go straight ahead along Rue Hoche, which leads past many fine shops to the octagonal Place Hoche, with a bronze statue of Lazare Hoche (1768–1797), the revolutionary general and companion of Napoleon, and then back to Place d'Armes with its cafés and restaurants. Continue in the same direction along Avenue Rockefeller, pass the Grandes and Petites Écuries, and cross Avenue de Sceaux to the fountain on the corner with Rue de Fontenay (a little to the left).

You are now in the Quartier St-Louis. Although there are still 17th-century houses here, most date from the 18th; the *hôtel* at no 10 has a mascaron. Walk along Rue de Fontenay and turn left into Rue du Jeu de Paume, where you will find the rather unprepossessing Salle du Jeu de Paume (real-tennis court), dating from 1686, the only such to have survived from the Ancien Régime (visitable by appointment). Here, on 20 June 1789, the representatives of the people (i.e., the members of the Third Estate of Parliament – the other two being the clergy and the aristocracy) swore they would not disperse until they had given France a new constitution . . . which they eventually did.

Walk on to the charming Rue du Vieux-Versailles; go left along it to Rue de Satory, another nice street, which you take to the right. At no 27 is the interesting Villa des Chevaux-Légers. Turn right and cross Rue de l'Orangerie (called Rue du Général Leclerc to your left) into Rue du Maréchal-Joffre. A little further along is the elegant Cathédrale St-Louis, built 1743–54 by Jacques Hardouin-Mansart de Lévy de Sargonne (1709–1776), a grandson of Hardouin-Mansart's. The cathedral is a fine recently renovated building with a superb organ (1761) by François Henri Clicquot (1732–1790) and a couple of works by François Boucher (1703–1770).

Leave the cathedral. On the other side of Rue du Maréchal-Joffre is the École Nationale Supérieur d'Horticulture et du Paysage, built by Hardouin-Mansart. Walk along the cathedral's eastern wall to Rue d'Anjou, the main street of the Carrés St-Louis, a group of low, picturesque 18th-century buildings set around four small squares. Take a stroll around the Carrés and then return to Rue Royale, go back across the wide diagonal Avenue de Sceaux, and so to the Versailles-Rive-Gauche station.

St-Germain-en-Laye

A wonderful walk in one of the most charming towns near Paris. It takes you to the celebrated Château de St-Germain, which also houses the Musée des Antiquités Nationales, and *via* the park, the St-Germain forest and the streets of the town to Église St-Louis, which contains the Old Pretender's Mausoleum.

Start and finish: **RER St-Germain-en-Laye.**
Length: **4.5km (2¾ miles).**
Time: **2hr.**
Refreshments: Buvettes **in the park; many cafés and brasseries in town.**
Which day: **Wednesday-Sunday, though on Sundays the town is a little dead while weekenders throng at the** *château* **and in the park and forest.**
To visit:
* **Musée des Antiquités Nationales: daily (not Tuesday) 09.45–12.00 and 13.30–17.15.**
* **Musée Départemental du Prieuré: daily (not Monday, Tuesday) 10.30–17.30.**

The forest of St Germain has long been renowned for its hunting, and it was with this in mind that Louis le Gros (Louis VI) built a castle here. In 1230–38 Louis IX (St Louis) added the Sainte Chapelle. The fortress itself, almost entirely razed during the Hundred Years' War by Edward III of England (reigned 1327–77), was restored by Charles V. François I was married here but decided the edifice was a little too medieval, and had it completely altered; Pierre de Chambiges (d1544), his architect, was succeeded by the great Philibert Delorme (c1510–1570).

Slowly St-Germain was becoming the royal residence, in preference to the Louvre. Henri II, who lived here with his queen, Catherine de' Medici (1519–1589), and his mistress, the celebrated Diane de Poitiers (1499–1566), determined that a new *château* be built within a stone's throw of the old one, and Francesco Primaticcio (1504–1570) was appointed to carry out the work. The *château* was finished under Henri IV by Jean Androuet de Cerceau (1585–1649), and the court then moved to St-Germain. Louis XIV, who was born here, initiated many modifications, including the transformation of the park and gardens by André Le Nôtre (1613–1700), but after he moved to Versailles the old *château* was left to the unfortunate Henrietta Maria (1609–1669) and later to his dethroned Stuart cousin James II (reigned 1685–8), the Old Pretender; James died at St-Germain, and is buried in Église St-Louis. Charles Stuart (1720–1788), the Young Pretender, also lived here.

Château-Neuf (new *château*) was given to and, all but the Pavillon Henri-IV, promptly demolished by the Comte d'Artois – later Charles X – who wanted to build something wild and wonderful. Napoleon had the Château Vieux converted to an army

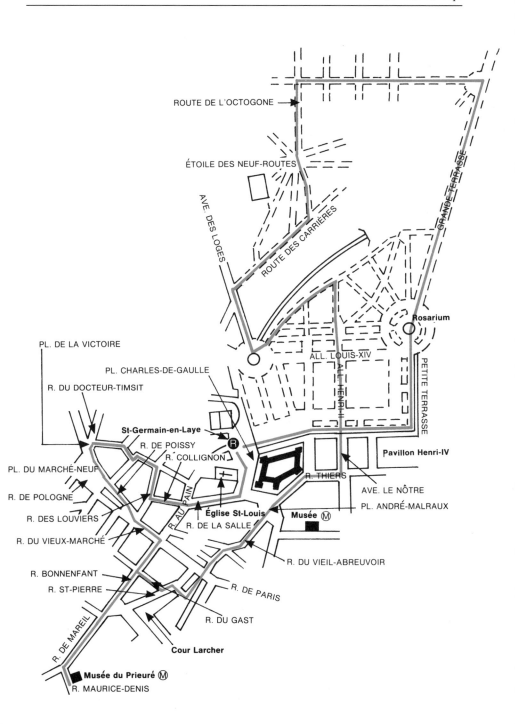

barracks, but Napoleon III finally gave it back some of its former glory by creating within its walls the Musée des Antiquités Nationales.

The château

Exit the station onto Place Charles-de-Gaulle; the old *château* and Église St-Louis are behind you.

The *château*, mostly Renaissance with 19th-century alterations, is a rather austere-looking building, lacking the grandeur of Fontainebleau and the splendour of Versailles. Perhaps it has kept too many of its medieval features – like the rather irregular pentagonal shape and the moats – for modern tastes. Most of it is now occupied by the museum.

It is a vast place and a vast museum: guidebooks are available at the entrance. The museum was entirely restored in the 1960s and makes a great visit, though the juxtaposition of the royal castle with the prehistoric objects is rather bizarre! The collection comprises fine examples of pottery, silverware, jewellery and other items from prehistoric times to the Gallo-Roman period and the Middle Ages. There is also a large room of comparative archaeology, containing artefacts from all over the world.

The remarkable Sainte Chapelle is virtually intact. It was built by the brilliant Pierre de Montreuil (d1267), who also built the Sainte Chapelle in the Île de la Cité, likewise instigated by Louis IX. Both are marvels of 13th-century Gothic architecture, sharing the same lightness and grace.

La Grande Terrasse

Leave the *château* and walk along the moat in the garden to the Petite Terrasse, where you will find the Pavillon Henri-IV, all that remains of the Château-Neuf. The pavilion became an hotel during the Restoration, and was very fashionable with artists and writers in the 19th century: here Alexandre Dumas père (1802–1870) wrote *Les Trois Mousquetaires* (1844) and *Le Comte de Monte-Cristo* (1844–5) and Jacques Offenbach (1819–1880) wrote many of his operettas. The St-Germain Treaty was signed in the pavilion in 1919. Today it is a good place for tea – meals are expensive.

Follow the Petite Terrasse to the Rond-Point du Rosarium, bordering the Jardin Anglais, created during the mid-19th-century restoration of the park and *château* by Eugène Millet (1819–1879) on the site of Le Nôtre's original gardens. Continue along the Grande Terrasse, a magnificent creation done by Le Nôtre in 1669–73. 30m (100ft) wide, it is nearly 2.5km (1½ miles) long – although we shall not go that far. Keep walking until you reach a junction: a gate on the left lets you out into the forest.

The forest covers some 3300 hectares (8000 acres) and is mostly planted with oaks, hornbeams, beeches and chestnuts. Take the central *allée*, pass the Chêne des Anglais on the right, cross the tarmac *allée* and take the third *allée* on the left, the Route de l'Octogone, which you follow to the Étoile des Neuf-Routes roundabout. Take the second or third path on the left to reach the tarmacked Route des Carrières, along which go right to reach Avenue des Loges, originally traced in Louis XIV's days.

Turn left into the avenue, follow it for a little while and then re-enter the park through the gates, take a sharp left and follow the crescent-shaped path that runs along the fence separating you from the old railway, which mutilated Le Nôtre's sumptuous gardens; on your right is the Jardin Anglais. Continue until you reach the Monument to the Dead; turn right into Allée Henri-II, which leads back towards the *château*. Cross Allée Louis-XIV and keep going to leave the park into Avenue Le Nôtre.

A walk in town

Take the first right into Rue Thiers, and walk along the *château* wall until you reach Place André-Malraux. Cross it diagonally to the delightful Rue du Vieil-Abreuvoir, which has several handsome houses, many 18th-century, notably the Hôtel de la Feuillade at no 24 and the Hôtel de la Marquise-de-Maintenon (Mme de Maintenon [1635–1719] later secretly married Louis XIV) at no 23. Pass Place Dauphine and then cross the busy Rue de Paris (St-Germain's high street) to the narrow entrance to Cour Larcher, which has cafés and a restaurant. Leave the *cour via* the narrow *passage* at the top right corner and emerge into Rue St-Pierre, which is a good shopping street. Turn left and then immediately right into the cobbled pedestrian Rue du Gast, which takes you to Rue Bonnenfant.

Turn left into Rue Bonnenfant, which soon becomes Rue de Mareil. When you come to a fork, turn left into Rue Maurice-Denis: the Musée du Prieuré is at no 2. It is situated in a fine 17th-century residence built for the Marquise de Montespan (1641–1707) as a shelter for the poor. The artist Maurice Denis (1870–1943) eventually bought the property in 1913, and it now houses a superb collection including paintings, drawings and prints by Denis himself, Paul Gauguin (1848–1903), Pierre Bonnard (1867–1947), Édouard Vuillard (1868–1940), Alphonse Mucha (1860–1939) and Piet Mondrian (1872–1944), and ceramics and glass by Émile Gallé (1846–1904), René Lalique (1860–1945), Alexandre Bigot (1862–1927) – of the Ceramic Hôtel (see p125) – the brothers Auguste (1853–1901) and Antonin (1864–1930) Daum and others. There is also furniture, including a screen decorated by Bonnard, and illustrated books, including the celebrated edition of *Le Morte d'Arthur* illustrated by Aubrey Beardsley (1872–1898). The chapel was entirely decorated by Denis.

Go back down Rue Bonnenfant, passing the entrance of Rue du Gast, and turn left at the bottom of the street into Rue du Vieux-Marché, which becomes Rue de Pologne and leads into Place du Marché-Neuf. Cross the *place,* turn right into Rue de Poissy and go down to Place de la Victoire, straight on into Rue du Docteur-Timsit and first right into Rue des Écuyers, with the Ancien Hôtel des Comtes-d'Auvergne at no 7. Keep on down to the end and turn right into the pedestrian Rue des Louviers, another shopping street. Take first left into Rue Collignon. Cross Rue au Pain; Claude Debussy (1862–1918) was born at no 2, now a small museum with a concert room.

Continue into Rue de la Salle, which takes you back towards Église St-Louis. The original church collapsed in 1681 and Louis XIV commissioned a new one; both Louis XV and Louis XVI altered it, and what is left is a rather odd-looking edifice in the shape of a Roman basilica. The Old Pretender's mausoleum, in the first side-chapel on the left, was built at the instigation of the British George V (reigned 1910–36).

The RER station is nearby.

Other Outings

Boat trips

The *bateaux mouches* (see p13) provide a beautiful and restful introduction to the city. They can be boarded as follows:

Bateaux-Mouches: Pont de l'Alma; tel 01 42 25 96 10
Bateaux Parisiens Tour Eiffel: Pont d'Iéna; tel 01 45 51 33 08
Vedettes du Pont-Neuf: Square du Vert-Galant (Île de la Cité); tel 01 46 33 98 38

La Défense

The '21st arrondissement of Paris' – an amazing 21st-century landscape dedicated to modern architecture – La Défense, 30 years in the making, is now almost entirely devoted to office and exhibition space. The most spectacular building is the Grande Arche, completed in 1989 and located along the historical axis of Paris formed by the Louvre, the Arc du Carrousel, the Obélisque and the Arc de Triomphe. Rapid lifts take you to the top of the building, where there are magnificent views over Paris and the western suburbs. Access is by RER to Défense station.

St-Denis Basilique

One of the first great Gothic buildings, this superb monument, Cathédrale de St-Denis, was the ancient burial place of the kings of France. The church was started in 1140 and completed, following the designs of the great Pierre de Montreuil (d1267), in 1281. Access is by train from Gare du Nord.

The sewers

Paris underground by boat! The huge sewer system of Paris is an incredible maze: over 2100km (1300 miles) of channels are passable. Entrance is from Quai d'Orsay, at the corner with Pont de l'Alma; visits are held daily (not Thursday and Friday), 11.00–17.00 in summer and 11.00–16.00 in winter, closed last three weeks in January. There are no tours during storms, after a heavy rainfall or when the river is in flood. Tel 01 43 20 14 40.

Practical Hints

Airports
Charles de Gaulle: tel 01 48 62 22 80; access via RER (line B2) from several stations, the best one being Châtelet-les Halles; there are also coach connections (Porte Maillot, Invalides). *Orly:* tel 01 49 75 15 15; coaches from the Air-France Terminal on Place des Invalides, or use a taxi.

Art galleries
Museums are listed below (p195) and at the head of each walk. However, there are also literally hundreds of private art galleries. They cluster mostly in Faubourg St-Honoré (see p98), around Beaubourg (see p70) and around St-Germain-des-Prés (see p65).

Buses
Going by bus has the obvious attraction that you can see something of the city as you go. The network is somewhat more complicated than the métro's, but connections are good. You can get a route-map from a tourist office. You must buy one ticket for up to two sections and two tickets thereafter. The métro is normally cheaper for long journeys.

Churches
Churches and other religious edifices are usually free and open daily 09.00–18.00. Some shut at lunchtime, and a few shut also at 17.00. Times may change now and again.

Cinemas
Cinemas are usually open 12.00–24.00 and cheaper at lunchtime. There are discounts for students (with a valid student card) and OAPs. The notation 'v.o.' indicates that a foreign film is in its 'original version' (i.e., subtitled rather than dubbed).

Consulates
Australia: 4 Rue Jean-Rey, 75015; tel 01 40 59 33 00
Canada: 35 Avenue Montaigne, 75008; tel 01 44 43 29 00
Eire: 4 rue Rude, 75016; tel 01 44 17 67 00
New Zealand: 7ter Rue Léonardo-de-Vinci, 75016; tel 01 45 01 43 43
UK: 35 Rue du Faubourg-St-Honoré, 75008; tel 01 44 51 31 00
USA: 2 Avenue Gabriel, 75008; tel 01 42 96 12 02 *and* 2 Rue St-Florentin, 75001; tel 01 43 12 22 22

Eating out
The adventurous-minded are recommended to explore the small restaurants around Montagne Ste-Geneviève and Place de la Contrescarpe (see pp 45 and 56), the Bastille (see p145), the Halles (see p75) and Montmartre (see p136). What follows is a very short selection of evening venues where you can expect good food and good atmosphere – needless to say, all have been tried and tested by myself. Especially at weekends, it is a good idea to make a reservation. Tipping is not necessary – a service charge of 15% is always added to the bill. Children are welcome in cafés and restaurants.

Brasserie Bofinger: 5 Rue de la Bastille, 75004; tel 01 42 72 87 82
Brasserie de l'Ile St-Louis: 55 Quai de Bourbon, 75004: tel 01 43 54 02 59
Brasserie Flo: 7 Cour des Petites-Écuries, 75010; tel 01 47 70 13 59
Brasserie Lipp: 151 Boulevard St-Germain, 75006; tel 01 45 48 53 91
Chez Denise (À la Tour de Monthléry): 5 Rue des Prouvaires, 75001; tel 01 42 36 21 82
Julien: 16 Rue du Faubourg-St-Denis, 75010; tel 01 47 70 12 06
L'Escargot: 38 Rue Montorgueil, 75001; tel 01 42 36 83 51
À la Pomponnette: 42 Rue Lepic, 75018; tel 01 46 06 08 36
Square Trousseau: 1 Rue Antoine-Vollon, 75012; tel 01 43 43 06 00
Terminus Nord: 23 Rue de Dunkerque, 75010; tel: 01 42 85 05 15

Another good idea is to treat yourself to breakfast at one of the city's grand hotels (you do not need to be a resident). Here are some you might try:

Bristol: 112 Rue du Faubourg-St-Honoré, 75008   George V: 33 Avenue George-V, 75008

Crillon: 10 Place de la Concorde, 75008   Ritz: 15, Place Vendôme, 75001

As a final note, most museums have their own restaurants and/or tea rooms; good examples include the terraced restaurants of the Musée d'Art Moderne and the Institut du Monde Arabe. Other restaurants also appear along the walks.

Health
EC nationals can get an El 1 1 form (available in the UK from any post office), which gives them cover (up to 75%) under their own Social Security system. However, the standard of health care available under this system can be poor; you have to pay at time of issue for things like drugs and then claim compensation back home for the cost; and the system can fall down if urgent attention is required (e.g., after a traffic accident). EC nationals, and certainly non-EC visitors, should therefore take out private health insurance, which is very cheap and covers all sorts of expensive but necessary 'extras' (e.g., getting your car home). In case of emergency, the following are useful:
SOS Médecins (emergency GP and hospital service): 01 43 07 77 77
24-hour chemist: Pharmacie des Champs-Élysées at 84 Avenue des Champs-Élysées; tel 01 45 62 02 41

Loos
The days of the *pissoir* or *vespasienne* have long gone. Public automatic pay loos are now dotted about reasonably liberally, as are underground public conveniences – indeed, the public loo at the Place de la Madeleine is one of Art Nouveau's premier monuments (see p115). In addition, there are loos at every museum, café, restaurant and hotel.

Markets
There are over 100 street markets offering a huge array of fresh food. The days on which they open differ. Here are a few to try:

Place d'Auteuil (see p163)   Rue Mouffetard (see p56)
Rue de Buci (see p106)   Rue Poncelet (see p126)

Some of the few remaining covered markets are:

Aligre, Place d'Aligre, 75012: Tuesday–Saturday, Sunday morning
Batignolles, 96 Rue Lemercier, 75017: Tuesday–Saturday, Sunday morning
Enfants Rouges, 39 Rue de Bretagne, 75003: Monday–Saturday, Sunday morning
Saint Quentin, 85bis Boulevard Magenta, 75010: Tuesday–Saturday, Sunday morning
Secrétan, 33 Avenue Secrétan, 75019: Monday–Saturday, Sunday morning

There are several flea-markets of interest:

Porte de Montreuil (access via métro Porte-de-Montreuil): Saturday, Sunday and
    Monday until 18.00
Porte de Vanves (Avenue Georges Lafenestre; access via métro Porte-de-Vanves):
    Saturday and Sunday; second-hand clothes, pictures, etc.
St Ouen (access via métro Porte-de-Clignancourt): Saturday, Sunday and Monday; the
    largest and best known flea market, actually comprising 16 distinct markets

Métro
A very simple and fast way to move around town. Fares are cheap when you buy a *carnet*
of 10 tickets (which can also be used on the bus). When you move to the RER network
– e.g., for the Versailles and St-Germain-en-Laye walks – different fares apply.

Museums
Of the 100 or so museums in Paris, some are rather obscure. All the major ones are visited
and briefly described during the course of one or other of the walks in this book, and
their opening times are given at the head of the relevant walk(s).

As a general rule national museums are shut on Tuesdays and City of Paris museums
on Mondays. All museums charge admission, though they are often free or half-price on
Sundays. You are advised to make the larger museums the object of a special visit. Here
are the addresses and telephone numbers of the major museums:

Assemblée Nationale (Palais Bourbon): Quai d'Orsay, 75007; tel 01 42 74 22 22
Catacombs: 1 Place Denfert-Rochereau, 75014; tel 01 43 22 47 63
Cite des Sciences de l'Industrie: Porte de la Villette, 30 Avenue Corentin-Cariou: 75019;
    tel 01 36 68 29 30 and 01 40 05 70 00
Centre Georges Pompidou: see Musée National d'Art Moderne below
Conciergerie: Île de la Cité, 1 Quai de l'Horloge, 75001; tel 01 43 54 30 06
Fondation Cartier pour l'art contemporain: 261 Boulevard Raspail, 75014;
    tel 01 42 18 56 51
Fondation Le Corbusier: 10 Square du Docteur-Blanche, 75016; tel 01 42 88 41 53
Maison de Balzac: 47 Rue Raynouard, 75016; tel 01 55 74 41 80
Maison de la Radio: 116 Avenue du President-Kennedy, 75016; tel 01 42 30 21 80
Maison Victor Hugo: 6 Place des Vosges, 75004; tel 01 42 72 10 16
Manufacture des Gobelins: 42 Avenue des Gobelins, 75013; tel 01 43 37 12 60
Musée d'Art Moderne de la Ville de Paris: 11 Avenue du Président-Wilson, 75016;
    tel 01 53 67 40 00
Musée de l'Armee: Hôtel des Invalides, Place des Invalides, 75007; tel 01 44 42 37 72
Musée de l'Assistance-Publique: 47 Quai de la Tournelle, 75005; tel 01 46 33 01 43

Musée Carnavalet: 23, Rue de Sévigné, 75003; tel 01 44 59 58 58
Musée Cernuschi: 7 Avenue Velasquez, 75008; tel 01 45 63 50 75
Musée de la Chasse et de la Nature: Hôtel Guénégaud, 60 Rue des Archives, 75003;
    tel 01 42 72 86 43
Musée de Cluny: 6 Place Paul-Painlevé, 75005; tel 01 53 73 78 00
Musée Cognacq-Jay: Hôtel Donon, 8 Rue Elzévir, 75003; tel 01 40 27 07 21
Musée Eugène Delacroix: 6 Place de Fürstenberg, 75006; tel 01 44 41 86 50
Musée Grévin: 10 Boulevard de Montmartre, 75009; tel 01 47 70 85 05
Musée Gustave Moreau: 14 Rue de la Rochefoucauld, 75009;
    tel 01 48 74 38 50
Musée Guimet: 6 Place d'Iéna, 75016; tel 01 56 52 53 00
Musée Jacquemart-André: 158 Boulevard Haussmann, 75008; tel 01 45 62 39 94
Musée de l'Homme: Palais de Chaillot, Place du Trocadéro-et-du-11-Novembre,
    75016; tel 01 44 05 72 00
Musée de l'Histoire de France: Archives Nationales, 60 Rue des Francs-Bourgeois,
    75003; tel 01 40 27 60 00
Musée du Louvre: Palais du Louvre, 75001; tel 01 40 20 53 17
Musée de la Marine: Palais de Chaillot, Place du Trocadéro-et-du-11-Novembre, 75016;
    tel 01 53 65 69 69
Musée Marmottan: 2 Rue Louis-Boilly, 75016; tel 01 44 96 50 33
Musée de la Mode et du Costume: Palais Galliera, 10 Avenue Pierre-1er-de-Serbie,
    75016; tel 01 56 52 86 00
Musée de Montmartre: 12 Rue Cortot, 75018; tel 01 46 06 61 11
Musée National d'Art Moderne: Rue St-Martin, 75004; tel 01 44 78 12 33
Musée National des Arts et Métiers: Conservatoire National des Arts et Métiers, 292
    Rue St-Martin, 75003; tel 01 40 27 22 20
Musée Nissim de Camondo: 63 Rue de Monceau, 75008; tel 01 45 63 26 32
Musée de l'Orangerie: Place de la Concorde, 75001; tel 01 42 97 50 12
Musée d'Orsay: 1 Rue de Bellechasse, 75007; tel 01 40 49 48 14
Musée du Petit Palais: 1 Avenue Dupuit; tel 01 44 51 19 31
Musée Picasso: Hôtel Salé, 5 Rue de Thorigny, 75003; tel 01 42 71 25 21
Musée Rodin: 77 Rue de Varenne, 75007; tel 01 44 18 61 10
Museum d'Histoire Naturelle: 57 Rue Cuvier, 75005; tel 01 40 79 36 00
Notre-Dame: 10 Rue du Cloître-Notre-Dame, Île de la Cité, 75004;
    tel 01 43 25 42 92
Opéra Palais Garnier: Place de l'Opéra, 75009; tel 01 40 17 35 35
Palais de la Découverte: Avenue Franklin-Roosevelt, 75008; tel 01 45 63 46 36
Panthéon: Place du Panthéon, 75005; tel 01 43 54 34 51
Sainte Chappelle: Île de la Cité, Boulevard du Palais, 75004; tel 01 53 73 78 51

Music
Concerts and other musical events can be booked at all FNAC and Virgin stores.

Newspapers and books in English
Most of the large kiosks have some Anglo-American titles. Here are some English-language bookshops.

Brentano's: 37 Avenue de l'Opéra and Rue Danielle-Casanova, 75002

Galigniani: 224 Rue de Rivoli, 75001
Shakespeare & Co.: 37 Rue de la Bûcherie, 75005
W.H. Smith: 248 Rue de Rivoli, 75001

Night-time
Paris is a great city for night-time walking. As Paris lights up, monuments acquire a different glow and a different quality, and the whole city a subtly different atmosphere. In particular, there are delightful strolls along the river. The action lasts until the early hours (especially on fine warm days) in these areas:

Bastille	Montmartre
Les Halles	Montparnasse
Montagne Ste-Geneviève and	St-Germain-des-Prés
Place de la Contrescarpe	St-Michel

Another surprisingly enjoyable evening activity is to go to one of the museums that open late; for example:

Art Moderne de la Ville de Paris:	Louvre: Monday and Wednesday
Wednesday	Orsay: Thursday
Beaubourg: daily	

Parks
Here is a selection of the finest parks (some quite small):

Parc des Buttes-Chaumont, 75019	Parc du Château de St-Germain-en-Laye
Parc Monceau, 75008	Parc du Château de Versailles
Parc Montsouris, 75014	Jardins du Luxembourg, 75006
Parc du Château de Fontainebleau	

The following, not visited in any of the walks, are certainly worth investigation:

Bois de Boulogne: access by métro to Porte Dauphine métro station; a flat rather busy place (too much traffic) but with the wonderful Jardin d'Acclimatation for children
Bois de Vincennes: diametrically opposite from the Bois de Boulogne; access by métro to Château-de-Vincennes station; superb lake and the celebrated Vincennes Zoo
Parc St-Cloud: best access is by car or taxi; several cafés and buvettes, bicycles for hire

Railway stations
Rail information: tel 0892 35 35 35 or www.sncf.com (with English link)
Paris Austerlitz: 7 Boulevard de l'Hôpital, 75013
Paris Est: Place du Trocadéro-et-du-11-Novembre, 75010
Paris Lyon: Rue de Lyon, Place Louis-Armand, 75012
Paris Montparnasse: 17 Boulevard de Vaugirard, 75015
Paris Nord: 19 Rue Dunkerque, 75010
Paris St-Lazare: 88 Rue St-Lazare, 75009

The RER
The Réseau Express Régional express network is a kind of super-métro run by the same body as governs the métro. Its stations are shown on the métro map.

Shopping

For a listing of shopping walks, see p10. See also the section on markets (p194). The major department stores are:

Bazar de l'Hôtel de Ville, 52–64 Rue de Rivoli, 75004
Bon Marché, 38 Rue de Sèvres, 75007
Galeries Lafayette, 40 Boulevard Haussmann, 75009
Printemps, 64 Boulevard Haussmann, 75009
Samaritaine, Pont Neuf and 75 Rue de Rivoli, 75001

Taxis

These are relatively cheap, depending on the time of day. In the rush hours the traffic is so congested that your ride may be prohibitively expensive. Evenings offer best value, even though fares go up around 10pm. A yellow light on a taxi roof indicates that it is available for hire. Taxi ranks are indicated by a navy-blue panel saying '*Tête de Station*'.

Telephone

There are public telephones in various places on the streets. Most require a phonecard, which you can purchase from post offices and tobacconists (who can also sell stamps); tobacconists are recognizable by their oval red 'TABAC' signs. To phone the UK, dial the prefix 00 44 followed by the number (omitting the 0 of the STD code). To phone the USA, dial the prefix 00 1 followed by the number. For the French provinces, dial 16 1 followed by the number. For Paris, dial the ten digits of the number.

Tourist Offices

French Government Tourist Office, 178 Piccadilly, London W1V OAL; tel 0891 244 123 French Government Tourist Office, 444 Madison Avenue, New York; tel 838 6798 Office du Tourisme de Paris, 127 Avenue des Champs-Élysées, 75008; tel 01 49 52 53 54 (There are also tourist offices at Paris's railway stations.)

What's on

Three magazines – *L'Officiel des Spectacles*, *Pariscope* and *7 à Paris* – all published on Wednesdays, provide the latest information on ballet, cinemas, concerts (classical and rock), exhibitions, operas, restaurants, sport, theatre, etc.

Where to stay

There are hundreds of hotels in Paris and your travel agent or the French Tourist Board will be able to advise you. Prices are calculated per room rather than per person. There is usually a supplement for breakfast. Below is a very brief selection of good mid-price hotels in the heart of the city:

Hôtel d'Angleterre: 44 Rue Jacob, 75006; tel 01 42 60 34 72
Hôtel le Colbert: 7 Rue Hôtel-Colbert, 75005; tel 01 43 25 85 65
Hôtel du Dragon: 36 Rue du Dragon, 75006; tel 01 45 48 51 05
Hôtel des Grandes-Écoles: 75 Rue du Cardinal-Lemoine, 75005; tel 01 43 26 79 23
Hôtel Récamier: 3bis Place St-Sulpice, 75006; tel 01 43 26 04 89

Glossary

Note: As with English, a single French word may have several meanings. The ones given here relate to the ways the words are used in this book, and are not intended to be comprehensive.

abbaye: abbey
allée: passage or alleyway
arc: arch
arrondissement: one of the 20 Parisian wards
avenue: approach or avenue
bistro: pub or café
boulevard: boulevard
brasserie: tavern
buvette: outside refreshment stall
café: bar
carrefour: crossroads
champ: field
charcutier: (1) pork-butcher, or (2) delicatessen
château: castle or mansion
chaussée: roadway
chemin: track or lane
cimetière: cemetery
cité: (1) city, or (2) alley with housing development on both sides
cour: courtyard
Cour d'Honneur: front courtyard
couvent: convent or monastery
école: school
église: church
espace: space or area, often with cultural connotations
faubourg: village absorbed by the city
folie: folly
fontaine: fountain

galerie: gallery or arcade
ginguette: cheap bar
hôpital: hospital or hospice
hôtel: mansion
île: island
impasse: blind alley
jardin: garden
jeu de boules: bowling alley
jeu de paume: real-tennis court
lycée: high-school or grammar school
mairie: town hall
marché: market
mascaron: grotesquely carved head
musée: museum
parc: park
parvis: unenclosed frontal courtyard
passage: arcade and/or alley
place: city square
pont: bridge
porte: gate
quartier: district or neighbourhood
restaurant: restaurant
rue: street
salle: hall
square: small public garden
terrasse: terrace
villa: (1) villa or (2) alley bordered with cottage-like houses
village: village
ville: town, borough or city

Index